SIMPLIFIED ACCOUNTING

COMMERCIAL PROPERTY MANAGEMENT FOR MANAGERS QUICKBOOKS® DESKTOP

GITA FAUST

**Commercial Property Management For Managers QuickBooks® Desktop
Simplified Accounting Solutions**
By Gita Faust

ISBN:-978-0-9964940-2-1
   0-9964940-2-2

Copyright © Gita Faust 2016 All Rights Reserved

Trademark
Intuit ®, Quicken ®, QuickBooks ®, and QuickBooks ® ProAdvisor ® are trademarks and service marks of Intuit Inc., registered in the United States and other countries.

The individual screen displays ("Screen Shots") are copyright images of Intuit, Inc.® The use of the Screen Shots © Intuit Inc.® is for purely illustrative purposes. The commentary provided with the Screen Shots © Intuit Inc.® is the copyright protected work of Gita Faust. Screen Shots © Intuit Inc.® All rights reserved. Displayed with the permission of Intuit Inc ®

This book is not sponsored or endorsed by Intuit, Inc.

Disclaimer
This book is intended for use with QuickBooks® Software. It is intended to help you start using QuickBooks® correctly. Most of the activities can also be accomplished in QuickBooks® Pro®, QuickBooks® Premier, QuickBooks® Premier, QuickBooks® Accountant 2015 and later versions, and QuickBooks® Enterprise Solutions v15.0 and later versions.

QuickBooks® software is not included with this manual. The computer files that are downloadable and may be used with your own QuickBooks® software.

Your own professional accountant or CPA should be consulted regarding the proper use of the QuickBooks® software, and this manual is intended for use as a software guide only. The author shall not be liable for any reliance on the statements and representations made in this manual, and the information provided herein is intended to be used in consultation with a professional accountant or CPA.

It is recommended that the methods provided in this manual be given one or more trial runs for related transaction prior to converting your bookkeeping system to QuickBooks®.

State laws and regulations related to property management may vary and this book is not intended to comply with any specific laws or regulations. All users of this guide book should seek their own legal advice regarding compliance with applicable laws or regulations.

The contents of this book are protected under registered copyright ©. No part of the text, tables, or exhibits in this book may be reproduced without written permission from Gita Faust.

Table of Contents

About the Author x
Introduction xi
How to Use This Manual xii

Section 1 Getting Started

Readme 2
Chapter 1 One or Multiple Files 3
Chapter 2 Files 5
    QuickBooks Software Versions 6
    Template Files 7
    File Extensions used in QuickBooks 8
Chapter 3 Restore and Backup 9
    Restore a File 10
    Backup or Copy a File 14
    Schedule Backups 19
Chapter 4 Finding Answers 25

Section 2 QuickBooks Basics

Gita's Best Friends 28
Chapter 5 Navigating QuickBooks 29
    Menu Bar 30
    Icon Bar 30
    Home Page 31
    Company Snapshot 32
    Viewing Your Open Screens (Windows) 33
    Closing Your Screens (Windows) 33
    Saving Transactions 34
    Transaction History 34

    Journal Entry 35

    Electronic Signatures 37

    Favorites Menu 38

    Search Feature 39

    Document Management 41

    Keyboard Shortcuts in QuickBooks 42

Chapter 6 Lists 43

    List of Lists 44

    Chart of Accounts 45

    Item List 46

    Class List 47

    Other Names List 48

    Lead Center 49

    Customer Center 50

    Vendor Center 51

    Employee Center 52

Chapter 7 Working with Lists 53

    Items 54

    Grouping Items 58

    Add, Edit, Delete, and Inactivate 60

    Activate List Names 61

    Merge Within Lists 62

    Moving Other Names 63

    Bank or Credit Card Register 64

Chapter 8 Notes, To Do List, and Reminders 65

Chapter 9 Recurring (Memorizing) Transactions 71

    Create Group 73

    Memorizing a Transaction 75

    Enter Memorized Transactions 77

    Change Frequency of a Memorized Transaction 78

    Update a Memorized Transaction 79

    Delete a Memorized Transaction 79

Chapter 10 Batch Invoicing 81

Chapter 11 What Others Owe You vs. What You Owe Others 87

Chapter 12 Cash or Accrual Basis 89

Chapter 13 Chart of Accounts 91

Chapter 14 Understanding Reporting 95

    Trial Balance 96

    Cash Flow 96

    Balance Sheet 97

    Profit & Loss 97

    Splits 98

    Undeposited Funds 98

Section 3 Your Company File

Chapter 15 Company File 101

    Open Your Company File 102

    Entity Type 103

    Company Information 104

    Users and Passwords 105

    Closing Date 110

    Chart of Accounts 112

    Credit Card Accounts 113

    Enter Your Company Name 114

    Custom Fields 115

    Late Fees 116

Chapter 16 Letters and Envelopes 119

Chapter 17 Templates 127

Chapter 18 Statements 133

Chapter 19 Categorizing Records 137

    Start-up Costs 139

    Organizational Expenses 139

    Gita's Transaction Rules 140

    Fixed vs. Variable Expenses 140

    Expenses vs. Items Tab 141

Overhead vs. Property 143
CAM vs. Non-CAM Expenses 144
Chapter 20 Taxes 145

Section 4 Manage Names

Gita's Naming Rule 132
Chapter 21 Owner's Equity 153
Chapter 22 Applicants 159
Chapter 23 Property Owners 161
Chapter 24 Properties 185
Chapter 25 CAM and Non-CAM 201
Chapter 26 Units 203
Chapter 27 Tenants 213
Chapter 28 Multi-Unit Tenants 227
Chapter 29 Vendors 231

Section 5 Balances

Chapter 30 Opening Balances 245
Chapter 31 Budgets and Forecasts 251
Chapter 32 Adding Prior Rents and CAM Expenses 257

Section 6 Manage Leases and Tenants

Chapter 33 Application Fees 263
Chapter 34 Leases 269
Chapter 35 Lease Abstract (Summary) 275
Chapter 36 Deposit and Last Month Rent 283
Chapter 37 Lease Commission 293
Chapter 38 Rent Roll 297
Chapter 39 Invoices 303
Chapter 40 Payments and Deposits 311

Chapter 41 Late Fees 319
Chapter 42 Pass Thru Charges 323
Chapter 43 Bounced Check 331
Chapter 44 Credit or Write Off 337
Chapter 45 Collections and Statements 343
Chapter 46 Vacancy Loss 347

Section 7 Manage Orders and Time

Chapter 47 Purchase Orders 353
Chapter 48 Work Orders 355
Chapter 49 Track Time and Tasks 367

Section 8 Manage Vendors

Chapter 50 Writing Checks 375
Chapter 51 Petty Cash 379
Chapter 52 Entering Bills 383
    Reimbursable Expenses 387
    Enter a Bill 388
    Credit Card Charges 393
    Pay Credit Card Balance 397
    Use Time to Enter Bills 400
    Recurring Bills 402
Chapter 53 Vendor Deposits 317
Chapter 54 Prepaid Expenses 409
Chapter 55 Markups 415
Chapter 56 Vendor Credits and Refunds 421
Chapter 57 Paying Bills 335
Chapter 58 Tax Payments 437
Chapter 59 Voiding a Check 443
Chapter 60 Vendor Bounced Check 447

Section 9 Manage Equity and Loans

Chapter 61 Investment, Draw, Personal Loans, and Reimbursements 453
Chapter 62 Line of Credit 457

Section 10 Manage Bank Accounts

Chapter 63 Transferring Funds 461
Chapter 64 Online Services 465
Chapter 65 Reconcile Accounts 471

Section 11 Manage Owners and Properties

Chapter 66 Management Fees 481
Chapter 67 Reserve Funds 495
Chapter 68 Reconcile Accounts 503

Section 12 It's a No Brainer!

Chapter 69 1099 Forms 515
Chapter 70 Rent Escalation 535
Chapter 71 Expense Recovery 539
Chapter 72 Customize Your Reports 553
Chapter 73 Customized Reports For You 563

Index 567

ACKNOWLEDGEMENTS

First, thanks go to my family. My husband, Robin, for all of the little things he does to make my life easier. His support for my business has inspired me to do my best and to push forward on those early mornings and late evenings. To my son, Justin, although a senior in a college spread his wings, he knows what he wants to do. Even though far, he is just a phone call away and is the one person I can always count on speaking his mind when discussing business.

As always, my greatest gratitude goes to my clients. Without questions and feedback from real estate investors and Accountants, I would not have the knowledge and background to write a book that fits the needs of so many readers in the field of real estate accounting and property management.

I am grateful for each and every question I receive, as such inquiries improve what I do. Also, for the expressions of thanks from those who have benefited from my accounting and management system. You make me never want to retire from this business!

Gita Faust

About the Author

Gita Faust is an accountant, author, speaker business consultant, entrepreneur and real estate investor bringing practical solutions to business owners, contractors, real estate investors, professionals and property managers. As a landlord herself, Gita adapted QuickBooks software to her needs, and in doing so, has helped over 10000 clients in the field of real estate accounting.

Gita is an expertly trained Intuit Certified ProAdvisor, who offers her vast and expert knowledge to clients all over the country. A trusted resource in the field of accounting for real estate professionals and the top QuickBooks software reseller in their niche industry.

Gita has brought her accounting background, business knowledge, and experience with real estate investing and rental properties together to author a series of books, which help various real estate professionals use QuickBooks for all of their accounting and management needs:

Gita has authored a NEW! Series Simplified Accounting Solutions for the QuickBooks Desktop and Online software which has taken the industry by storm.

INTRODUCTION

Flip Real Estate with QuickBooks Desktop gives you the tools you need to confidently set up and manage the finances of your real estate investing business.

Many people think accounting is about numbers and equations in spreadsheets. While this is certainly part of the profession, the most important aspect for small business owners understands how the numbers influence the big picture of your business. This book will help you select and implement the appropriate accounting and management system based on the goals and objectives of your business.

I have worked in accounting for many years, and I have yet to find off-the-shelf financial software that is easy to use as QuickBooks. It is even better if you do not think about it as accounting software, but as an easy way to compile data and produce reports.

This manual summarizes the process of managing properties using QuickBooks. It will dispel any fears you may have by systematically showing you how to utilize simple workflows and procedures.

Following the steps in this book will save you countless hours and possible money spent on consulting, seminars, and customization of your files and reports.

Purchasing QuickBooks for your business is relatively inexpensive compared to industry-specific software, and this manual will show you how to maximize its potential.

By providing instructions on how to enter transactions and analyze your, income, and properties with hundreds of reports, I will recommend the best solutions for managing properties with QuickBooks. I will also help you organize money you receive and spend on behalf of the owner.

This comprehensive manual will answer 95% of your questions, and for anything else, feel free to contact me.

Gita Faust

How to Use This Manual

This Manual is intended to teach you how to use QuickBooks for your real estate investing business. It is suggested that you go through the book in order, from beginning to end. Do not skip parts because you believe you know that material. Finish the entire section before proceeding to the next section. Enter all of the information for one property and run the suggested reports. Once you have reviewed the manual in its entirety and set up at least one property, you will be ready to repeat the steps to enter data for all of your other properties.

Throughout the Manual, you will be instructed to open various windows and enter information. The following definitions will help you navigate the steps:

Icon: A small picture that indicates a function.

Click: Indicates you should place your mouse cursor over the word or icons indicated in the instructions and press the left button on your mouse.

Select: Refers to either choosing a selection from a list or moving your mouse cursor over the word indicated in the instructions to highlight it for an additional menu or list of choices.

Enter: Usually refers to the actual typing of data. For example, "Enter the address" means to type the address into the area instructed. This does not mean press the "Enter" key. You will be instructed to press the Enter key when that is necessary.

Screen: Refers to the image you are looking at on your computer monitor. The instructions will tell you to open individual QuickBooks screens and how to open the screen.

Screen Shot: A picture of a QuickBooks screen reproduced in this Manual.

Field: The places on the screen, which appear as empty rectangles with words above or to the left, indicating the names of the fields.

Data: The information you type into the empty boxes next to the field is called data and may include property addresses, names, monthly amounts due, etc. Some books refer to fields as data fields, but we do not want to confuse this with our term, Field Data Tables.

Drop down menu: To enter some data, there may be prefilled choices from which you choose the most appropriate option. Often, there is a drop down menu for fields. When clicked, it will display options.

Field Data Tables: Throughout the Manual, you will be given guidelines as to what should be entered into QuickBooks to track your information. Typing the correct information in the appropriate places will enable you to develop reports. These reports will summarize the information in an orderly fashion, allowing you to manage properties and your money efficiently.

You will see Field Data Tables, like the sample below, listing the name of each field on a screen in the left column and what data to type into the corresponding field in the right column. These tables appear below many screens that have fields for data entry.

Field	Data
Customer	Enter the Property Name
Date	Enter the date you wish to make the payment

In the example above, we are instructing you to enter a property name in the field labeled "Customer" and to enter the date you wish to make the payment in the field labeled "Date."

Tab: Use the tab key to move from field to field on a screen.

TIP, NOTE, and **IMPORTANT:** In certain areas, additional information or cautions are provided to emphasize the importance of a concept or a limitation. This information is often found in a box, bold printed, or otherwise made more visible.

IMPORTANT

This manual is intended to help you start using QuickBooks correctly. You will be on the fast track to improving your business and saving time when you implement Gita Faust's system for accounting and management of your real estate investing business. Enter transactions as per our instructions to get results as we have outlined.

With Purchase: You are Entitled

Good news! With the purchase of the book, you are entitled to the following:

- Bonus! Define Your Business
- A downloadable, customized QuickBooks file with reports
- Access to our how to videos for Your Business

Claim: Send Proof of Purchase

To request your file and learn how to access additional resources, send an email to support@RealEstateAccounting.com with the following information:

1. Your order number (include a copy of your receipt)
2. The exact title of the book you purchased
3. The email provided at the time of purchase (files are sent to that email only)
4. The QuickBooks version you are using (including year and country)

SECTION 1

GETTING STARTED

This manual is designed for QuickBooks users of all levels: basic, intermediate and advanced users. Some readers may have more experience, and others may be using QuickBooks for the first time.

Whichever category you fall into, we recommend that you read each chapter even though you may believe that you can skip one. This is because many chapters are interrelated and include specific instructions, which build on one another.

To start, you will learn how to copy the template file, as well as backup and restore files. Upon opening our custom designed template, you will enter basic information about your Company and begin to apply best business practices.

README

The author does not imply or instruct that QuickBooks will automatically calculate percentage rent, base year and expense stop, gross up, rent escalation, expense recovery, and CAM.

However, if you enter transactions per her instruction, you can view reports and create your template for additional calculations.

CHAPTER 1 ONE OR MULTIPLE FILES

Before working with the provided QuickBooks template file, decide how you will manage your back office accounting for rental properties.

You can use one QuickBooks file to manage all properties or multiple files, one file for each property, depending on your agreement with the property owner.

Property Management

One QuickBooks file may be created for all of the owners, in which you would enter all money received and spent on behalf of the owners. This would include tenant management, expenses for the unit, and all disbursement of owner's funds.

QuickBooks Files Needed (2): Management and Office

Your Rental Office

In another scenario, a file may be created for all your office accounting. This file is a combination of payments that are not the responsibility of the owner, such as payroll, office supplies, and other items necessary to run the business. We recommend opening an additional bank account.

QuickBooks Files Needed (2): Management and Office

Property Management and Rental Office

One file includes all property management and office money received and spent. It is, in theory, a combination of both #1 and #2.

QuickBooks Files Needed (1): Combination

File For Each Owner

We do not recommend multiple files unless the owner pays you three times more than your current management fees for all the extra work. Having multiple files can be more time consuming for day-to-day management as you will have to open and close each property QuickBooks file to enter transactions. There is a higher chance of error with the possibility of entering data into the wrong company file. You would also need to open and maintain bank accounts for each property.

QuickBooks Files Needed (Multiple): per Property Owner and Office

The decision is yours, but to be honest – Keep one file for everything.

IMPORTANT
We strongly suggest you consult with a real estate CPA and/or attorney.

CHAPTER 2 TEMPLATE FILES

A template file, including a Chart of Accounts and hundreds of memorized reports and transactions, is included with the purchase of this manual. The template file is a QuickBooks file customized for the accounting and management of your properties.

Objectives

Upon completion of this chapter, you will be able to:

- Understand QuickBooks Software
- View and Download the Template File
- Access the Define Your Business Bonus
- Learn QuickBooks File Extensions

QUICKBOOKS SOFTWARE VERSIONS

You will need to have QuickBooks Desktop software installed on your computer.

To use QuickBooks for accounting and management, we recommend you purchase one of the following:

- QuickBooks Pro
- QuickBooks Premier
- QuickBooks Premier Accountant
- Intuit Enterprise Accountant, which includes Intuit Statement Writer and QODBC (QODBC is a report writing tool for accessing the data in your QuickBooks files)

Before you start using this manual, you should be aware of QuickBooks Intuit software limitations. You can view reports, export reports into Excel, and create your templates for additional calculation, but QuickBooks will not automatically calculate percentage unless you create a process for it. We have addressed this the best we can.

We recommend hosting your software and data in "the cloud" or a secure online server with on-demand access. We offer cloud solutions, which provide online access to your QuickBooks software and files 24/7.

Contact our support team with any questions you may have. We are your one-stop shop for real estate and property management needs. We offer report customization, custom programming and will answer your questions about purchasing software, hosting, document management, and automating your office.

TEMPLATE FILES

Template files are only available for the US desktop versions of Pro, Premier, and Enterprise at this time.

> **IMPORTANT**
> We follow the Sunset Policy, put forth by Intuit, which does not support software and offer a template file that is more than three years old.
>
> Read more at http://support.quickbooks.intuit.com/support/articles/INF12842.

> **NOTE**
> If you are using a previous version, you should still be able to restore the file. If not, send us an email with the following information:
>
> 1. Your order number (include a copy of your receipt)
> 2. The exact title of the book you purchased
> 3. The email provided at the time of purchase (files are sent to that email only)
> 4. The QuickBooks version you are using (including year
> 5. Send an email to support@realestateaccounting.com

You will receive an email with the files to download. If you do not receive the email or have difficulties or questions about the download, contact the author, providing the information listed above. We will gladly help you get started, or answer any questions you may have.

When you download the template file, you will receive complete instructions including the file password. If you are using a newer version of QuickBooks, follow the prompts to update the restored file.

TEMPLATE FILES

FILE EXTENSIONS USED IN QUICKBOOKS

The following table describes the QuickBooks file extensions:

Extension	File type	Description
.DES	QuickBooks form template	QuickBooks provides a variety of templates that you can use for your forms.
.IIF	Intuit Interchange Format File	You can import and export lists and/or transactions using text files with an .IIF extension.
.ND	QuickBooks Network Data File	A configuration file that allows access to the QuickBooks company file. Do not delete this configuration file.
.QBA	Accountant's Copy working file	When you export your QuickBooks data for your accountant's review, the accountant restores the export file on his or her computer as a file with a .QBA extension.
.QBA.TLG	Transaction log file (for Accountant's Copy)	When you back up an Accountant's Copy, QuickBooks starts a log of transactions that you have entered since the last time you backed up. The file is created during backup provided you have set a verification level. In the case of accidental loss of data, Technical Support can use your most recent backup in conjunction with the transaction log file to recover your data.
.QBB	QuickBooks backup file	When you back up your company file, QuickBooks saves the backup file with a .QBB extension. To open a .QBB file, go to the File menu and click **Restore**.
.QBM	QuickBooks portable company file	When you want to e-mail or move a company file, QuickBooks creates a compressed version of the company file with a .QBM extension.
.QBR	Report template	When you export the template for a memorized report, QuickBooks saves the file with a .QBR extension.
.QBW	QuickBooks for Windows company file	When you create a company file, QuickBooks saves the file with a .QBW extension. For example, if you enter MyBusiness as the company name, QuickBooks saves the file as MyBusiness.QBW.
.QBW.TLG	Transaction log file (for QuickBooks company file)	When you back up your company file, QuickBooks starts a log of transactions that you have entered since the last time you backed up. In the case of accidental loss of data, Technical Support can use your most recent backup in conjunction with the transaction log file to recover your data. This log file is also used if you sync your QuickBooks data with certain online services using Intuit Sync Manager. This allows ongoing syncs to happen much more quickly than the initial full upload of QuickBooks data into your online services.
.QBX	Accountant's Copy (export file)	When you export your QuickBooks data for your accountant's review, QuickBooks creates an Accountant's Copy with a .QBX extension.
.QBY	Accountant's Copy (import file)	When your accountant is finished making changes in an Accountant's Copy, he or she provides you with a .QBY file to be imported into your company file.

Table 1 File Extensions Used in QuickBooks

CHAPTER 3 RESTORE AND BACKUP

Creating backups will help you to avoid data corruption, errors of your data file, and data loss due to machine failure. A good policy is to perform backups on a weekly, monthly, <u>and</u> annual basis.

You can schedule backups that take place at these regular intervals, even when you are away from your desk. Your computer must be on and your data file must be closed. You will then be prepared to restore a backup, if and when it becomes necessary.

To ensure your backup file is not corrupted, restore the file and check the balances.

Objectives

Upon completion of this chapter, you will be able to:

- Restore Your File
- Backup Your File
- Copy a File
- Schedule Automatic Backups

RESTORE A FILE

> **IMPORTANT**
> To best use this manual, we recommend you restore and use the template file provided. If you do not have the template file, refer to the chapter on Files to learn how to request it.

After copying or downloading the files included, restore appropriate backup files.

A backup is a copy of your file which is stored on a removable storage device such as rewriteable CD/DVD, external hard drive, or a memory stick.

Under certain circumstances, you may need to restore a QuickBooks data file from a backup copy. The process differs depending on whether the backup file is saved in a local or remote location.

Restoring a backup uncompresses the file and creates a new company file using the backup data.

If you saved your company file using an online service, you must restore it to that same service.

RESTORE AND BACKUP

To restore the template file:

- Click **File** on the Menu Bar
- Click Open or Restore Company...

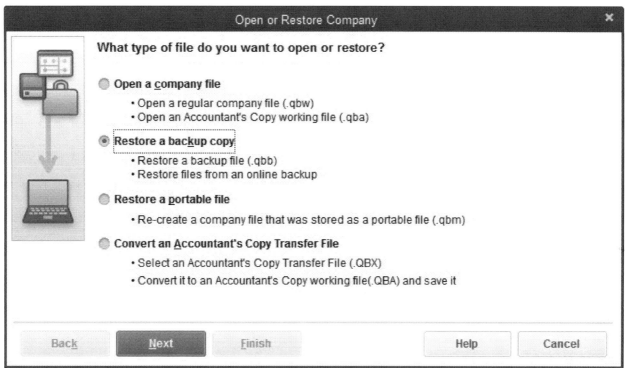
Screen Shot 1 Open or Restore Company

- Select Restore a backup copy
- Click Next
- Select Local backup
- Click **Next**

Restore and Backup

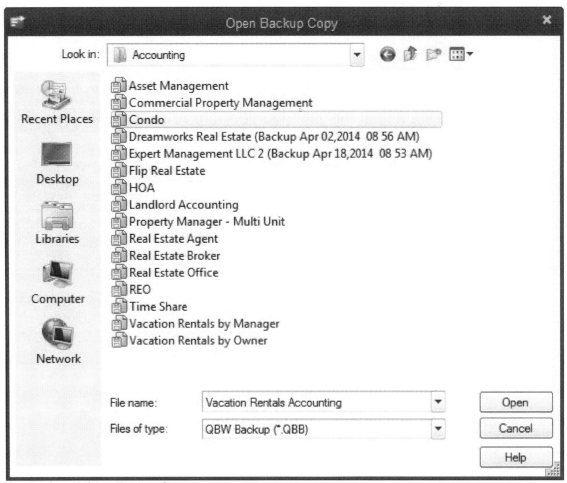

Screen Shot 2 Open Backup Copy

- Open the folder that contains the downloaded or copied file
- Select the file
- Click **Open**
- Click **Next**
- Double-click on the folder in which you would like to save the file
- Rename the file to your Company's name
- Click **Save**

Restore and Backup

It may take a few minutes to restore, update, and convert the file and data. A window advising you to update the company file for a new version may appear.

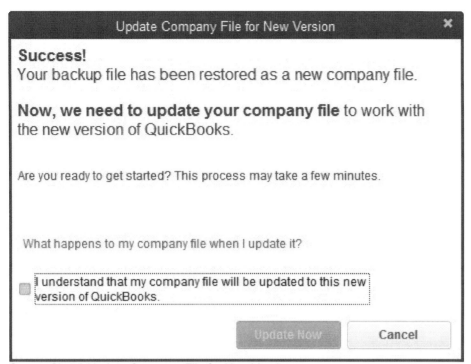

Screen Shot 3 Update Company File for New Version

- Select the box indicating you understand the file will be updated
- Click Update Now
- Click **Yes** to verify, convert, and rebuild the data
-
- This step will create a working file with the file extension .QBW.

BACKUP OR COPY A FILE

You may wish to create a copy of your backup file, portable file, or an accountant's copy.

IMPORTANT
To backup, the Loan Manager file manually, search for a file with extension *.lmr.

The process to create a backup and portable file are the same. However, when creating the portable file, the time and date stamp will not auto-populate in the file name, so you must manually add this information.

To backup or copy your file:

- Click **File** on the Menu Bar
- Select Create Copy…

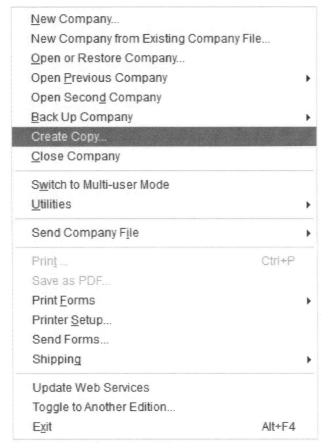

Screen Shot 4 Create Local Backup

RESTORE AND BACKUP

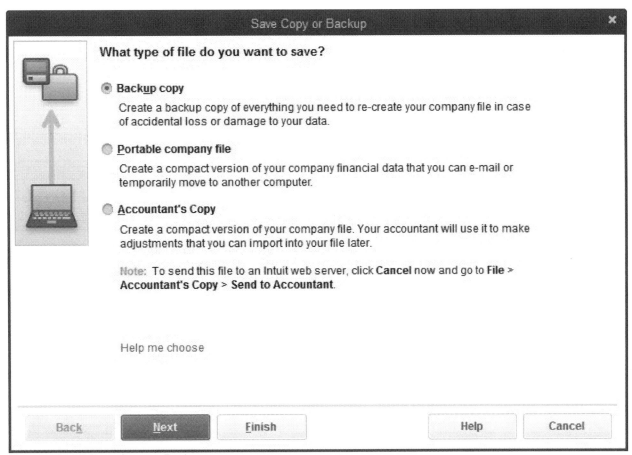
Screen Shot 5 Save Copy or Backup

- Select the type of file you want to create
- Click **Next**
- Click **Local backup**
- Click **Next**

RESTORE AND BACKUP

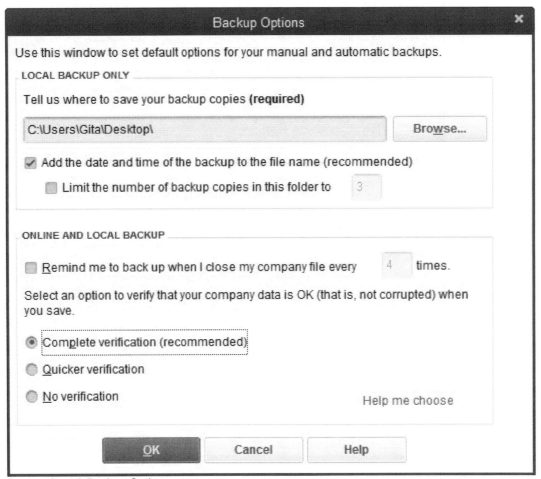
Screen Shot 6 Backup Options

- Click **Browse...** to choose the location to save the backup file
- Check the box Add the date and time of the backup to the file name (recommended)
- Select Complete verification (recommended)
- Click **OK**

RESTORE AND BACKUP

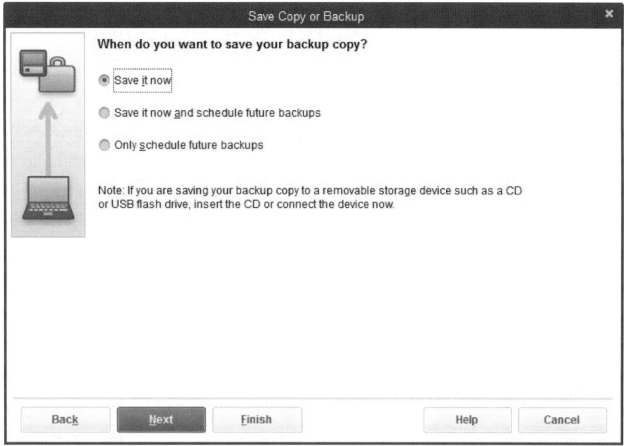

Screen Shot 7 Save Copy or Backup When to Save

- Select Save it now
- Click **Next**

NOTE
Select Save it now and schedule future backups or Only schedule future backups to schedule future automatic backups. Refer to the section on Schedule Backups at the end of this chapter.

Restore and Backup

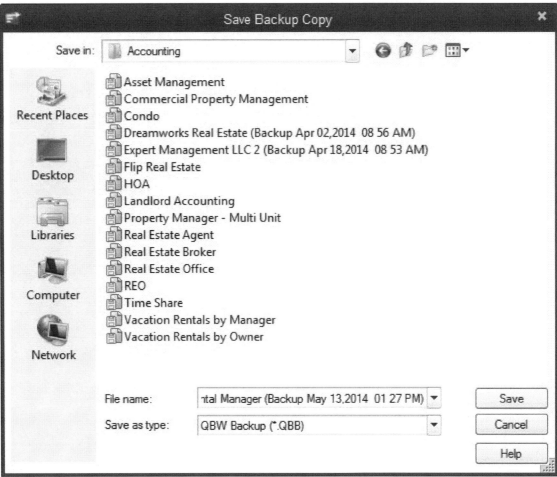

Screen Shot 8 Save Backup Copy

- Click **Save**

QuickBooks confirms when the backup is complete.

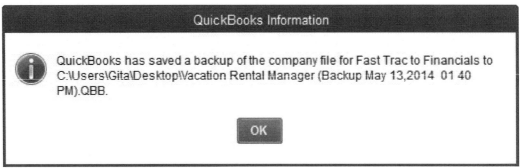

Screen Shot 9 QuickBooks Information

- Click **OK**

SCHEDULE BACKUPS

Schedule backups to be sure you do not lose important information.

To schedule future automatic backups:

- From the Create Backup screen, select either Save it now and schedule future backups or Only schedule future backups
- Click **Next**

Screen Shot 10 Create Backup When to Save

Restore and Backup

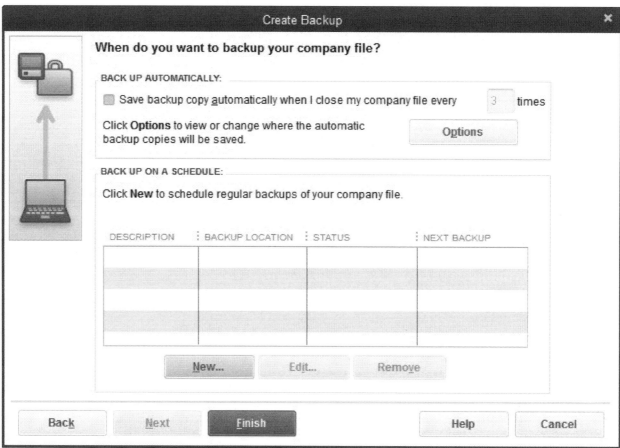

Screen Shot 11 Create Backup When to Backup

- Click **Options** at the top of the screen

RESTORE AND BACKUP

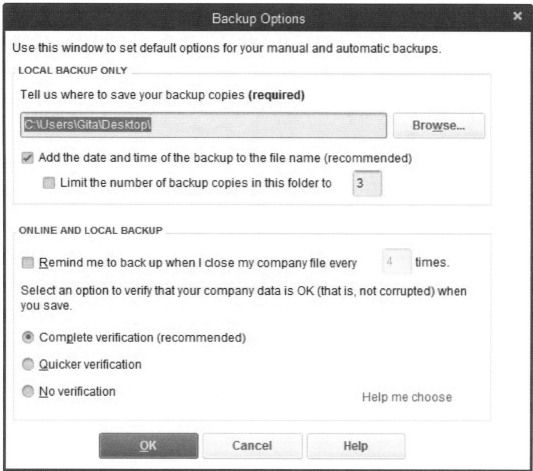

Screen Shot 12 Backup Options

- Click **Browse...** to choose the location to save the backup file
- Check the box, Add the date and time of the backup to the file name (recommended)
- Select Complete verification (recommended)
- Click **OK**

Restore and Backup

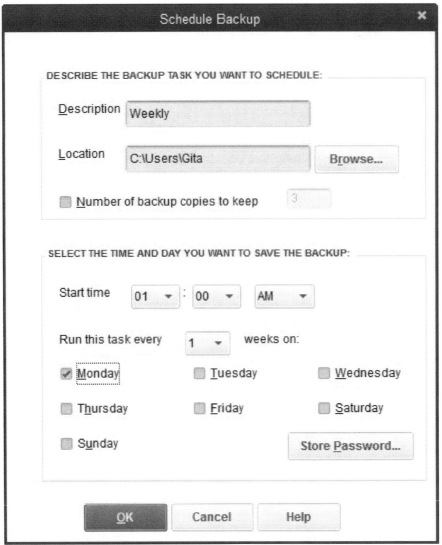

Screen Shot 13 Schedule Backup

- Enter a name for the backup in the Description field
- Browse to the location of where you want the file to be saved
- Select the time and frequency for which you want to save the backup
- Click Store Password

RESTORE AND BACKUP

The Store Windows Password window appears.

Screen Shot 14 Store Windows Password

- Enter the username and password you use to login to your computer
- Click **OK**

RESTORE AND BACKUP

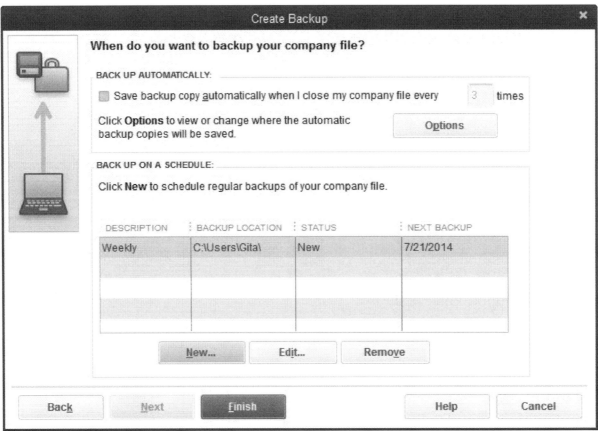

Screen Shot 15 Create Backup When to Backup with Scheduled Details

- Confirm the details of your scheduled backup
- Click **Finish**

QuickBooks confirms the backups have been scheduled.

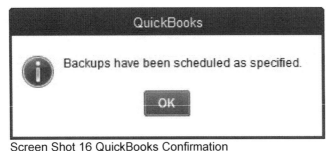

Screen Shot 16 QuickBooks Confirmation

- Click **OK**

Commercial Property Management for Managers: QuickBooks Desktop

CHAPTER 4 FINDING ANSWERS

Situations may arise for which you need additional assistance. There are many resources available to help answer your questions or address your concerns.

QuickBooks is powerful and easy to use but can be a challenge for those in the real estate and property management business.

Objectives

Upon completion of this chapter, you will be able to:

- Find Answers in QuickBooks
- Contact the Author
- Ask for a Local QuickBooks Advisor and/or a Certified QuickBooks ProAdvisor

FINDING ANSWERS

To find answers to your questions in QuickBooks:

- Click **Help** on the Menu Bar
- Click Live Community or QuickBooks Help

If you are looking for an experienced real estate and property management accountant or QuickBooks advisor, contact the author, who can refer you to a local experienced real estate or property management advisor.

NEED HELP?

Gita Faust, with her team, helps clients stay relevant in the industry, by providing knowledge, procedures, processes, and tools to enhance your business and analyze financials.

We offer **traditional accounting services** with a twist. Let us help you look for **hidden profits**— changes you can make to **improve your bottom line**.

We are here to help you save time and money. We can help you achieve your dreams with the services listed below and more.

- Bookkeeping
- Setup and Training
- Custom Application
- Data Conversion
- Data Transfer
- File Review
- File Cleanup

- Hosting Data Files
- Integration
- Programming
- Reporting
- Support
- Training

Our clientele includes small to medium to large sized businesses, from one to 30 users, and various industries from construction, retail, manufacturing, wholesale to nonprofit and e-commerce.

Plan for the future! Measure the consequences on profitability, working capital, cash flow, and returns on invested dollars. Let us help you streamline your business and get to the next level!

To contact the author, Gita Faust and her team, who will gladly assist you:

- Visit www.RealEstateAccounting.com
- Email support@RealEstateAccounting.com

SECTION 2

QUICKBOOKS BASICS

Before you dig into customizing your company's file and using QuickBooks for your financial recording, you need to understand the basic layout and functions of the software. Although QuickBooks is user-friendly, becoming acquainted with its various functions will help you to improve the efficiency of your daily operations.

In the following chapters, we will explore both basic functions and special features of QuickBooks. You will see how easily adaptable the software is for managing your finances on a cash or accrual basis, and how it allows you to produce basic financial reports for your Company easily. You will learn how to use the time management tools within QuickBooks, as well as familiarize yourself with some basic and advanced transactions such as invoicing, reconciling, and deposits.

Gita's Rules—she makes them and then breaks them. For now, you should follow the tips and rules provided in this chapter. They are intended to supplement the content of this manual and serve as a reference guide.

Gita's Best Friends

Tab Key: Within a form, press the Tab Key to move from one field to the next.

Esc Key: Press the Esc Key to close the current window.

Right-click: Within a list or form, right-click to apply an action to the selected name or transaction.

Double-click: Double-click a name or amount to edit a name or open a transaction type.

Magnifying Glass: Within a report, double-click on the magnifying glass to view a detailed transaction breakdown or to open a form or list.

Search: Look for any character/s or number in your file. Just like you would search in Google.

CHAPTER 5 NAVIGATING QUICKBOOKS

The QuickBooks workspace gives you fast access to the features and reports you use most. Customize your view of the workspace to reflect how you move through QuickBooks, find features, and switch between windows. There are many ways to easily access QuickBooks data and process transactions through menus, shortcut lists, navigators, and the Icon Bar.

Objectives

Upon completion of this chapter, you will be able to:

- Navigate the Menu Bar
- View the Icon Bar
- View the Home Page
- Customize the Company Snapshot
- View Open Screens and Close Your Screens
- Save Transactions
- View Transaction History
- View and Add a Journal Entry and an Electronic Signature
- Customize Favorites
- Use the Search Feature
- Navigate Document Management
- View Keyboard Shortcuts

Navigating QuickBooks

Menu Bar

The Menu Bar can be used to access any form, activity, list, or report in QuickBooks. Click on any item on the Menu Bar to expand function.

File Edit View Lists Favorites Accountant Company Customers Vendors Employees Inventory Banking Reports Window Help
Screen Shot 17 Menu Bar

Icon Bar

The Icon Bar gives you one-click access to many QuickBooks features. Notice the file provided to you already has a customized Icon Bar.

To view the Icon Bar:

- Click **View** on the Menu Bar
- Click Top Icon Bar

Screen Shot 18 Icon Bar

HOME PAGE

The Home Page gives you a picture of your day-to-day business transactions, your Company Finances, Banking, Customers, Vendors, Employees, and more.

To view the Home Page:

- Click **Company** on the Menu Bar
- Select Home Page

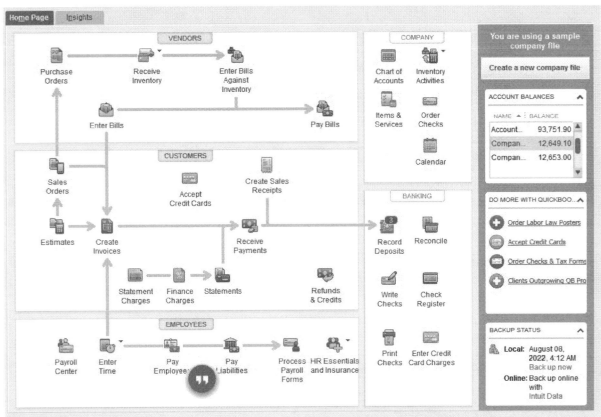

Screen Shot 19 Home Page

COMPANY SNAPSHOT

The Company Snapshot provides real-time company information, from income and expense trends to accounts receivable and accounts payable, account balances, and more. You can customize the content and details displayed in the snapshot.

To view your Company Snapshot:

- Click **Company** on the Menu Bar
- Select Company Snapshot

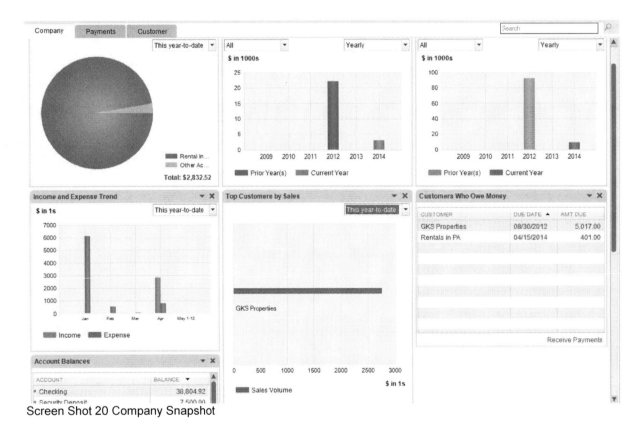

Screen Shot 20 Company Snapshot

VIEWING YOUR OPEN SCREENS (WINDOWS)

The Open Windows box appears on the left of your screen when you have one or more open screens (windows). For example, you may have a data entry screen open while you also have multiple forms open. You can only see one screen at a time, but you can see the list of screens in the Open Windows box. Select the screen you wish to view to switch from one to another.

To view the Open Windows box:

- Click **View** on the Menu Bar
- Select Open Window List

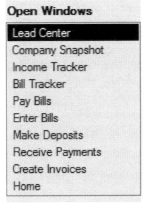

Screen Shot 21 Open Windows

CLOSING YOUR SCREENS (WINDOWS)

To completely close a window and remove it from Open Windows box, hit **Esc** (the escape key) on your keyboard while viewing the window. If you have made any changes, you will have the option to save before closing.

SAVING TRANSACTIONS

Click **Save & Close** to save the current transaction and close the window.

Click **Save & New** to save the current transaction and open a new window to enter the next transaction.

TRANSACTION HISTORY

To view Transaction History, select reports and click **Transaction History** on the top of the transaction screen.

Screen Shot 22 Transaction History

JOURNAL ENTRY

In accounting, journal entries are used to record transactions. The amounts are debited from one account and credited to another account. For day-to-day transactions, we do not recommend using journal entries aside from the year-end adjustments.

QuickBooks automatically creates journal entries from the information entered on invoices, bills, checks, and other forms.

To view a journal entry for any transaction, click **Journal** on the top of the transaction screen. Account names, as well as debit and credit amounts, appear.

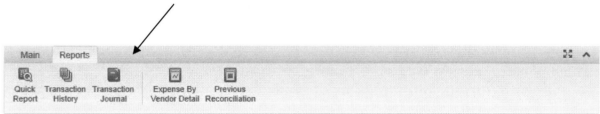

Screen Shot 23 Transaction Journal

NAVIGATING QUICKBOOKS

To Add a Journal Entry

To add a journal entry:

- Click **Company** on the Menu Bar
- Click **Make General Journal Entries…**

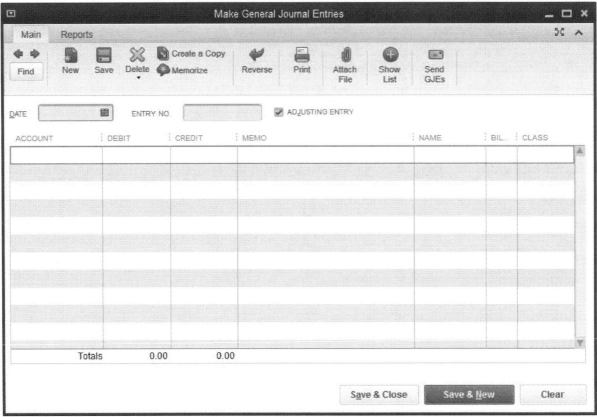
Screen Shot 24 Make General Journal Entries

The amounts in the Debit column must equal the amounts in the Credit column. Specify Name and Class where appropriate.

ELECTRONIC SIGNATURES

To add an electronic signature on a check:

- Click **File**
- Click **Printer Setup…**
- Select Check/PayCheck for Form Name
- Click **Signature** on far bottom right
- Click **File** to upload the file

Screen Shot 25 Signature

- Click **OK**

NAVIGATING QUICKBOOKS

FAVORITES MENU

Customize the Favorites Menu with your most frequently used functions to work faster and easily access tasks in a list format.

To customize your Favorites:

- Click **Favorites** on the Menu Bar
- Click **Customize Favorites…**
- Select the items to add to Favorites Menu
- Click **Add**

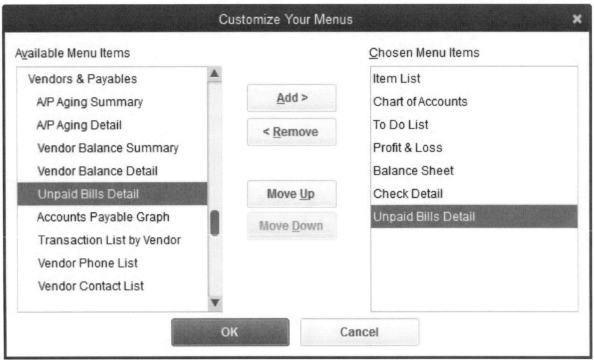

Screen Shot 26 Customize Your Menus

- Click **OK**

Commercial Property Management for Managers: QuickBooks Desktop

NAVIGATING QUICKBOOKS

To view the updated list:

- Click **Favorites** on the Menu Bar
- Select a specific category

Screen Shot 27 View Favorites

SEARCH FEATURE

In 2011, QuickBooks implemented a new Search feature, which is similar to the Google search feature.

To use the Search feature:

- Click **View** on the Menu Bar
- Click **Search Box**

Screen Shot 28 Search Feature

Search the file by typing keyword(s) in the search field. If it has been entered in QuickBooks, it will be found.

Alternatively, type keyword(s) directly to the search box on the Icon Bar (on the far right of the screen).

Navigating QuickBooks

For example, when we perform a search for Home Depot, all the related records are located:

Screen Shot 29 Search Results

Hold the cursor over each record for a list of available functions.

DOCUMENT MANAGEMENT

Add or scan any document to a form, list, or transaction in QuickBooks.

> **NOTE**
> Click 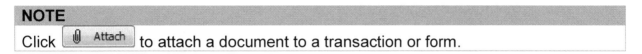 to attach a document to a transaction or form.

To view the Doc Center:

- Click **Company**
- Select Documents
- Click **Doc Center**

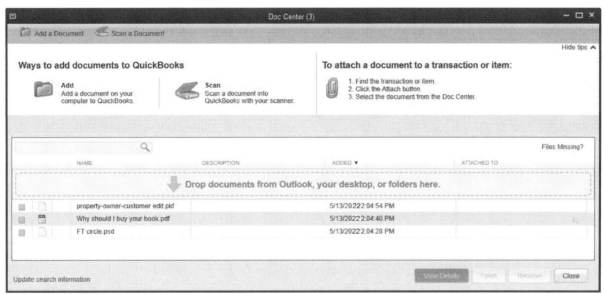
Screen Shot 30 Doc Center

KEYBOARD SHORTCUTS IN QUICKBOOKS

The following are the most common keyboard shortcuts in QuickBooks:

Key	Date
+ (plus key)	Next day
- (minus key)	Previous day
T	Today

Key	Editing
Ctrl + E	Edit transaction selected in register
Ctrl + Del	Delete line from detail area
Ctrl + Ins	Insert line in detail area
Ctrl + X	Cut selected characters
Ctrl + C	Copy selected characters
Ctrl + V	Paste, cut, or copied characters
Ctrl + Z	Undo changes made in a field

Key	Numbers
+ (plus key)	Increase check or another form number by one
- (minus key)	Decrease check or another form number by one

Key	Activity
Ctrl + A	Account list, display chart of accounts
Ctrl + W	Check, write
Ctrl + J	Customer:Job list, display
Ctrl + D	Delete check, invoice, transaction, or item from list
Ctrl + E	Edit lists or registers
Ctrl + F	Find transaction
Ctrl + H	History of A/R or A/P transaction
Ctrl + I	Invoice, create
Ctrl + L	List (for current field), display
Ctrl + N	New invoice, bill, check, or list item
Ctrl + P	Print
Ctrl + R	Register, display
Ctrl + Y	Transaction journal, display

Key	Memorize Transaction
Ctrl + M	Memorize transaction or report
Ctrl + T	Memorize transaction list, display

Key	Moving around a window
Tab	Next field

CHAPTER 6 LISTS

Lists are the framework of QuickBooks. Lists are helpful for completing everyday business tasks like writing checks or contacting vendors. Lists contain vital information such as names, addresses, and account numbers, which conveniently prefill on forms. This saves you time and reduces typing errors. If necessary, you can also change the information directly on the form.

In this chapter, we will give a brief introduction of each list and show you how to view them. The functions of each will be elaborated on later in the manual.

Objectives

Upon completion of this chapter, you will be able to:

- View List of Lists
- View Chart of Accounts
- View Item List
- View Class List
- View Other Names List
- View Lead Center
- View Customer Center
- View Vendor Center
- View Employee Center

LIST OF LISTS

Lists are easy to set up in QuickBooks but some Lists, such as the Chart of Accounts, Item List, and Class List, require careful planning.

To view the list of Lists:

- Click **Lists** on the Menu Bar
- Select Customer and Vendor Profile Lists, as needed, for additional lists

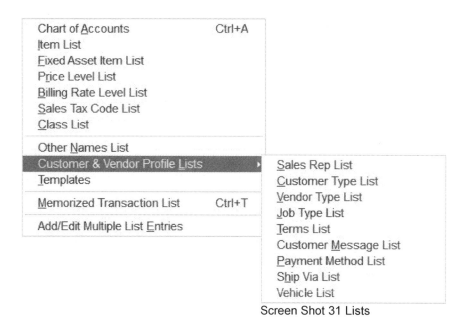

Screen Shot 31 Lists

CHART OF ACCOUNTS

The Chart of Accounts is a list of all Assets, Liabilities, Equity, Income, and Expenses. The template file is customized to manage your company and includes relevant accounts. Refer to the chapter on Files for more information.

To view the Chart of Accounts:

- Click **Lists** on the Menu Bar
- Select Chart of Accounts

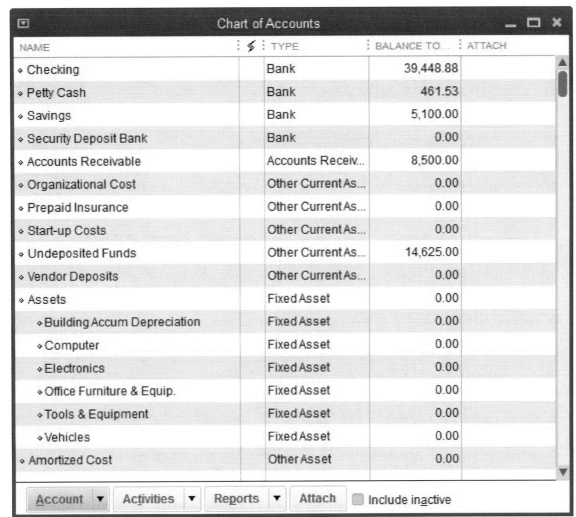

Screen Shot 32 Chart of Accounts List

Commercial Property Management for Managers: QuickBooks Desktop

ITEM LIST

The Item List is used to identify goods and services provided or received. Always use the Service Item type for services you provide or purchase like specialized labor, consulting, or professional fees. Use Inventory to track quantity on hand for objects you buy and sell.

Items are used to categorize transactions. Each item is associated with a description and is linked to an account in the Chart of Accounts.

To view the Item List:

- Click **Lists** on the Menu Bar
- Select Item List

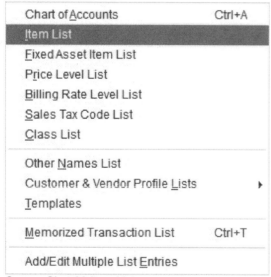
Screen Shot 33 Item List

Fixed Asset Item List is only available in QuickBooks Accountant and Enterprise versions.

Price Level List and Billing Rate Level List is only available in QuickBooks Premier, Accountant and Enterprise versions.

CLASS LIST

The Class List identifies properties and your company's overhead. Each and every transaction MUST specify a Class (whether it is a specific property name or Your Company).

The Overhead class relates to business transactions which cannot be applied to a specific property. Things like office expenses, telephone, computers, bank service charges, furniture, equipment, loans, and utilities for the office.

To view the Class List:

- Click **Lists** on the Menu Bar
- Select Class List

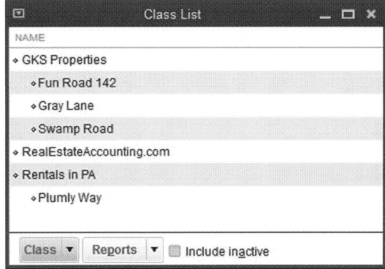
Screen Shot 34 Class List

LISTS

OTHER NAMES LIST

IMPORTANT
DO NOT USE OTHER NAMES. The names on the Other Names List do not always reflect on reports. For example, the Vendor Summary report does not show transactions from the Other Names List.

To view the Other Names List:

- Click **Lists** on the Menu Bar
- Select Other Names List

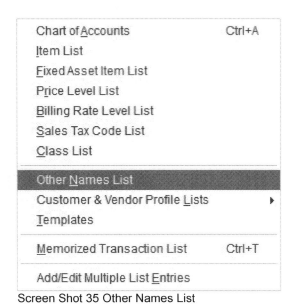
Screen Shot 35 Other Names List

TIP
You can select names from the Other Names List when you write checks or enter credit card charges but not when entering bills or work orders.

Commercial Property Management for Managers: QuickBooks Desktop

LISTS

LEAD CENTER

Lead is a potential prospect. You may wish to keep track of contact information and interactions as a part of your sales strategy. Manage your leads with the Lead Center in QuickBooks.

To view and add leads:

- Click **Company** on Icon Bar
- Select Lead Center

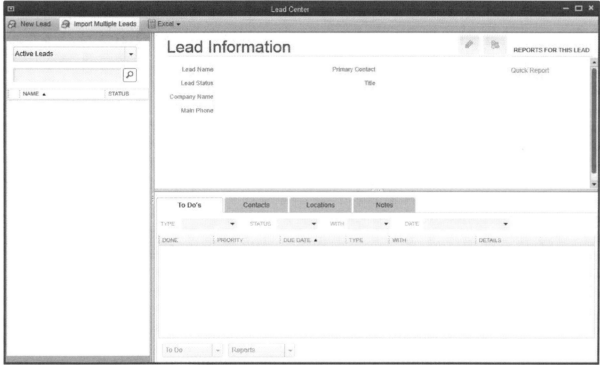

Screen Shot 36 Lead Center

Add or import Leads to track contact information, their specification, and other notes, as well as associate related tasks and priorities.

LISTS

CUSTOMER CENTER

The Customer Center is a central location for managing properties and units. The Customer Center easily organizes contact information, transaction history, to do list, notes, emails, collection center and income tracker.

To view the Customer Center:

- Click **Customer** on the Menu Bar
- Select Customer Center

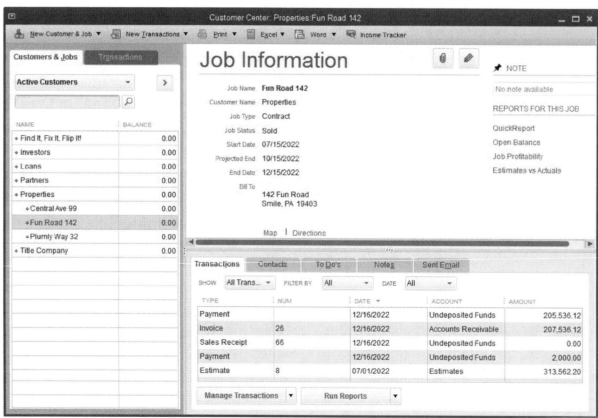
Screen Shot 37 Customer Center

Commercial Property Management for Managers: QuickBooks Desktop

LISTS

VENDOR CENTER

The Vendor Center displays people or companies you have paid or will pay for services, labor, and materials. Access the Vendor Center to view contact information, transaction history, balances, to do list, notes, emails and bill tracker.

To take a look at the Vendor Center:

- Click **Vendors** on the Menu Bar
- Select Vendor Center

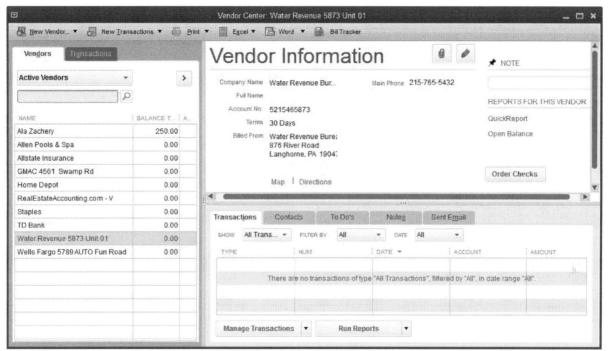
Screen Shot 38 Vendor Center

Commercial Property Management for Managers: QuickBooks Desktop

LISTS

EMPLOYEE CENTER

The Employee Center displays payroll and personal information for employees.

To take a look at the Employee Center:

- Click **Employees** on the Menu Bar
- Select Employee Center

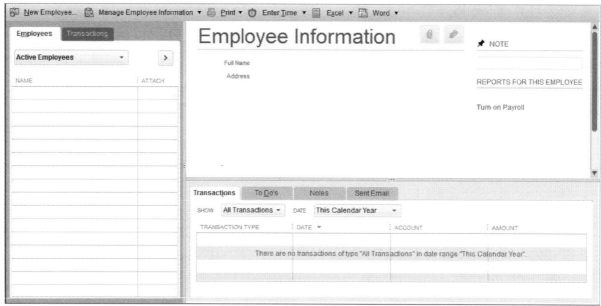
Screen Shot 39 Employee Center

NOTE
We will not be covering the functions of the Employee Center in the manual.

Commercial Property Management for Managers: QuickBooks Desktop

CHAPTER 7 WORKING WITH LISTS

QuickBooks lists are customizable for your business needs. When working with any of the lists, the same procedures apply for adding, editing, deleting, or inactivating list items.

Objectives

Upon completion of this chapter, you will be able to:

- Understanding Items
- View, Add, Edit, Delete, and Group Items
- Add, Edit, Delete, and Inactivate Names
- Activate Names
- Merge within Lists
- Move Other Names
- Add Custom Fields
- View Registers

ITEMS

Items provide a quick means of data entry and organize behind the scenes accounting. QuickBooks Items represent everything on a sale or purchase form; for example, services and products you sell or things you buy. You use Items when you create invoices, write checks, create purchase orders, or buy new equipment.

Consider how much detail you want to track on your invoices and statements, and set up your Items with that level in mind. Refer to the table below for types of Items.

Use this type	For
Services	Services you charge for or purchase. This includes specialized labor, consulting hours, and professional fees.
Inventory Part	Goods you purchase track as inventory and resell.
Non-Inventory Part	Goods you buy, but do not track (such as office supplies), or materials you buy for a specific job that you charge back to your customer.
Other Charge	Includes miscellaneous labor, materials, or part charges such as delivery charges, setup fees, service charges, bounced checks, late fees, opening balance, reimbursable expenses, retainers, surcharges, gift certificates, prepayments, retainers, sales tax, and shipping and handling fees.
Subtotal	Totals all items above it on a form, up to the last subtotal. Useful for applying a percentage discount or surcharge to many Items.
Group	Associates individual Items that often appear together on invoices, purchase orders, and so on, so that all Items in the group can be added to the form at one time.
Discount	Subtract a percentage or fixed amount from a total or subtotal. Do not use this Item type for an early payment discount.
Sales Tax Item	Used to calculate a single sales tax at a specific rate that you pay to a single tax agency.
Sales Tax Group	Used to calculate and individually track two or more sales tax items that apply to the same sale (the customer only sees the total sales tax).

Table 2 Types of Items

New Item

Link each Item to an Expense and/or Income account. If you change any Items in the template file, check the reports for accuracy.

To create a new Item:

- Click **Lists** on the Menu Bar
- Select Item List

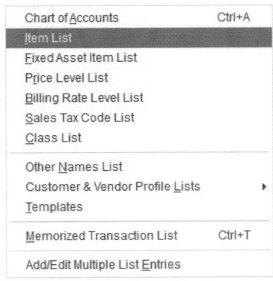

Screen Shot 40 Item List

- Right-click on the Item and select New

Working with Lists

The New Item window appears.

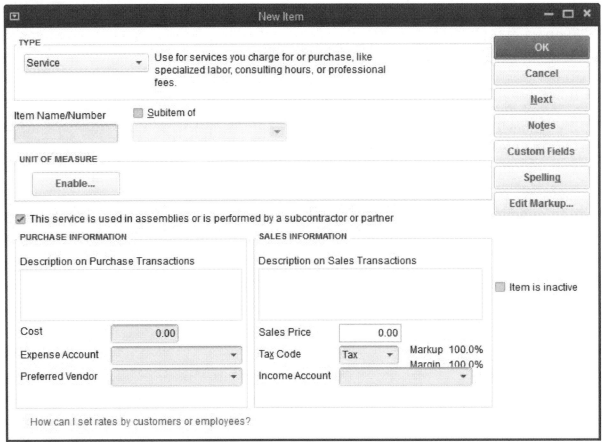

Screen Shot 41 New Item

WORKING WITH LISTS

- Complete the fields as follows:

Field	Data
Type	Select from drop down menu
Item Name/Number	Name
Subitem of	As needed
(The following sentence will be different depending on the Item type you selected) This item is used in assemblies or is a reimbursable charge	Check the box, as needed
Purchase Information	
Description on Purchase Transactions	If you use the same description for all transactions, enter when creating the Item. If not, leave it blank. You can change it in the future if needed.
Cost	ZERO
Expense Account	Select from drop down menu
Preferred Vendor	As needed
Sales Information	
Description on Sales Transactions	If you use the same description for all transactions, enter when creating the Item. If not, leave it blank. You can change it in the future if needed.
Sales Price	As needed – Leave blank if the amount changes each time you use this Item
Tax Code	As needed
Income Account	Select from drop down menu
Click **OK** to add and close or **Next** to enter another Item	

Table 3 New Item

NOTE
If you change an Item description on one form, be aware it may not update the on all forms and reports.

Commercial Property Management for Managers: QuickBooks Desktop

WORKING WITH LISTS

GROUPING ITEMS

Create an Item Group to easily enter multiple Items that are frequently recorded together in a particular transaction. For example, you may have to pay tax on a rental to different tax authorities (city and state). Create a group to avoid entering multiple separate line Items.

To create an Item Group:

- Click **Lists** on the Menu Bar
- Select Item List
- Right-click on the Item and select New

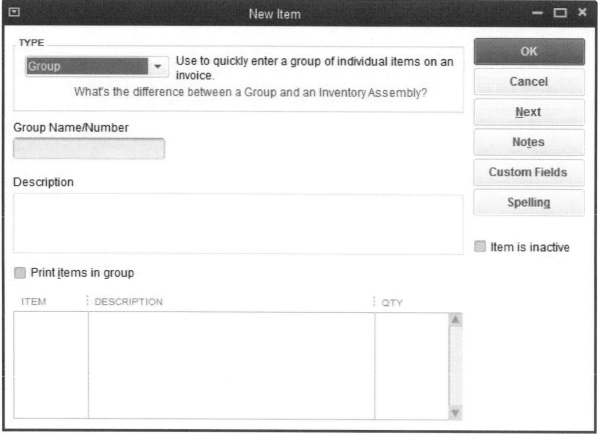

Screen Shot 42 New Item Group

WORKING WITH LISTS

- Complete the fields as follows:

Field	Data
Type	Select Group from drop down menu
Group Name/Number	Name
Description	As needed
Print items in group	If you select Print items in the group, each Item will be listed on the printed sales transaction. Note: If any Items in the group are Subitems, they will not be printed. If you do not select this option, a single line group Item will appear on the printed sales transaction.
Group Information	
Item	Select Items from the drop down menu
Description	Prefills
Qty	As needed
Click **OK** to add and close or **Next** to enter another group Item	

Table 4 New Item Group

ADD, EDIT, DELETE, AND INACTIVATE

To add, edit, delete, or inactivate:

- Click **Lists** on the Menu Bar
- Select a list
- Right-click on the list and select the function you wish to perform

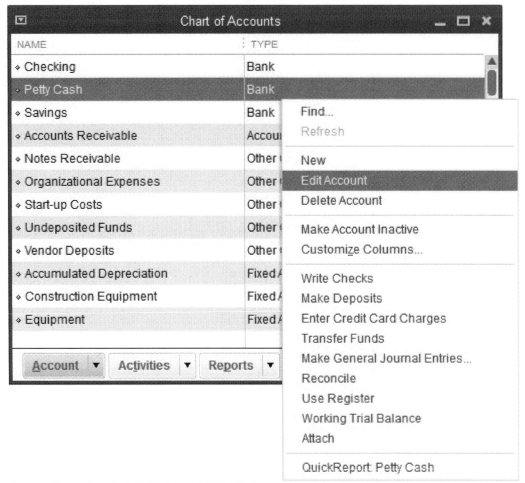

Screen Shot 43 Add, Edit, Delete, and Inactivate

If you inactivate an account, all subaccounts are also inactivated and will be hidden from the list. To view inactive accounts, click on the box **Include inactive** or select All Customers (or All Vendors) from the drop down menu.

Activate List Names

To reactivate an Item that was inactivated or hidden, you must first view the containing list.

To reactivate an Item:

- Open the list containing the Item
- Select All Customers (or All Vendors) from the drop down menu
- Click on the **x** next to the name to reactivate it

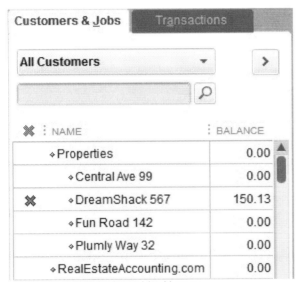

Screen Shot 44 Activate List Names

MERGE WITHIN LISTS

Use the Merge Feature when you have two list items you would like to merge; for example, two misspelled names or two accounts that should be the same.

You can merge names within each list such as Chart of Accounts, Item List, Customer & Vendor Profile Lists, and Other Names List. Duplicate names in the Customer Center and Vendor Center can also be merged.

To merge items on a list:

- Edit the name to exactly match the other name
- Click **OK**
- Click **Yes** when asked if you would like to merge them

Screen Shot 45 Merge

WARNING
Merging accounts is irreversible. If you are not sure, do NOT click **Yes**.

MOVING OTHER NAMES

You can move a name from the Other Names List to any of the other three lists (Customers, Vendors, or Employees), but not the other way around.

For instance, Home Depot, a vendor, was originally entered on the Other Names List in error and should be moved to the Vendor List.

To move a name from the Other Names List to the Vendor List:

- Click **Lists** on the Menu Bar
- Select Other Names List
- Right-click on the name
- Select Edit Other Name
- Click **Change Type…**
- Select the correct type of name
- Click **OK**

WARNING
Name types cannot be changed once you click **OK**. Therefore, if you are not sure, DO NOT make the change.

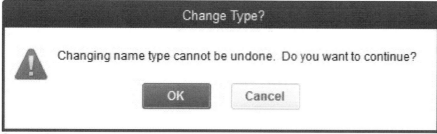

Screen Shot 46 Change Type?

- Click **OK** to change the name type or **Cancel** if you do NOT want to change the name type

BANK OR CREDIT CARD REGISTER

A register is a list of all transactions for a particular account. On paper, the checking or savings account register displays each deposit and check by date. In QuickBooks, the register can be sorted by date, payee, type of transaction, etc.

To view a bank or credit card register:

- Click **Banking** on the Menu Bar
- Click **Use Register**
- Select the correct account
- Click **OK**

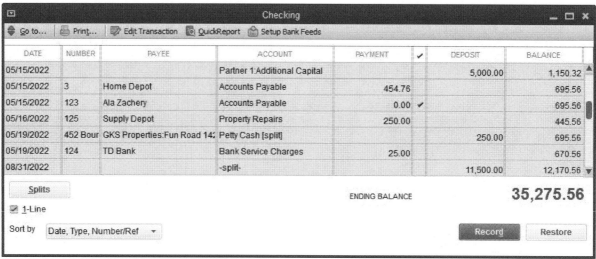

Screen Shot 47 Bank or Credit Card Register

CHAPTER 8 NOTES, TO DO LIST, AND REMINDERS

Keeping track of conversations or notes for your properties, units, vendors, and employees is just as important as tracking finances for seamless business operations. QuickBooks allows you to manage tasks and interactions with Notes, To Do List, and Reminders.

Objectives

Upon completion of this chapter, you will be able to:

- Enter Notes
- View Calendar
- View To-Do List
- Enter a Reminder
- Edit a Reminder
- Complete, Inactivate, or Delete a Reminder
- View Reports

NOTES

To record customer or vendor notes, conversations, and details:

- Click **Customers** or **Vendors** on the Icon Bar
- Select the customer or vendor for whom you would like to record notes
- On the right, click the **Notes** tab
- Right-click and select Add New, Edit Selected Note, or Delete Selected Note

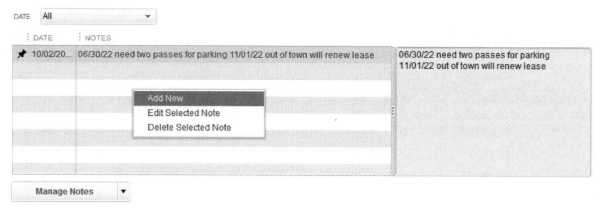

Screen Shot 48 Notes

Notes, To Do List, and Reminders

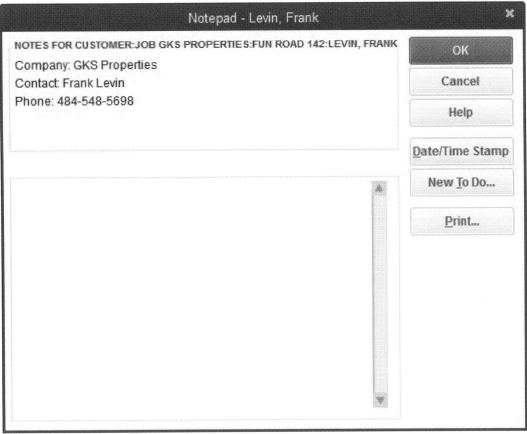

Screen Shot 49 Notepad

- View name and contact information
- Click **Date/Time Stamp** to enter today's date
- Enter notes
- Click **New To Do…** and enter the contact person's name
- Click **OK**

IMPORTANT
Be sure to add the contact person's name as a New To Do, so that it appears accurately on your reports.

NOTES, TO DO LIST, AND REMINDERS

REPORTS FOR NOTES

To view related reports:

- Click **MemRpts** on the Icon Bar
- Select by double-clicking the following under Notes:
    - Property Notes
    - To Do Notes
    - Unit Notes
    - Vendor Notes

CALENDAR

After you add you're your transactions and To Do tasks, you can view everything, OK almost everything on your Calendar right within QuickBooks.

To view calendar:

- Click **Company** on the Icon Bar
- Select Calendar

Commercial Property Management for Managers: QuickBooks Desktop

TO DO LIST

The To Do List displays scheduled reminders that require future action. You can also add reminders to the To Do List when memorizing transactions. Refer to the chapter on Recurring Transactions.

To enter, edit, or delete a reminder on the To Do List:

- Click **Company**
- Select To Do List

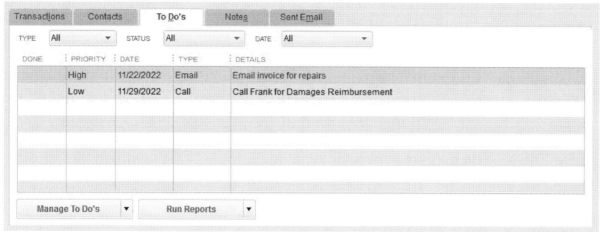

Screen Shot 50 New To Do List

- Right-click on the screen
- Select New To Do, Edit Selected To Do, or Delete Selected To Do
- Enter details
- Click **OK**

COMPLETE, INACTIVATE, OR DELETE A REMINDER

After the action is taken on the reminder, you can change the status of an Item.

To change the status of a To Do List Reminder:

- Click **To Do** on the Icon Bar
- Double-click on the note you want to complete
- Change the status to Active, Done, or Inactive in the lower left portion of the window
- Click **OK**

To delete a To Do List Reminder:

- Click **To Do** on the Icon Bar
- Right-click on the note you want to delete
- Select Delete Selected To Do
- Click **OK**

REPORTS FOR TO DO LIST

To view related reports:

- Click **MemRpts** on the Icon Bar
- Select by double-clicking the following under To Do List:
    - To Do Notes
    - To Do Notes – Active
    - To Do Notes – All
    - To Do Notes – Completed
    - To Do Notes – Not Active
    - To Do Notes – Not Completed

Chapter 9 Recurring (Memorizing) Transactions

Recurring Transactions are transactions that occur periodically (monthly, quarterly, or annually) such as a telephone bill or annual maintenance.

Set up recurring transactions so that you are reminded to enter data for essential transactions. Save or memorize recurring transactions such as invoices, sales receipts, credit memos, bills, checks, credit card charges, and journal entries, so you do not have to re-enter them repeatedly.

Objectives

Upon completion of this chapter, you will be able to:

- Group Transactions
- Memorize Transactions
- Set the Frequency of a Memorized Transaction
- Update or Delete a Memorized Transaction
- Print a Memorized Transaction List
- View Reports

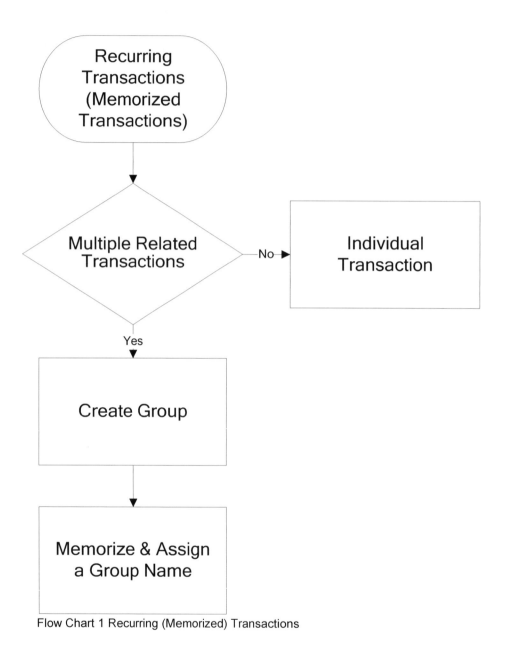

Flow Chart 1 Recurring (Memorized) Transactions

CREATE GROUP

Create a group for transactions that occur with the same frequency with the property or vendor's name and percentage. Bills may need to be allocated to each property and would be in the same group. Name groups by property or a category (insurance, real estate tax). The goal is to easily find and enter transactions by changing only the date, number, and amount.

To create a group:

- Click **Lists** on the Menu Bar
- Select Memorized Transaction List
- Click **Memorized Transaction**
- Select New Group

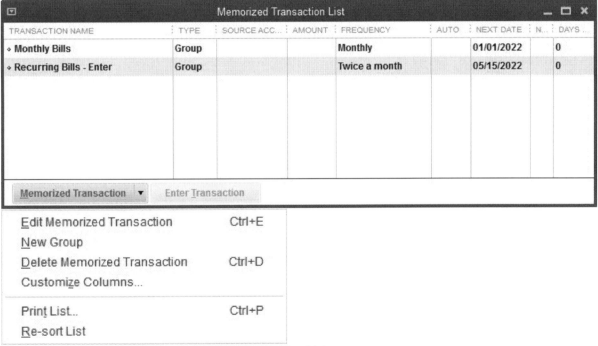

Screen Shot 51 New Group from Memorized Transaction List

Recurring Transactions

The New Memorized Transaction Group screen appears.

Screen Shot 52 New Memorized Transaction Group

- Complete the fields as follows:

Field	Data
Name	A descriptive name you will recognize easily
	Choose from Add to my Reminders List, Do Not Remind Me, or Automate Transaction Entry and select the appropriate fields
How Often	Select from drop down menu
Next Date	Date of the next transaction you want to be entered
Number Remaining	Number of times you want the transaction to be entered (use 999 for indefinite transactions)
Days In Advance To Enter	10 (because you may receive payment before the due date)
Click **OK**	

Table 5 New Memorized Transaction Group

MEMORIZING A TRANSACTION

To create individual recurring transactions:

- After you enter an invoice, bill, check, credit memo, or credit card charge, right-click on the form
- Select Memorize (name of form)

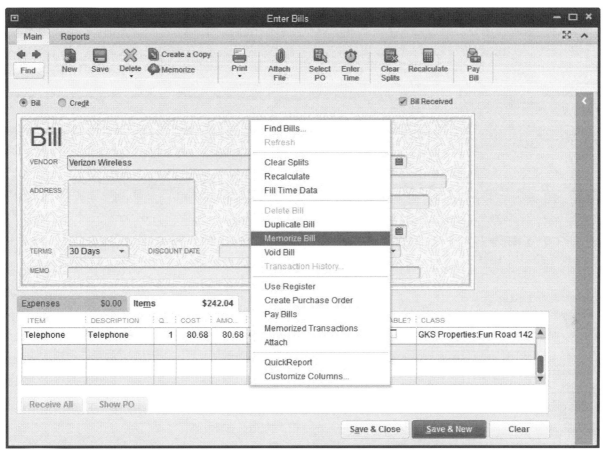

Screen Shot 53 Memorize a Transaction

IMPORTANT
Add to my Reminders List: Use when the description and amount may change
Do Not Remind Me: Use for informational purposes only
Automate Transaction Entry: Use when the description and amount remain the same
Add to Group: Use when grouping transactions

RECURRING TRANSACTIONS

Let's say you want to set up a memorized transaction for Verizon Wireless. You provide phone service to the property, for the same amount each month, and wish to memorize the bill to be automatically entered in QuickBooks.

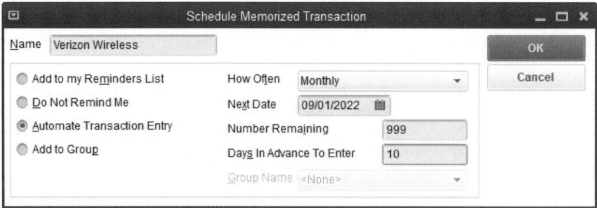

Screen Shot 54 Memorize Transaction

- Complete the fields as follows:

Field	Data
Name	Depends on transaction
	Choose from Add to my Reminders List, Do Not Remind Me, or Automate Transaction Entry and select the appropriate fields
How Often	Select from drop down menu
Next Date	Date of the next transaction you want to be entered
Number Remaining	Number of times you want the transaction to be entered (or use 999 for indefinite transactions)
Days In Advance To Enter	10 (because you may receive payment before the due date)
Group Name	Insert group name (only if With Transactions in Group is selected)
Click **OK**	

Table 6 Memorize Transaction

Commercial Property Management for Managers: QuickBooks Desktop

RECURRING TRANSACTIONS

ENTER MEMORIZED TRANSACTIONS

When you open the file on the day the memorized transaction is due; the following screen appears as a reminder to enter memorized transactions.

- Click **Enter Checked Now** or **Enter All Later**

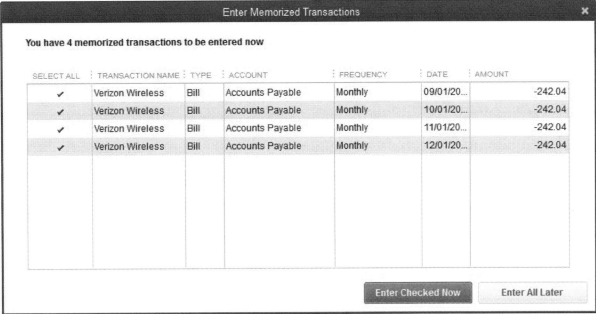

Screen Shot 55 Enter Memorized Transactions

If you choose Enter All Later, the same screen will appear every time you open QuickBooks until you enter the memorized transactions. If you Select Enter Checked Now, QuickBooks confirms the number of transactions entered.

You do have the option to enter one transaction at a time. Notice the date and number remaining will update when you select the transaction from the list.

To view the Transaction Detail by Account report, go to Reports > Accountant & Taxes, and change to the current date. Alternatively, you many check the Customer Center or Vendor Center to view transactions entered.

Commercial Property Management for Managers: QuickBooks Desktop

CHANGE FREQUENCY OF A MEMORIZED TRANSACTION

To change the frequency of a memorized transaction:

- Click **Lists** on the Menu Bar
- Select Memorized Transaction List
- Right-click on the group or transaction and select Edit Memorized Transaction
- Change the scheduling
- Click **OK**

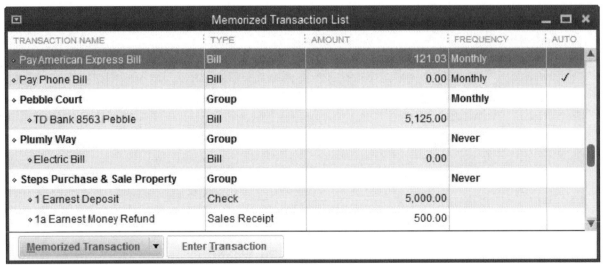
Screen Shot 56 Edit Memorized Transaction

Update a Memorized Transaction

To change line items, amounts, or other details of a memorized transaction:

- Click **Lists** on the Menu Bar
- Select Memorized Transaction List
- Double-click to open the transaction
- Make the necessary changes
- Right-click and select Memorize (name of form)
- Click **Replace**
- Click **Clear** to avoid recording the transaction

Delete a Memorized Transaction

To delete a memorized transaction:

- Click **MemTx** on the Icon Bar

OR

- Click **Lists** on the Menu Bar
- Select Memorized Transaction List
- Right-click on the transaction and select Delete Memorized Transaction
- Click **OK**

PRINT MEMORIZED TRANSACTION LIST

To print a memorized transaction list:

- Click **MemTx** on the Icon Bar

OR

- Click **Lists** on the Menu Bar
- Select Memorized Transaction List
- Click **Memorized Report** on the bottom right of the screen
- Select Print List…
- Click **Print**

REPORTS FOR ENTERED TRANSACTIONS

To view related reports:

- Click **MemRpts** on the Icon Bar
- Select by double-clicking the following:
    - General Ledger under Accountant
    - Profit & Loss by Property under Company
    - Profit & Loss by Overhead under Company

CHAPTER 10 BATCH INVOICING

Batch Invoicing allows you to create an invoice with the same date, item, description, property name (Class), and amount for more than one tenant. This saves time entering each invoice separately. All invoices within a batch must have the same date, item, description, property name (Class), and amount.

> **IMPORTANT**
> When you create batch invoices, you will be able to link only one property (Class).
>
> Terms of payment will be prefilled from the Customer:Job center.

Objectives

Upon completion of this chapter, you will be able to:

- Create Billing Groups
- Create Batch Invoices

CREATE A BILLING GROUP

Create a Billing Group with the group of names that receive invoices on a regular basis. It saves the time taken to enter each invoice individually. Occasionally, you may choose not to invoice a particular customer in the group. If so, you can easily remove the name.

You have the option to select only the Customer:Job names to include them in the batch invoice process.

To create a billing group:

- Click on **Billing Group** (on the right top column)

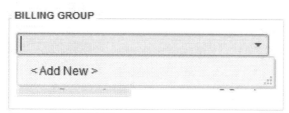

Screen Shot 57 Billing Group

- Click on the arrow to expand the drop down menu and select Add New

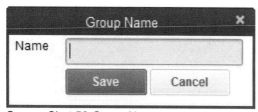

Screen Shot 58 Group Name

- Add the name for future reference
- Click **Save**

BATCH INVOICING

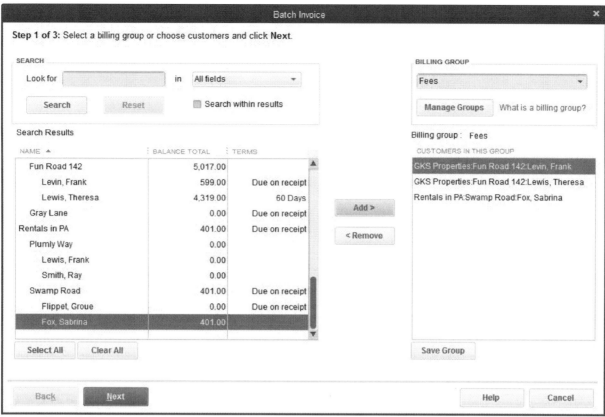

Screen Shot 59 Batch Invoice 1

- Hold the CTRL key and select the name and click the **Add** button OR Select each name one at a time on the right column and click the **Add** button located between the two columns
- Click **Save Group**

BATCH INVOICING

CREATE A BATCH INVOICE

> **IMPORTANT**
> Before creating batch invoices, you MUST have the terms, sales tax, and payment method updated for each Customer. If you do not have these items updated, click **Customer:Job** to update these details. Refer to the section on Manage Names.

To create a batch invoice:

- Click **Customers** on the Menu Bar
- Select Create Batch Invoices

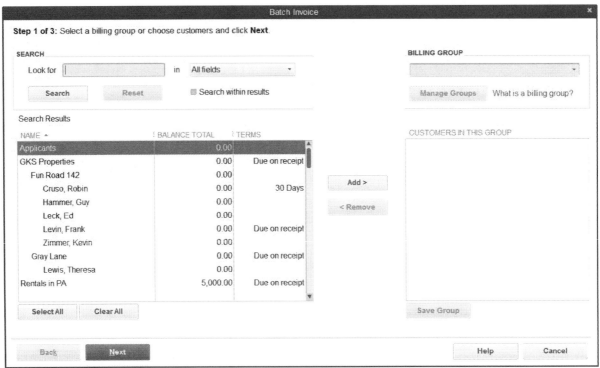

Screen Shot 60 Batch Invoice 2

- Hold the CTRL key and select the name and click the **Add** button OR Select each name one at a time on the right column and click the **Add** button located between the two columns or a billing group
- Click **Next**

Commercial Property Management for Managers: QuickBooks Desktop 84

BATCH INVOICING

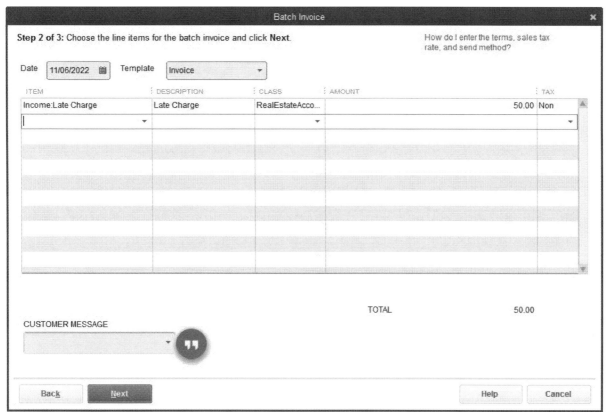

Screen Shot 61 Choose Line Items

- Complete the fields as follows:

Field	Data
Date	Date of the invoice
Template	Default
Item	As needed
Description	
Class	Property Name
Amount	As needed
Tax	
Customer Message	
Click **Next** to review the list	

Table 7 Choose Line Items

> **NOTE**
> Invoices that are unmarked for mail or email can be viewed in the Open Invoices Report. In the Open Invoices Report, simply double-click on the invoice you wish to print or email.

BATCH INVOICING

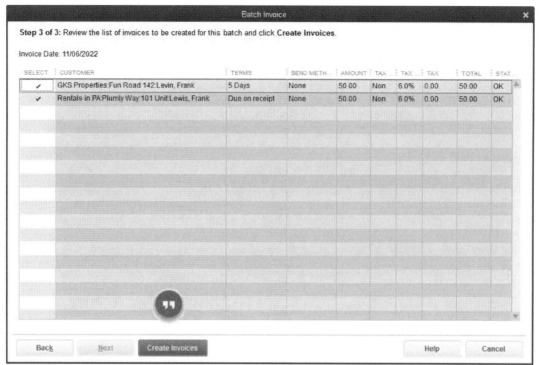

Screen Shot 62 Review Invoices

- Unselect customers, if needed, by clicking the corresponding checkmark in the first column
- Click **Create Invoices**

The Batch Invoice Summary box appears.

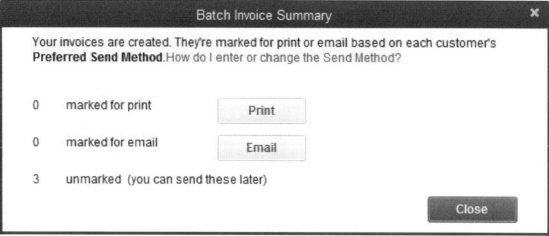

Screen Shot 63 Batch Invoice Summary

- Click **Close**

CHAPTER 11 WHAT OTHERS OWE YOU VS. WHAT YOU OWE OTHERS

Many people view invoices and bills as the same thing. The same can be said for payments and pay bills. They certainly resemble each other; however, in QuickBooks, they refer to two different things.

Others Owe You	You Owe Others
Invoice	Bill
Payment (of an invoice)	Pay Bills
Sales Receipts (charge and payment received)	Check, Credit Card Charge
Statement (all transactions or just open balances)	

Table 8 What Others Owe You vs. What You Owe Others

Objectives

Upon completion of this chapter, you will be able to:

- Track What Others Owe You
- Track What You Owe Others

TRACKING WHAT OTHERS OWE YOU

Invoices are created by YOU and track what OTHERS owe YOU. For example, you would create an invoice in QuickBooks to reflect that a customer owes you money for services. The invoice is created some time before the customer pays the amount due on the invoice. Although you may choose not to mail invoices to the customer, you still create them in QuickBooks, so the records will correctly indicate that there is an outstanding balance. Of course, if you create an invoice, you will be able to print and mail it or e-mail it.

A **Payment** is used in QuickBooks to indicate that OTHERS paid YOU for an invoice.

Sales Receipts reflect a charge and payment received in one transaction. You would create a sales receipt when the customer pays you the full amount of a charge at the time the charge is made. An example is a violation fee.

Statements are created in QuickBooks to summarize the history of a customer account, including invoices, payments, and credits that have occurred during a given period. You can also choose to create a short statement, which shows only invoices that are not paid in full. The statement shows the "bottom line" amount due and can be printed and mailed or e-mailed to customers.

TRACKING WHAT YOU OWE OTHERS

Bills are created by OTHERS and track what YOU owe OTHERS. For example, if you hire a vendor to make a repair, the vendor presents you with a bill, reflecting money that you owe him. You can re-create the vendor's bill in QuickBooks to keep track of what you owe him and what type of work was performed. Later, you would write a check to the vendor for that amount and QuickBooks matches the two.

Pay Bills is the QuickBooks function where you to pay what YOU owe OTHERS as it is reflected on a bill.

Write Checks is a method of paying others. You may also pay others by credit card or online payments.

To avoid confusing these terms, refer to the table at the beginning of the chapter.

CHAPTER 12 CASH OR ACCRUAL BASIS

Before implementing any accounting system, you must decide to track cash flow on either cash or an accrual basis. If you are not sure which method to use, consult with your accountant.

Objectives

Upon completion of this chapter, you will be able to:

- Understand Cash Basis
- Understand Accrual Basis

Cash Basis

On a cash basis, revenue is reported when cash is received, and expenses are reported when cash is paid out.

Accrual Basis

Under an accrual basis, revenue is reported at the time it is earned, even if cash is not yet received, and expenses are reported at the time they are incurred, even if they are not yet paid for.

To illustrate the difference between the two, let us assume that on January 1st, Joe, a plumber, provided a service that totaled $400. The customer did not have the money that day and sent Joe a check on January 15th. On a cash basis, the revenue for the job would be recorded when the payment was received on January 15th. In an accrual-based system, the revenue for the job would be recorded January 1st, regardless of whether or not Joe received payment from the customer that day.

Most people think of numbers and equations on spreadsheets when they think of accounting, which is certainly an aspect of the business. However, the most important aspect for small business owners is understanding how those numbers make up the big picture for your business. Deciding whether to use a Cash or Accrual system is vital.

> **IMPORTANT**
> We recommend you use the accrual method. If you do, you will be able to view reports on both a cash and accrual basis.

CHAPTER 13 CHART OF ACCOUNTS

The Chart of Accounts is a complete list of accounts and balances used to track how much money a business has, owes, earns, and spends. All companies should follow a systematic method of assigning account numbers to identify each account name, although it is not necessary to use numbers in QuickBooks.

Objectives

Upon completion of this chapter, you will be able to:

- Define Account Numbers
- Define Assets
- Define Liabilities
- Define Equity
- Define Income or Revenue
- Define Expenses
- Define Other Income
- Define Other Expenses

Account Numbers

The rule of thumb for account number assignments is shown below:

- 1000-1999 Assets
- 2000-2999 Liabilities
- 3000-3999 Capital, Equity
- 4000-4999 Income, Revenue
- 5000-6999 Expenses
- 7000-7999 Other Income
- 8000-8999 Other Expenses

Assets

Assets are things owned by the business, from office equipment to properties.

Current Assets

Current Assets are cash, bank accounts, and accounts receivables (the total of amounts owed to the business by its customers for goods and services sold to them on credit).

Fixed Assets

Fixed Assets are items held by the business, such as equipment, buildings, and land, which may be sold at a future date.

Other Assets

Other Assets are items neither Current or Fixed Assets such as Goodwill, Long-term notes receivable, deposits paid.

LIABILITIES

Liabilities are the business's debts, borrowed amounts, accounts payable (money owed to creditors for goods and services bought on credit), loans, lines of credit, and notes payable.

CURRENT LIABILITIES

Current Liabilities are monies owed for less than a year.

LONG TERM LIABILITIES

Long-Term Liabilities are monies owed for more than a year.

EQUITY

Equity is the interest in business assets that remains after deducting its liabilities.

Assets – Liabilities = Net Worth or Ownership Equity

INCOME

Income, or revenue, is money received in exchange for goods or services provided to customers. Rent received, payments for cleaning, or payments for amenities are examples of a landlord's income.

EXPENSES

Expenses are costs incurred to run your Company, such as printing and advertising costs.

OTHER INCOME

Other Income is revenue, earned from other means, but not by selling services. An example of Other Income is bank interest.

OTHER EXPENSES

Other Expenses are bad debt expenses, such as invoices that were never paid.

CHAPTER 14 UNDERSTANDING REPORTING

The beauty of using QuickBooks to manage properties is instantaneous financial analysis with customized reports. Examining these reports allows you to make sound decisions, discover areas of the operation that require attention, and check the status of your business for planning and tax purposes.

View pre-billed reports in the Reports Center. We have included memorized reports, which you can view by selecting MemRpts on the Icon Bar.

Objectives

Upon completion of this chapter, you will be able to:

- Understand a Trial Balance
- Understand a Cash Flow Report
- Understand a Balance Sheet Report
- Understand a Profit & Loss Report by Property and/or Overhead
- Understand Splits
- Understand Undeposited Funds

UNDERSTANDING REPORTING

TRIAL BALANCE

A Trial Balance is a list of general ledger accounts with the ending balances of each account. Balances will be in either the Debit column or Credit column depending on the type of account. Check the Trial Balance for errors before producing financial statements such as the Profit & Loss report, Balance Sheet, and Statement of Cash Flows.

> **NOTE**
> Assets = Liability + Owner's Equity
> Debits = Credits
>
> Assets are increased by debits and decreased by credits. Debits decreased Liabilities and Owner's Equity and increased by credits.

To view the Trial Balance:

- Click **Reports** on the Menu Bar
- Select Memorized Reports
- Select Accountant
- Select Trial Balance

REPORT: CASH FLOW

The Cash Flow report shows a company's flow of cash over a period. The money coming into the business is called cash inflow while money going out from the business is called cash outflow. This report shows the increase or decrease of cash supply during a period and how much cash remains on hand at the end of that period.

To view the Cash Flow report:

- Click **MemRpts** on the Icon Bar
- Double-click Cash Flow under Accountant
- Customize reports by filtering for each Property (Class)

REPORT: BALANCE SHEET

A Balance Sheet shows a company's financial condition as of a single point in time, such as December 31st of the past year. A Balance Sheet displays assets, liabilities, and owner's equity.

> **IMPORTANT**
> The Balance Sheet by Class report is only available in the Premier and Enterprise versions of QuickBooks.
>
> **YOU WILL HAVE TO REVIEW THE REPORT FOR ACCURACY AND MAKE ADJUSTMENTS AS YOU DEEM NECESSARY.**

To view the Balance Sheet by Class report:

- Click **Reports** on the Menu Bar
- Select Company & Financial
- Select Balance Sheet by Class

REPORT: PROFIT & LOSS

The Profit & Loss by Class report is particularly important for each property. This report is sometimes referred to as an income statement and shows if the business made or lost money over a period (either by month, quarter, or year).

You must supply a beginning and end date to produce a Profit & Loss report.

> **IMPORTANT**
> The Profit & Loss by Overhead report is a condensed report which reflects your Company's income and expenses.

To view the Profit & Loss or the Profit & Loss by Class report:

- Click **Reports** on the Menu Bar
- Select Memorized Reports
- Select Accountant
- Select Profit & Loss or Profit & Loss by Class

SPLITS

A split column on a report displays multiple accounts, customers, jobs, or classes used in a transaction. If you create an invoice with two line items, the reports and register display -SPLIT-. If you had used only one line item, the name of the item or account would show. When viewing reports, double-click -SPLIT- to view additional transaction details.

ITEM	DESCRIPTION	PROPERTY NAME	AMOU...	TAX
Income Rental:Rent	Rent	GKS Properties:Fun Road 142	6,600.00	Tax
Income Rental:Cleaning	Cleaning	GKS Properties:Fun Road 142	125.00	Non

Screen Shot 64 Invoice with Two Line Items

www.RealEstateAccounting.com

Type	Date	Num	Name	Split
Dec 16, 22				
Invoice	12/16/2022	26	Properties:Fun Road 142	-SPLIT-

Report 1 Split Transaction

UNDEPOSITED FUNDS

After receiving payment, funds are held in a holding account in QuickBooks. It is equivalent to holding checks in a safe before depositing them into a bank account. When viewing reports, funds that have not been deposited into a bank account are held in the Undeposited Funds account.

www.RealEstateAccounting.com

Type	Num	Date	Memo	Account	Amount
Payment		03/17/2022		Undeposited Funds	-25,000.00

Report 2 Transactions by Account Undeposited Funds

SECTION 3

YOUR COMPANY FILE

To prepare for entering your information into the template file, gather all company information, including your tax ID number. Depending on your state, rent may be taxable, requiring you to file the appropriate sales tax and tax returns. These city and county returns are typically due monthly, quarterly, or annually.

Once you have your Company's information together, we will show you how to modify the template file and customize settings based on your business procedures. Having the correct settings and entering data and transactions appropriately produces accurate reports.

COMPANY INFORMATION CHECKLIST

Company Information
☐ Company Name and Address
☐ Phone Number, Fax Number, Email, and Website
☐ Type of Entity
☐ EIN No.

Checklist 1 Company Information

YOUR COMPANY FILE

REQUIRED DOCUMENTS

You need to gather business and bank documents to set up the QuickBooks file accurately. Collecting these papers before setting up your file will save you time and energy as you will have all of the necessary information at hand.

REQUIRED DOCUMENTS CHECKLIST

Required Documents
☐ Outstanding Tenant Invoices, Credits and over Payments
☐ Paid Security Deposit, Pet Deposit, Last Month Rent and CAM
☐ Outstanding Deposit Money
☐ Outstanding Reserve Funds
☐ Unpaid Owners Funds
☐ Bills and Receipts from Vendors
☐ Open Work Orders
☐ Bank Statement
☐ Credit Card Statements
☐ Personal Money Spent
☐ Uncleared Checks and Deposits
☐ Balance Sheet from Prior Year (for each property and your business)
☐ Profit and Loss Statement (if you are starting the file mid-year)

Checklist 2 Required Documents

CHAPTER 15 COMPANY FILE

The template file is customized for your real estate investing business who buys and sells properties. To make it your own, you will need to personalize it for your business. Customizing the file with user accounts, company closing dates, specialty fields, and other details will maximize the capability for your business. These business customizations also create a professional brand for the customers and vendors you work with, facilitating more business opportunities.

Objectives

Upon completion of this chapter, you will be able to:

- Open your Company File
- Understand Your Entity Type
- Enter Company Details
- Change Users and Passwords
- Set a Closing Date
- Delete or Inactivate Accounts
- Set up Credit Card Accounts
- Enter Your Company Name
- Customize Fields
- Get Ready for Late Fees

OPEN YOUR COMPANY FILE

To open your file:

- Open QuickBooks
- Click **File** on the Menu Bar
- Select Open or Restore Company…

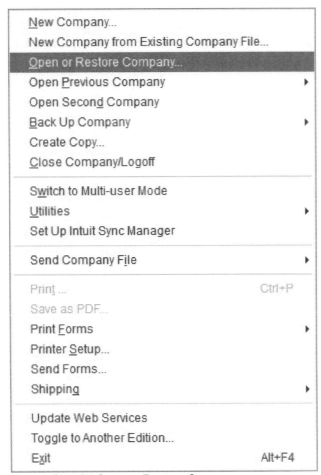

Screen Shot 65 Open or Restore Company

- Click **Open a Company File**
- Click **Next**
- Follow the prompts to open the file
- Browse to and open your previously renamed Company File

ENTITY TYPE

Depending on your entity type, select the correct accounts in the Chart of Accounts. Refer to the chapter on Working with Lists.

Sole Proprietorship

A sole proprietorship is an unincorporated company owned by one person. When an owner invests money from his or her personal funds, it should be posted to the Investment account, and withdrawals of funds should be posted to Draws.

Partnership

A partnership is an unincorporated company owned by two or more persons. Each partner may invest in the partnership, draw funds, and receive a specific share of profit. When a partner loans money from his personal funds, it should be posted to the Investment account, and withdrawals of funds should be posted to Draws. The share of profit should be recorded to the Distribution account.

Corporation

A corporation is owned by its shareholders or stockholders.

COMPANY FILE

COMPANY INFORMATION

Your Company information is identified and printed on invoices, sales receipts, checks, forms, statements, and financial reports.

TIP
It is strongly recommended that the administrator password for the data file be changed AFTER you enter your Company information.

To enter company information:

- Click **Company** on the Menu Bar
- Select My Company
- Click on the pencil icon located on the top, right corner of the screen
- Enter Contact, Legal, Company, Report, Payroll Information and Ship To Address details corresponding to the descriptions listed to the left of each input field
- Click **Ship To Address…** to add your shipping information
- Click **OK**

TIP
Use the TAB KEY to advance to the next field.

Screen Shot 66 My Company

Commercial Property Management for Managers: QuickBooks Desktop

COMPANY FILE

USERS AND PASSWORDS

For your security, you should always have a password for the data file. Do not use common personal information such as family names or pets.

The administrator can assign system users, passwords, and specific user access. The administrator has full access to your Company's information. Change the administrator password and set up different passwords for each user.

Administrator Password

To change the administrator password:

- Click **Company** on the Menu Bar
- Select Set Up Users and Passwords
- Click **Change Your Password**…
- Complete the form
- Click **OK**

Screen Shot 67 Change QuickBooks Password

COMPANY FILE

Add or Change User Names and Passwords

The instructions below are for the Pro and Premier versions only. If you are using the Enterprise version, contact the author for information.

The template file includes five usernames with blank passwords.

To change a username:

- Click **Company** on the Menu Bar
- Select Set Up Users and Passwords
- Click **Set Up Users**...
- Enter the administrator password to confirm changes

The User List window appears.

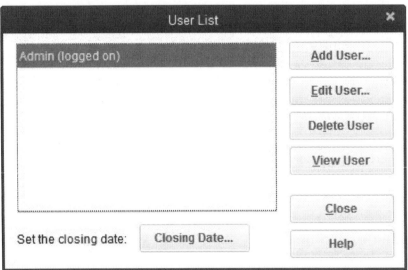

Screen Shot 68 User List

- Select the user name you are changing
- Click **Add User…** or **Edit User…**

Commercial Property Management for Managers: QuickBooks Desktop   106

COMPANY FILE

Screen Shot 69 User Name and Password

- Enter the desired username and password
- Click **Next**

COMPANY FILE

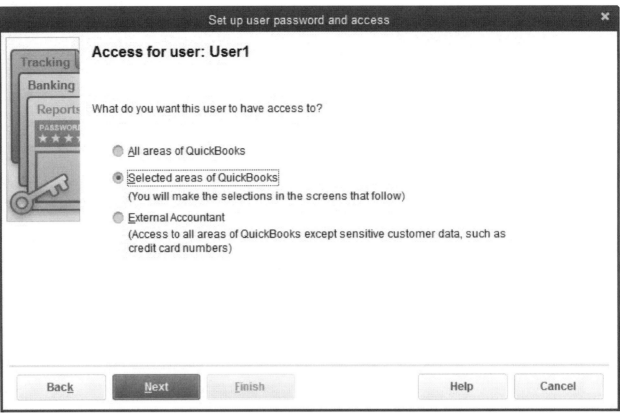
Screen Shot 70 Access for User

- Select the appropriate level of access
- Click **Next**
- Follow the prompts to complete

As Administrator, you have the option of adding users and giving users access to any or all of these areas:

- Sales and Accounts Receivable
- Purchase and Accounts Payable
- Checking and Credit Cards
- Inventory
- Time Tracking
- Payroll and Employees
- Sensitive Accounting Activities
- Sensitive Financial Report
- Changing or Deleting Transactions
- Changing Closed Transactions

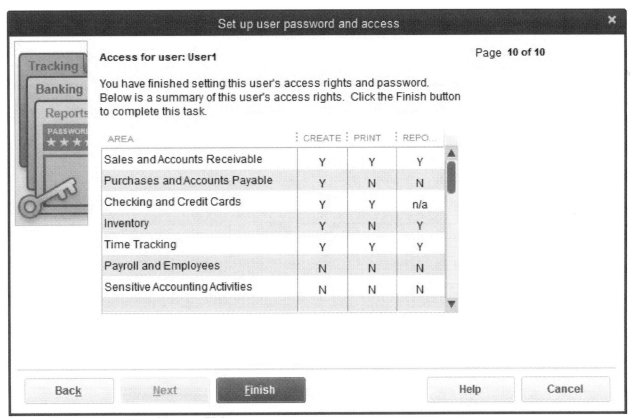

Screen Shot 71 Summary of Access Rights

- Click **Finish**

COMPANY FILE

CLOSING DATE

Set a closing date with a separate password after you reconcile your accounts. Any changes made on or before the closing date changes the financial reports.

IMPORTANT
The closing date password should be different from the administrator password. The closing date password applies to all users.

To set a closing date:

- Click **Company** on the Menu Bar
- Select Set Closing Date…

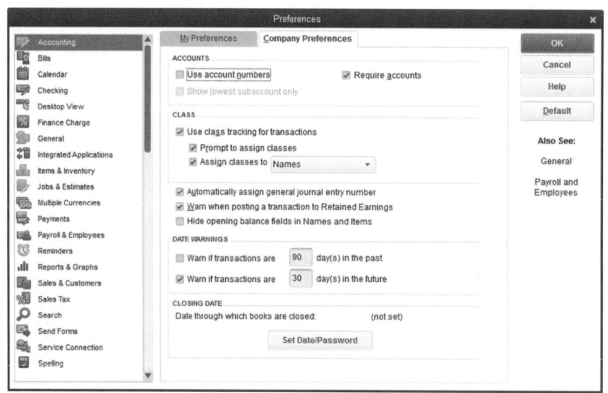

Screen Shot 72 Closing Date Preferences

- Click **Set Date/Password**
- Change Closing Date and Password
- Click **OK**

Commercial Property Management for Managers: QuickBooks Desktop

COMPANY FILE

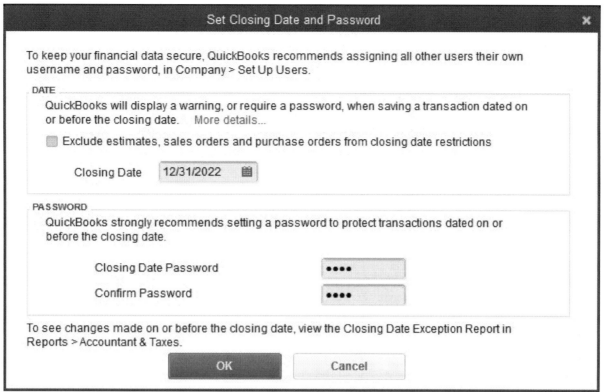

Screen Shot 73 Set Closing Date and Password

When adding, editing, or deleting transactions dated on or before the closing date, QuickBooks displays a warning and requires a password. The following screen appears.

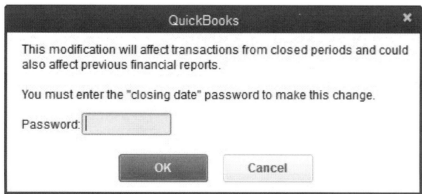

Screen Shot 74 QuickBooks Password Request

- Enter Password
- Click **OK**

Commercial Property Management for Managers: QuickBooks Desktop

COMPANY FILE

CHART OF ACCOUNTS

There may be one or more accounts that you do not need. You can delete or inactivate these accounts to simplify the list.

To inactivate accounts on the Chart of Accounts:

- Click **Accnt** on the Icon Bar

Screen Shot 75 Inactivate Chart of Accounts

- Right-click on account and select Delete Account or Make Account Inactive

When you inactivate the main account, all subaccounts will also become inactive. To view an inactive account, click on the **Include Inactive** box on the bottom of the screen.

Commercial Property Management for Managers: QuickBooks Desktop

COMPANY FILE

SET UP CREDIT CARD ACCOUNTS

If you have only one credit card holder, create a credit card account by entering the name of the card and the last four digits of the account number.

If multiple employees have company credit cards, create an account for the credit card company and a subaccount for each cardholder. Again, name the account with the last four digits of the card number and in this case, the cardholder's name as well. In addition to the subaccounts, add another subaccount, named Payments Only. This subaccount will only be used when you make a payment to the credit card company to reduce the balance on the statement.

To add a new credit card account:

- Click **Lists** on the Menu Bar
- Select Chart of Accounts
- Right-click on any account
- Select New
- Select the Credit Card name and click **Continue**
- Enter the Account Name
- Click **Save & Close** or **Save & New** to enter another account

The Chart of Accounts should match the example below:

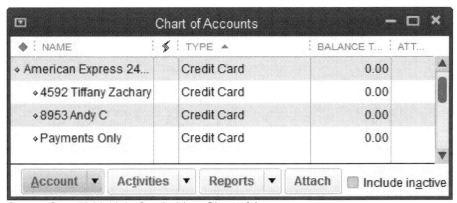
Screen Shot 76 Multiple Cardholders Chart of Accounts

NOTE
If the Online Services window appears, refer to the chapter on Online Services.

Commercial Property Management for Managers: QuickBooks Desktop   113

ENTER YOUR COMPANY NAME

All transactions must have a Customer:Job name and a Class, but what about overhead expenses?

When expenses are related to your business and cannot be attributable to a specific property, you will select your Company as both the Customer:Job and the Class. It is important that you set up your Company Name as such.

To enter your Company as a Customer:Job:

- Click **Customers** on the Icon Bar
- Select Customer Center
- Right-click Overhead
- Select Edit Customer:Job
- Change the Customer Name to your Company name

To enter your Company as a Class:

- Click **Lists** on the Icon Bar
- Select Class List
- Right-click on Overhead
- Select New or Edit Class and update to reflect your Company name

CUSTOM FIELDS

Use Custom Fields to track unique details about each customer, vendor and employee.

Create additional data fields (Define Fields) to track specifics by Customer further:Job, Vendor, and Employee.

In Pro/Premier, although there is a total of 15 custom fields, you cannot have more than 7 per category. For example, you could only have seven custom fields for customers, 7 for vendors and 1 for the employee.

In Enterprise Solutions, although there is a total of 30 customer fields, you cannot have more than 12 per category. For example, you could only have 12 custom fields for customers, 12 for vendors and 6 for the employee.

Only in the Enterprise Solutions fields can be formatted by text, date, numeric, and other characters.

To add custom fields:

- Click **Customer Center** or **Vendors** on the Icon Bar
- Right-click on a name and select Edit
- Click **Additional Info** tab
- Click **Define Fields**
- Enter labels or custom fields
- Click the column under Cust, Vend or Empl to identify whom the labels apply to
- Click **OK**

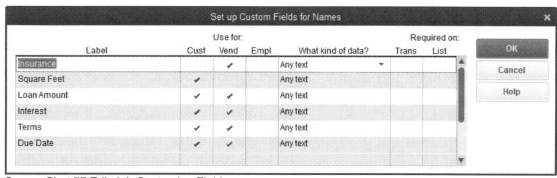

Screen Shot 77 Edit Job Customize Fields

COMPANY FILE

LATE FEES

To customize late fees:

- Click **Customers** on the Menu Bar
- Select Assess Finance Charges
- Click **Settings**

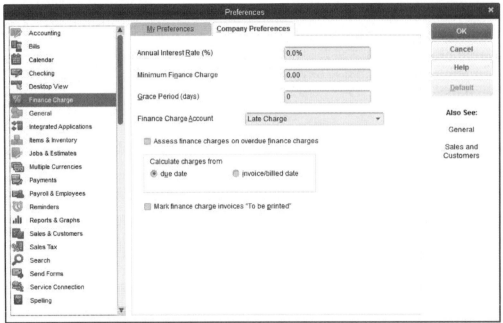

Screen Shot 78 Late Fee Preferences

COMPANY FILE

- Complete the fields as follows:

Field	Data
Annual Interest Rate (%)	Leave blank
Minimum Finance Charge	Late fee amount
Grace Period (days)	Grace period (days) minus one (For example, $15^{th} - 1 = 14^{th}$)
Finance Charge Account	Late Fees
	Click the box, **Assess finance charges on overdue finance charges**, if desired
Calculate charges from	Select due date or invoice/billed date
	Click the box; **Mark finance charge invoices "To be printed."**
Click **OK**	

Table 9 Late Fee Preferences

COMPANY FILE

CHAPTER 16 LETTERS AND ENVELOPES

You may want to send letters to all of your customers and vendors informing them of a new regulation, or instead, send a letter to one name Using both QuickBooks and Microsoft Word, you can create customized letters and envelopes for the customer, vendor, or employee notices. Create a new letter template from scratch, convert an existing Microsoft Word document into a QuickBooks template, or edit an existing template.

Objectives

Upon completion of this chapter, you will be able to:

- Create, View, or Edit a QuickBooks Letter Template
- Customize Letters
- Print Letters and Envelopes

CREATE QUICKBOOKS LETTER TEMPLATE

To prepare a letter template:

- Click **Company** on the Menu Bar
- Select Prepare Letters with Envelopes
- Click **Customize Letter Templates…**

Screen Shot 79 Customize Letter Templates

The Find Letter Templates window appears.

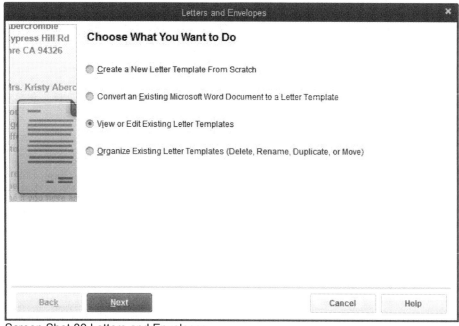
Screen Shot 80 Letters and Envelopes

- Select View or Edit Existing Letter Templates (or choose one)
- Follow the prompts to create a type of letter template

Letters and Envelopes

Screen Shot 81 Add-Ins Tab

- The Microsoft Word – Add-Ins tab opens.
- Select and insert the Company, Customer, and Collection fields within the letter

CREATE LETTER FOR A CUSTOMER, VENDOR, OR EMPLOYEE

You can send letters from an existing template or customize your letter to send to a single recipient or multiple recipients.

Create letters and envelopes for customers, vendors, or employees, including agreement letters and statements. To create a letter for a Vendor, open the Vendor Center. To create a letter for an Employee, open the Employee Center.

To create a letter and envelope for a vendor:

- Click **Vendors** on the Menu Bar
- Select Vendor Center
- Select a name
- Click on the **Word** Menu

> Prepare Letter to AARBO Roofing
> Prepare Vendor Letters...
> Customize Letter Templates...

Screen Shot 82 Word Menu

Vendor Letters

To prepare letters for customers:

- Click **Prepare Vendor Letters…**

Screen Shot 83 Review and Edit Recipients for Vendor

- Click the left column with check marks to select vendor recipients for the letter
- Click **Next**

LETTERS AND ENVELOPES

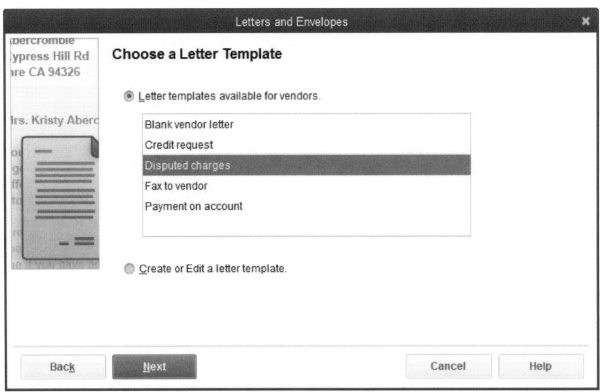

Screen Shot 84 Choose a Letter Template

- Select Letter templates available for customers/jobs
- Select your preferred letter from the list
- Click **Next**

LETTERS AND ENVELOPES

- Enter your name and title to customize the letter

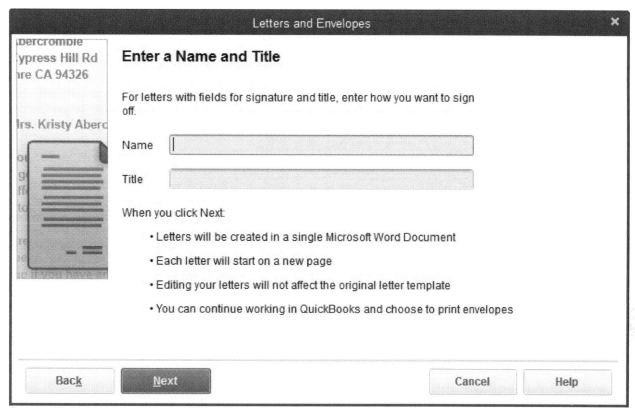

Screen Shot 85 Enter a Name and Title

- Click **Next**

Letters and Envelopes

The letters open in Microsoft Word. You can edit the letters without editing the template. Double-check the document to make sure that no required information is missing. Print the letters from the Microsoft Word Print menu.

RealEstateAccounting.com
PO Box 456
Smile, PA 18940

December 13, 2022

AARBO Roofing
Joe Schmo
PO Box 110
Smile, PA 18940

To Whom It May Concern,

Re: Account **MISSING*INFORMATION**

We have received an invoice that we believe contains incorrect charges. Would you please contact me with the current balance you have on file? I'd like to straighten this out as soon as possible, and will wait to send the check until I hear from you.

Thank you for your prompt attention to this matter.

Sincerely,

RealEstateAccounting.com

Screen Shot 86 Sample Letter

Print the letters. We recommend on purchasing single or double window envelopes to mail the letter rather than printing the envelope from QuickBooks.

CHAPTER 17 TEMPLATES

From basic forms invoices, statements and purchase orders, the Templates List is the place to start customizing forms to fit your needs.

> **NOTE**
> If you use an online booking site, most correspondence is likely sent and recorded via the software. In this case, customizing templates in QuickBooks is not necessary. Go ahead and skip this chapter.

Objectives

Upon completion of this chapter, you will be able to:

- Create Forms
- Customize Templates

FORMS

Customize Templates for documents sent to customers and vendors.

If you own multiple properties, customize templates for each property, with the property name and contact information as letterhead. Name the templates by property street address.

> **TIP**
> If your invoices and statements have different names and addresses than your Company, create additional templates for each address.

To view, customize, or create a new template:

- Click **Lists** on the Menu Bar
- Select Templates
- Right-click on a name and select New, Edit, Delete, or Inactivate

> **NOTE**
> We have included a template for an invoice, sales receipt, credit memo, and work order. Simply duplicate or change as needed.

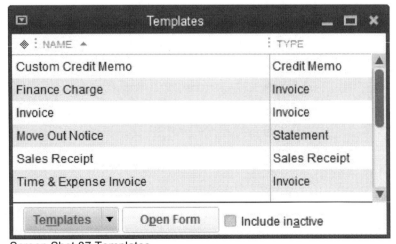
Screen Shot 87 Templates

The Select Template Type window appears.

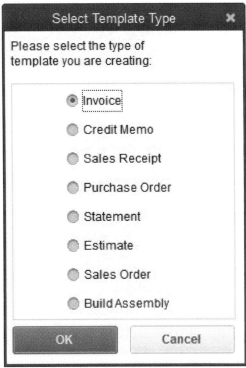

Screen Shot 88 Select Template Type

- Select the type of template you would like to create

TEMPLATES

A blank template opens, or you can customize an existing template for your business needs.

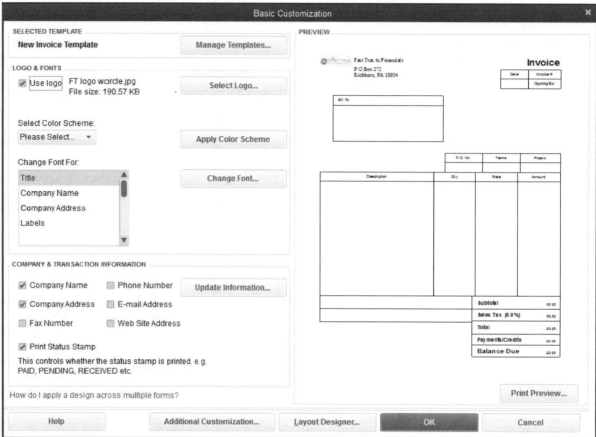

Screen Shot 89 Basic Customization

To add a logo to the template form:

- Select Use Logo by marking the corresponding checkbox
- Click **Select Logo…**

TEMPLATES

- Browse to the image and click **Open** to attach
- Apply the color scheme and fonts, as needed
- Click **Additional Customization…**

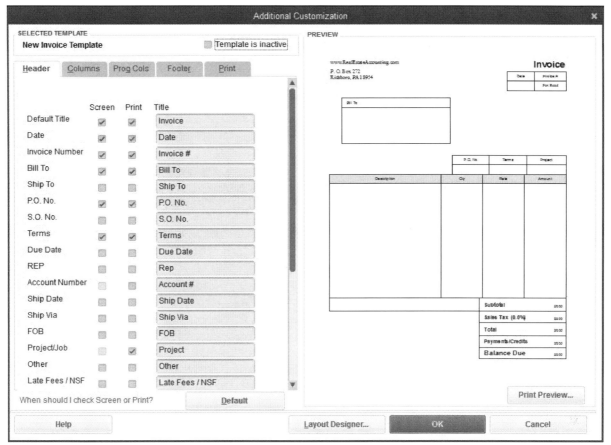

Screen Shot 90 Additional Customization

- Make changes, as needed
- Click **Layout Designer…** to customize the template's format

IMPORTANT
Remember to correctly use the Due Date field, depending on if you are tracking balances in QuickBooks. Refer to the chapter on Categorizing Records.

TEMPLATES

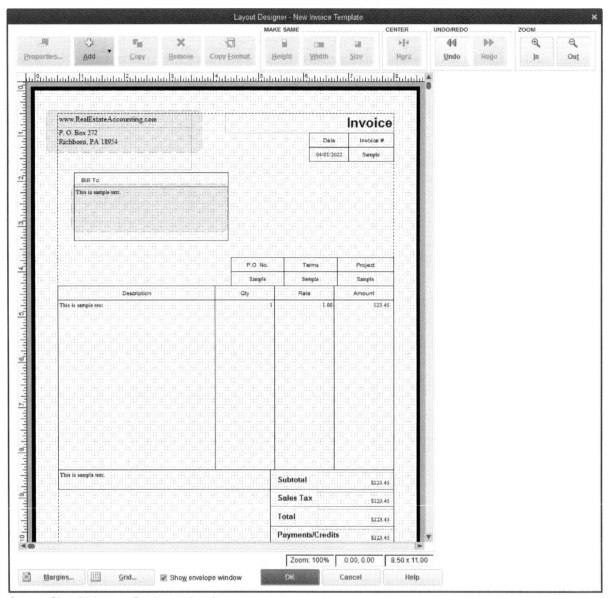

Screen Shot 91 Layout Designer - Invoice

- Make changes, as needed
- Click **OK** three times to save

CHAPTER 18 STATEMENTS

Sometimes you want to send statements to tenants to remind them of overdue balances. A statement summarizes a tenant's account by listing recent invoices, credit memos, and payments in summary or detail.

Objectives

Upon completion of this chapter, you will be able to:

- Customize Statement
- Create Tenant Statements

STATEMENTS

To create tenant statements:

- Click **Customers** on the Menu Bar
- Select Create Statements…

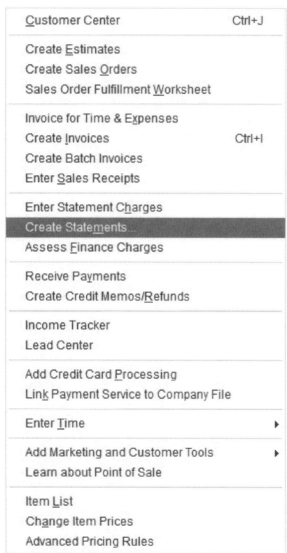
Screen Shot 92 Select Create Statements...

STATEMENTS

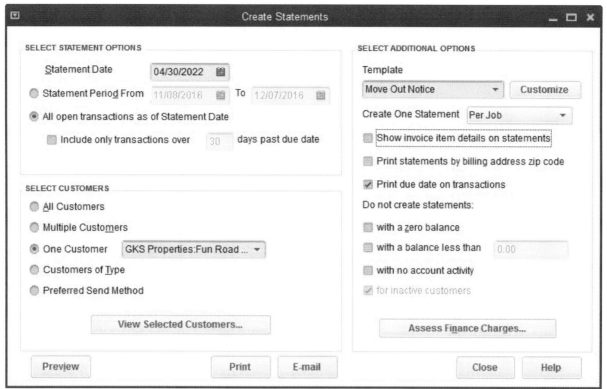

Screen Shot 93 Create Statements

- Complete the fields as follows:

Field	Data
Select Statement Options	
Statement Date	Today's date
	Select all open transactions as of Statement Date
Select Customers	
	Select Multiple Customers, One Customer, or Customers of Type (must select Tenant name from drop down menu)
Select Additional Options	
Template	Select the appropriate template or customize your statement
Create One Statement	Per Customer or Per Job (by property or tenant)
Options	As needed
Select Print due date on transactions under Template	
Click **Preview**, **Print,** or **E-mail**	

Table 10 Create Statements

Commercial Property Management for Managers: QuickBooks Desktop   135

CUSTOMIZE STATEMENT

We have provided a customized template. You can further customize statements for your business before beginning to create and use them.

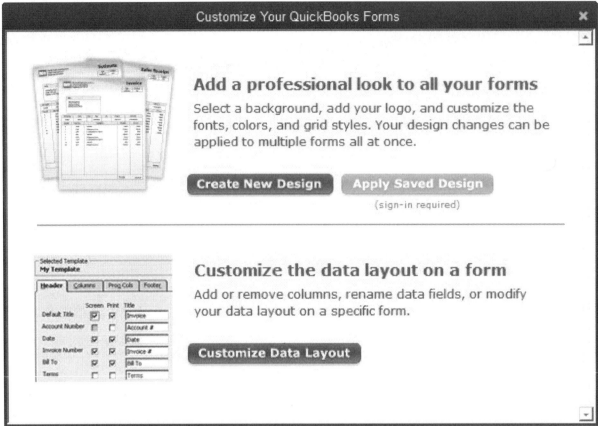

Screen Shot 94 Additional Customization

Follow the prompts, and you will be able to customize the layout and the header, columns, footer, and print.

CHAPTER 19 CATEGORIZING RECORDS

Items represent everything bought or sold in the course of doing business. This includes products and services. Items help you to analyze business operations and transactions, such as invoices, checks, and purchases for a particular property (Class).

Expenses relating to your overall business and administrative costs are often referred to as Overhead (Your Company). Enter and track items and expenses as you want them to appear in your reports.

Objectives

Upon completion of this chapter, you will be able to:

- Track Start-up Costs and Organizational Expenses
- Gita's Transaction Rules
- Distinguish between Fixed and Variable Expenses
- Understand the Expenses and Items Tabs
- Understand Item Types
- Categorize Overhead and Property Expenses
- Differentiate between CAM and Non-CAM Expenses

MEMORIZE THIS CHAPTER

As you set up your business, you should be aware of tax policies for new ventures. Track start-up costs and organizational expenses, such as training employees, advertising, and related travel, as some of these costs may be tax deductible. Check the IRS website for more details.

Start-up Costs

Start-up costs are amounts paid or incurred to create a business or to investigate the creation or acquisition of business.

Start-up costs may include market analysis, advertisements, salaries and wages for training instructors, web design costs, travel expenses to meet potential suppliers or customers, as well as salaries and fees for executives.

When recording start-up costs, use the Start-up Costs asset account and your Company as the Customer:Job and Class.

Organizational Expenses

Organizational expenses are amounts paid or incurred to set up a business's entity.

Organizational expenses for a sole proprietorship or single-member LLC are direct costs incurred to register a fictitious name or DBA (doing business as).

Organizational expenses for a partnership are direct costs incurred to create a partnership, such as legal fees for negotiation and preparation of the partnership agreement, accounting fees, and partnership filing fees.

Organizational expenses for a corporation are direct costs incurred to create a corporation such as salaries of temporary directors, organizational meetings, state incorporation fees, and the cost of related legal services.

When recording organizational expenses, use the Organizational Expenses asset account and your Company as the Customer:Job and Class.

CATEGORIZING RECORDS

GITA'S TRANSACTION RULES

Entering data in transaction fields helps you to retrace your steps when communicating with a vendor. The Ref. No. fields and Check No. field are especially important.

The Ref. No. field appears on bills and credit card transactions. If there is no bill number provided by the Vendor, enter the date of the invoice in Year-Month-Day format. For example, you may receive a bill without a number to reference on May 3, 2014. The Ref. No. should be entered as 2014-05-03. For credit card transactions, we recommend leaving the Ref. No. field blank.

If you did not write a physical check to make a payment, follow the procedure to Assign Check Numbers. Enter a payment method as the Check No. from those listed below:

- ACH
- Debit
- Direct Deposit
- EFT
- Online
- Paypal
- Phone

FIXED VS. VARIABLE EXPENSES

Operating expenses are those costs incurred to maintain your business.

Fixed expenses are those items that keep your office operational and have a specific cost, such as insurance or rent.

Variable expenses are items that vary, such as office supplies, your telephone bill, meal, and entertainment costs.

Few expenses can be both fixed and variable; however, some administrative expenses can fall into both categories.

EXPENSES TAB VS. ITEMS TAB

When you enter bills, enter a credit card charge, or write a check, categorize the cost as either an Expense or an Item.

> **NOTE**
> Be sure to enter data in the Customer:Job and Class fields to classify the Expense or Item related to.

Notice that the Expenses and Items tabs are located about half-way down the screen on the bill check credit card charge and credit forms.

Expenses Tab: Used for Overhead or costs not related to a specific property, such as auto expenses, office expenses, loans, etc.

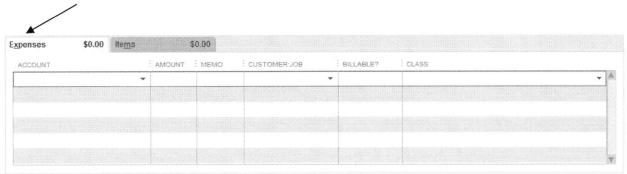
Screen Shot 95 Expenses Tab

Items Tab: Used for costs specific to property, such as utility bills, labor, and materials for repairs, capital improvements, etc.

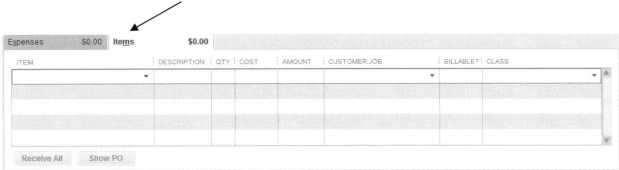
Screen Shot 96 Items Tab

TWO TYPES OF ITEMS

There are two types of Items used for one time entry in QuickBooks.

Income only items are used on invoices or sales receipts and show as income on the Profit & Loss report. When using these, the Item may be a negative or positive amount.

Items used for **both income and expenses** related to a property and your Company can be entered on invoices, sales receipts, bills, checks, or credit card transactions.

An example of an Item used for both income and expenses is when you spend money on utilities, and the same amount is charged on an invoice for reimbursement.

OVERHEAD VS. PROPERTY

To distinguish between overhead and property expenses or income, ask yourself whether the money received or spent was for a particular property.

Customer:Job

The Customer:Job field tracks all money related to property or Your Company (Overhead). Refer to CAM vs. Non-CAM Expenses

Billable?

When do you add a check mark in the Billable? column?

- Only if you are going to invoice the owner or the tenant, for the amount you in entered in the line item. Refer to chapter Markup and Pass Thru Charges
- DO NOT add a check mark if you are going to deduct the expenses from owner proceed check. As you are receiving and paying on behalf of the owner's fund.

Class

The Class tracks the owner's name and Your Company (Overhead). The Subclass tracks the property name that belongs to the real estate investor.

A property management company always collects and spends money on behalf of the owner. Make a decision with only three questions:

- Is the income and expense owner's money?
- Are you going to deduct the expense from rent collected?
- Do you collect money in advance or reserve fund for the expenses?

If you said yes to one or all select the property name as the class. If you said no to all the questions select Your Company (Overhead).

CAM vs. Non-CAM Expenses

Common Area Maintenance (CAM) expenses are any costs incurred to maintain common areas. Depending on your lease agreement, the tenant may be liable for expenses incurred.

Once the expenses are assigned to a specific property, determine whether the expenses can be billed to a particular tenant. If you know the exact amount the tenant is responsible for, then assign the expenses to the Tenant (Customer:Job).

CAM Expenses

CAM expense is calculated on an accrual basis. It is very important to enter Invoices for tenants and Bills for vendors.

CAM expenses can be reconciled monthly, quarterly, semi-annually, or annually.

Tenants pay either a percentage, fixed amount, or an amount specified by the lease agreement. After reconciling, tenants are charged or credited the difference between the actual and estimated amounts.

Categorize CAM expenses incurred:

- The expense incurred and is calculated at the end of the year; add CAM as "Customer:Job" and uncheck the Billable? box
- Expenses incurred which is the exact amount to be charged to the Tenant, add the tenant's name as "Customer:Job" and add a check mark on the Billable? Box

Non-CAM Expenses

Non-CAM expenses are any expenses incurred that are not included in calculating CAM for the tenants.

- The expense incurred and is not considered as CAM; add Non-CAM, Unit or Tenant as "Customer:Job" and uncheck the Billable? box

CHAPTER 20 TAX

Sales and tax may be charged to tenants for rentals. These required taxes are established by city, state, county, and local authorities and may be referred to as sales, rental room, or occupancy tax. Most of the time the taxes are grouped together as one line item.

Objectives

Upon completion of this chapter, you will be able to:

- Add and Change Tax Settings
- Set up Tax for Multiple Authorities
- Understand Tax Code
- Assign Taxes to Amenities

UPDATE TAX PREFERENCES

Be sure to include all taxes you are required to collect from tenants. In QuickBooks, we use the term Sales Tax for tracking all tax details.

To add, change, and verify the sales tax:

- Click **Edit** on the Menu Bar
- Select Preferences...
- Select Sales Tax
- Click the **Company Preferences** tab

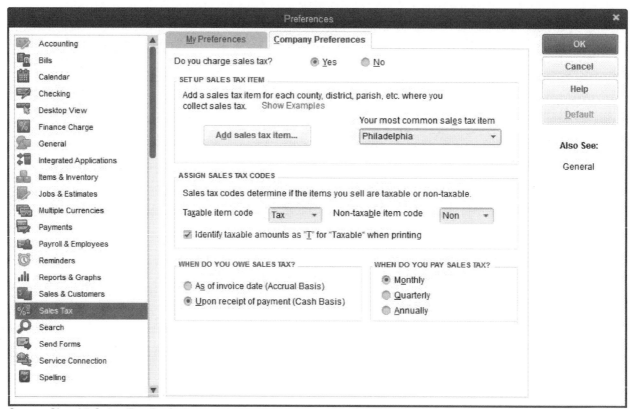

Screen Shot 97 Sales Tax Preferences

- Click **Add Sales Tax Item...**

TAX

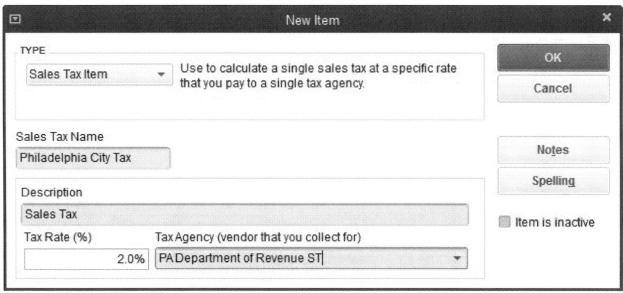

Screen Shot 98 New Item Sales Tax

- Make selections based on how and how often you pay taxes. Enter the Sales Tax Name, Description, Tax Rate, and Tax Agency
- Click **OK**

IMPORTANT
When entering deposits such as pet, or security, change them to non-taxable. All deposits received will show on one line (Non) on the Sales Tax Liability report.

Sales Tax Code

Each Customer and Item you create is automatically tagged in QuickBooks as taxable or non-taxable.

To change the tax code:

- Click **Lists** on the Menu Bar
- Select Sales Tax Code List
- Double-click on the sales tax Item you want to change
- Click **OK**

SALES TAX GROUP

In some situations, a property may be subject to tax from multiple authorities. For example, a property in the city of Philadelphia would be subject to Pennsylvania's sales tax of 6% and Philadelphia's city tax of 2%, totaling 8%. To track revenue and sales tax for each authority easily, create a sales tax group.

To create a sales tax group:

- Click **Lists** on the Menu Bar
- Select Item List
- Right-click on the list name and select New
- Select Sales Tax Group from the drop down menu
- Enter Group Name/Number and description
- Add the sales tax Items from the drop down menu

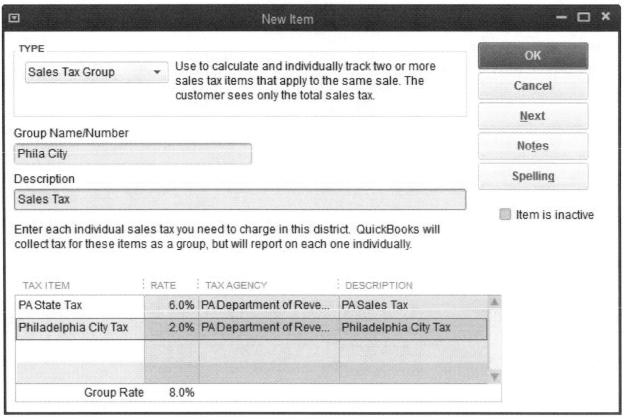

Screen Shot 99 New Item Sales Tax Group

- Click **OK**

SECTION 4

MANAGE NAMES

Now that you have learned the basic layout of QuickBooks and have restored your Company's file, you are ready to enter property owners, properties, units, and tenants.

We are "tweaking" QuickBooks' use of Customer:Job in the following manner:

- Property Owner as a Customer
- Property as a Job of a Property Owner (Customer) (optional)
- Unit as a Job of a Property (Job) (only if there are multiple units)
- Tenant as a Job of a Unit (Job) (optional)
- CAM as a Job of a Property (Job)
- Non-CAM as a Job of a Property (Job)

To understand this better, let's say you are a contractor. You have several customers or real estate investors, and for each customer, you have multiple jobs. Similarly, we are using Customer and Job to mean property owner, property, unit, and tenant, respectively.

For each Customer (Property Owner) and Job (Property), there are multiple Jobs (Units), and you have new and old Jobs (Tenants) for the same unit. You may have multiple units in one building with multiple tenants at one time, or you may have homes or offices with one resident at a time, but there are still multiple tenants over the course of time. This is how the relationship between property owners, properties, units, and tenants fits into QuickBooks' Customer and Job setup.

Additionally, you will learn to enter vendors, equity holders, and financiers. By adding and organizing these players correctly in QuickBooks, you will be able to record transactions and evaluate your business through specific reporting.

When entering names, you may wish to abbreviate them, as shown below under the Abbreviated Names heading. The reason for this is that when you create forms, the entire name may not be visible, due to space restrictions.

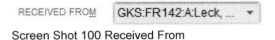
Screen Shot 100 Received From

Either method will yield to the name printing exactly as it is keyed into QuickBooks.

Abbreviated Names

NAME	BALANCE
◆ GKS	0.00
◆FR142	0.00
◆A Unit	0.00
◆Cruso, Robin	0.00
◆Leck, Ed	0.00
◆B Unit	0.00
◆Levin, Frank	0.00
◆Zimmer, Kevin	0.00
◆C Unit	0.00
◆Hammer, Guy	0.00
◆Smith, Ray	0.00
◆GrayL	0.00

Screen Shot 101 Names Abbreviated

Regular Names

NAME	BALANCE
◆ GKS Properties LLC	0.00
◆Fun Road 142	0.00
◆A Unit	0.00
◆Cruso, Robin	0.00
◆Leck, Ed	0.00
◆B Unit	0.00
◆Levin, Frank	0.00
◆Zimmer, Kevin	0.00
◆C Unit	0.00
◆Hammer, Guy	0.00
◆Smith, Ray	0.00
◆Gray Lane	0.00

Screen Shot 102 Names Regular

Before entering names, gather the following pertinent details about property owners, properties, units, and tenants. Entering this information in QuickBooks will save you time as you can easily access it.

MANAGE NAMES

PROPERTY OWNER CHECKLIST

Property Owner
☑ Contact Information: Name, Address, Phone No., Fax No. & Email
☑ Agreement Letter
☑ W-9 Form – Available on www.irs.gov
☑ Payment Information
☑ Loan Balances and Documents
☑ Reserve Fund Amount by Owner or Property
☑ Vendor Insurances

Checklist 3 Property Owner

PROPERTY CHECKLIST

Property
☑ Budget
☑ Property Address
☑ Square Feet - Rentable Space vs. Usable Space
☑ No. of Units
☑ Contracts, Licenses, Inspections & Permits
☑ List of Contractors and Vendors including Contact Information
☑ Deposits with Contractors & Utility Companies
☑ Insurance & Policies
☑ Open Work Orders
☑ Details of Unpaid Bills

Checklist 4 Property

Commercial Property Management for Managers: QuickBooks Desktop

Units Checklist

Unit
☑ Square Feet
☑ Budget by Unit
☑ Open Work Orders
☑ Equipment & Fixtures- locations, serial no., warranties, etc.

Checklist 5 Units

Tenant Checklist

Tenant
☑ Copy of Lease
☑ Lease Abstract & Rent Roll
☑ Lease Addendum
☑ Tenant Improvements
☑ Rent & CAM Expenses - Prior Years and Year-to-Date
☑ Security Deposit
☑ Details of Unpaid Balances
☑ Insurance Certificate

Checklist 6 Tenant

CHAPTER 21 OWNER'S EQUITY

Equity owner may very well be the heart and soul of your business. If you enter them accurately into QuickBooks, you will be able to track cash flow and maintain good records for equity in either a sole proprietorship, partnership, or a corporation. If you are not sure in which category your business fits, refer to the chapter on Company File.

Objectives

Upon completion of this chapter, you will be able to:

- Enter an Equity Owner
- Enter a Partner
- Enter a Shareholder
- Customize Reports

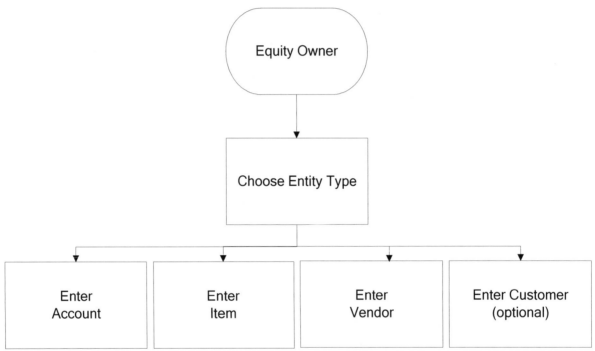

Flow Chart 2 Equity Owner

Entity Type

Depending on your entity type, select the correct accounts in the Chart of Accounts. Refer to the chapter on Working with Lists.

Sole Proprietorship

Enter the following Owner's Equity Accounts and Items:

- Draws
- Investment

Partnership

Enter the following Partner's Equity Accounts and Items for each partner:

- Distribution
- Draws
- Investment

Corporation

Enter the following Liability and Equity Accounts and Items for each shareholder:

- Loan from Shareholders (as a Long Term Liability account)
- Additional Paid in Capital (as an Equity account)

The following as Equity Accounts:

- Paid in Capital
- Dividends Paid
- Common Stock
- Net Profit & Loss

EXAMPLE

According to your entity type add and change accounts as shown in the example below. Refer to chapter Chart of Accounts

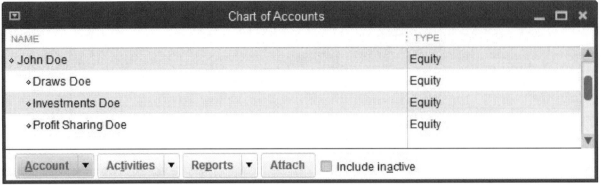
Screen Shot 103 Equity Accounts

According to your entity type add and change items as shown in the example below. Refer to the chapter on Working with Items to add items names and link them to the corresponding accounts.

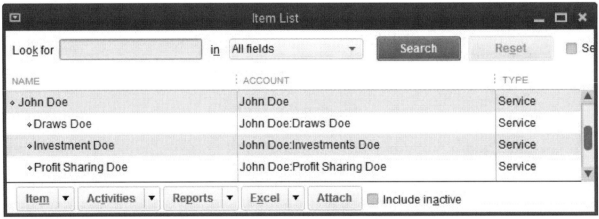
Screen Shot 104 Equity Items

OWNER'S EQUITY

AS A VENDOR

Enter each owner, partner, or shareholder as a Vendor to account for all money deposited, withdrawn, and distributed.

To add an equity partner as a Vendor:

- Click **Vendors** on the Icon Bar
- Right-click in the list and click **New Vendor**

For more information, refer to the chapter on Vendors.

CUSTOMIZE REPORTS

Several memorized reports for sole proprietorships, partnerships, and corporations are included in the template file.

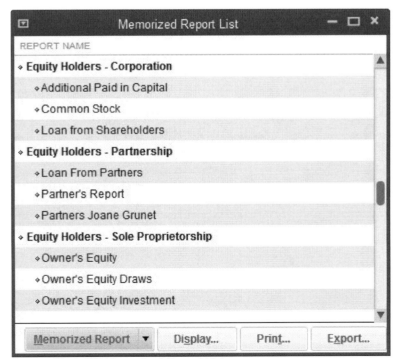

Screen Shot 105 Memorized Report List

Customize equity owner reports as needed.

To customize a report:

- Click **MemRpts** on the Icon Bar
- Double-click on the report
- Click **Customize Report**
- Modify the report to your requirements in the filters and header/footer tabs
- Click **OK**

Memorize customized reports under the appropriate report group. Refer to the chapter on Customizing Reports.

DELETE REPORTS

Delete the additional reports after determining your Company's entity type.

> **NOTE**
> Delete all reports under a heading before deleting the report group. You cannot remove a memorized report group that contains reports.

To delete reports:

- Click **MemRpts** on the Icon Bar
- Right-click on the report and click **Delete Memorized Report**

CHAPTER 22 APPLICANTS

Prospective tenants must submit an application for the property management company to check credit history and run a background check.

Objectives

Upon completion of this chapter, you will be able to:

- Enter Applicant

APPLICANT NAME

You have two options to enter the Applicant name:

- If the application was denied use the name "Applicant" as Customer
- If the application was approved and tenant signs the lease, add the name as Tenant. Refer to chapter Tenants.

If you do not want to keep track of each payment received you can use the Applicant name as Customer and track the applicant's name by entering the name in the description field.

CHAPTER 23 PROPERTY OWNERS

An owner is a person or entity (holding company) who owns property in their name or under a corporate name. Rather than maintain separate QuickBooks files for properties under different EIN numbers, you may want to track all rent, managing of tenants, and maintenance of the properties in one file, making it easier to handle day-to-day operations.

If you choose to use one QuickBooks file, or you have separate companies, follow the steps outlined in this chapter to enter each one. You will be able to quickly view and analyze referenced reports for each owner or Your Company on a periodic basis by tracking transactions for its properties and tenants.

Objectives

Upon completion of this chapter, you will be able to:

- Enter Holding Companies as Property Owners
- View Property Owner Information
- Group Property Owners
- Customize and Memorize Reports
- View Reports

PROPERTY OWNERS

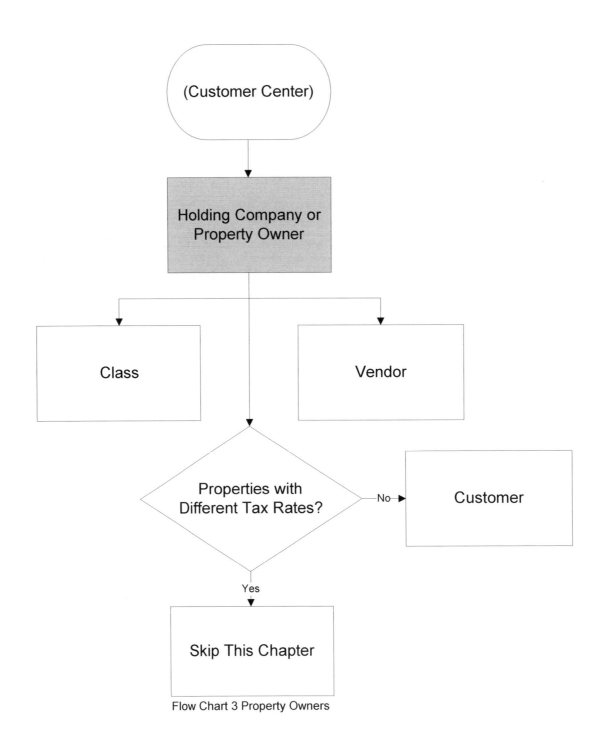

Flow Chart 3 Property Owners

THREE STEPS TO OWNER

Add the owner as:

- Vendor
- Customer
- Class

For concise reporting, enter each property owner as both a Class and a Customer. The name should be entered the same.

If there is only one owner for all the properties, you can skip the Property Owners chapter and start with the Property chapter.

> **TIP**
> The Property Owner's name should be in last name, first name format or simply listed as the holding company's name.

PROPERTY OWNER AS VENDOR

Enter each property owner as a Vendor to any payments and follow the instructions on adding a new vendor. Refer to chapter Vendors.

The only difference would be:

- Add " – PO" at the end of the vendor name
- Change the Vendor Type to Property Owner
- Remember to add the 1099 details

PROPERTY OWNERS

PROPERTY OWNER AS A CLASS

Enter each property owner as a Class to analyze the income and expenses for each one's associated properties.

> **TIP**
> Use the Your Company class for transactions that are not related to a particular property. Examples of overhead expenses are office expenses, purchase of computers or equipment, bank service charges, and utilities for the office.

The image below displays how the Class List should look in QuickBooks. In this example, the company name is GKS Properties.

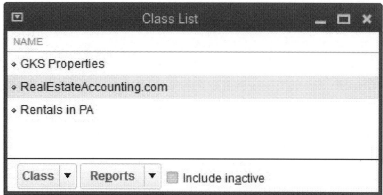
Screen Shot 106 Class List

Commercial Property Management for Managers: QuickBooks Desktop

PROPERTY OWNERS

To enter a property owner as a Class:

- Click **Lists** on the Menu Bar
- Select Class List
- Right-click on a Class name within the list
- Select New

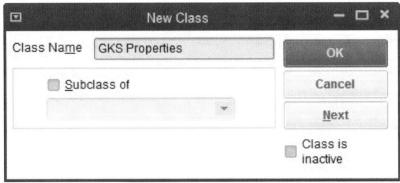
Screen Shot 107 Property Owner as a Class

- Complete the fields as follows:

Field	Data
Class Name	Property Owner or Holding Company Name
Click **OK** or **Next** to enter another property owner	

Table 11 Property Owner as a Class

Commercial Property Management for Managers: QuickBooks Desktop

PROPERTY OWNER AS A CUSTOMER

IMPORTANT
When you select the tax code for a property owner, the data flows through to all of the properties, units, and tenants related to that owner.

If you have multiple properties under one holding company, but the properties are in different locations, the rental tax percent may be different. If that is the case, it is not necessary to enter the property owner as a Customer.

If the taxes are the same for all the properties owned by the same company, enter the holding company as a Customer to list all property, unit, and tenant (optional) details for each.

The image below displays how property owners (as Customers) should look in QuickBooks. In this example, the company name is GKS Properties.

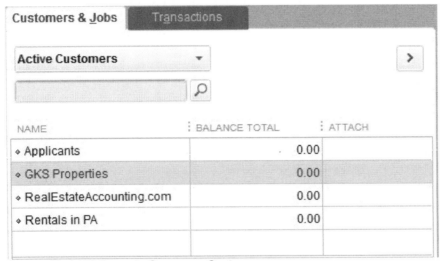

Screen Shot 108 Property Owners as Customers

PROPERTY OWNERS

To enter a property owner as a Customer:

- Click **Tenants** on the Icon Bar or **Customer Center** on the Menu Bar
- Right-click on any name
- Select New Customer

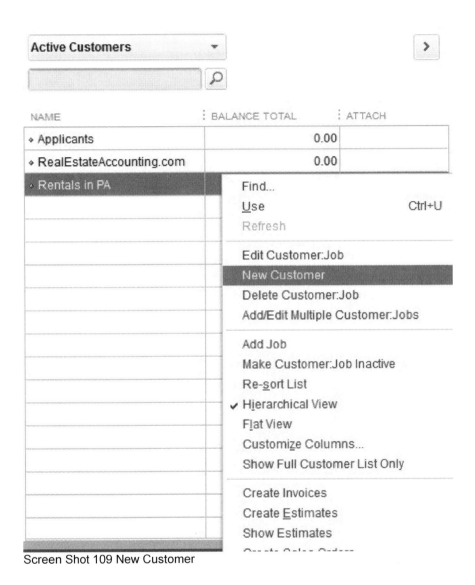

Screen Shot 109 New Customer

Commercial Property Management for Managers: QuickBooks Desktop 167

Address Info

Screen Shot 110 Property Owner Address Info

PROPERTY OWNERS

- Complete the fields as follows:

Field	Data
Customer Name	Property Owner or Holding Company Name
Opening Balance	Leave blank
as of	Leave as is
Address Info	
Company Name	Prefills
Full Name	
Mr./Ms./…	As needed
First	First name
M.I.	Middle initial
Last	Last name
Job Title	Title
Main Phone	Click the drop down arrow to select the type of data you want to track
Main Email	
Work Phone	✓ Main Phone
CC Email	Home Phone
Mobile	Alt. Phone
Website	Alt. Mobile
Fax	Alt. Fax
Other 1	Alt. Email 1
	Alt. Email 2
	LinkedIn
	Facebook
	Twitter
	URL 1
	URL 2
	URL 3
	URL 4
	Skype ID
	Other 2
	Other 3
	Screen Shot 111 Field drop down
Address Details	
Invoice/Bill To	Address of the Owner
Ship To	Leave blank
Click **Payment Settings** tab	

Table 12 Property Owner Address Info

Commercial Property Management for Managers: QuickBooks Desktop

Payment Settings

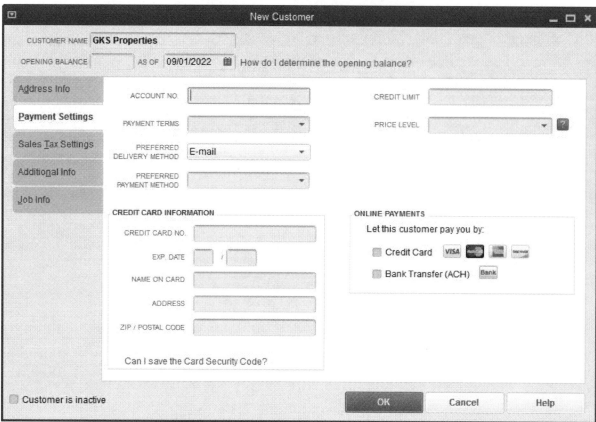

Screen Shot 112 Property Owner Payment Settings

PROPERTY OWNERS

- Complete the fields as follows:

Field	Data
Account Number	Leave blank unless you are tracking the account number
Credit Limit	As needed
Payment Terms	
Price Level	
Preferred Delivery Method	
Preferred Payment Method	
Credit Card Information	As needed
Credit Card No	
Exp. Date	
Name on Card	
Address	
Zip/Postal Code	
Click **Sales Tax Settings** tab	

Table 13 Property Owner Payment Settings

Sales Tax Settings

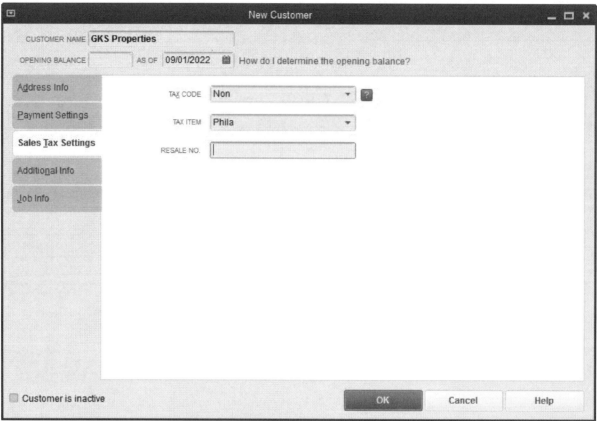

Screen Shot 113 Property Owner Sales Tax Settings

- Complete the fields as follows:

Field	Data
Tax Code	Taxable or Non-Taxable
Tax Item	If taxable, select correct sales tax item or group
Resale No.	Leave blank
Click **Additional Info** tab	

Table 14 Property Owner Sales Tax Settings

PROPERTY OWNERS

Additional Info

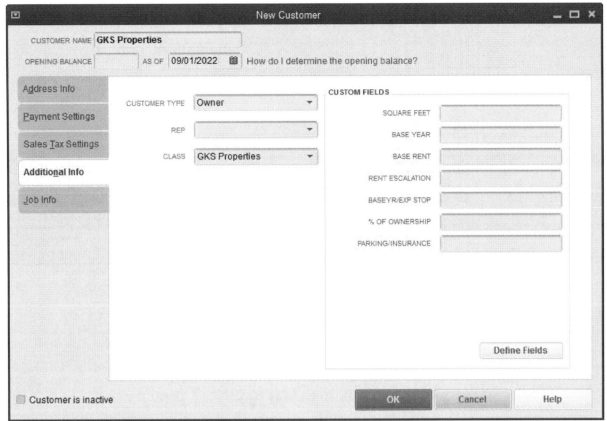

Screen Shot 114 Property Owner Additional Info

- Complete the fields as follows:

Field	Data
Customer Type	Owner
Rep	As needed
Class	Select Owner name (only in Enterprise version)
Custom Fields	As needed
Click **OK**	

Table 15 Property Owner Additional Info

Class: Only available in Enterprise version. When you enter a transaction selecting an owner (Customer) name, the owner name (Class) will prefill.

Custom Fields: There are 12 custom fields available in the Enterprise version and the type of data you can enter by amount, date, numbers, text and multi-choice which makes it easy to filter and report.

PROPERTY OWNER INFORMATION

To view a property owner's information:

- Click **Tenants** on the Icon Bar

Screen Shot 115 Property Owner Information

REPORT: OWNER LIST

To view a detailed list of property owners:

- Click **MemRpts** on the Icon Bar
- Double-click Owner List under Lists

www.RealEstateAccounting.com
Property Owner List

Customer	First Name	Last Name	Main Phone	Main Email	Street1	Street2	City	State	Zip
GKS Properties	John	Smith	123-456-45...	gks@gmail.com	John Smith	140 Liberty Avenue	Norristown	PA	19403
Rentals in PA	Zach	Groney	215-985-57...	rentalspa@gmail.c...	Zach Groney	85 S West Road	Elden	PA	19874

Report 3 Owner List

ADD PROPERTY OWNER GROUP

It is important that property owners, properties, units, tenants, and vendors be organized and easy to find when viewing reports related to them.

Set up your QuickBooks file to group related information, transactions, and reports for each owner by adding a group for each in both the Memorized Transaction List and in the Memorized Report List.

To set up a group for each owner in the Memorized Transaction List:

- Click **Lists** on the Menu Bar
- Select Memorized Transaction List
- Right-click on the list and select New Group
- Enter the name of the owner
- Select Do Not Remind Me
- Click **OK**

To set up a group for each owner in the Memorized Report List:

- Click **Reports** on the Menu Bar
- Under Memorized Reports, select Memorized Report List
- Click **Memorized Report** on the bottom left of the screen
- Select New Group
- Enter the name of the owner
- Click **OK**

CUSTOMIZE AND MEMORIZE REPORTS

The success of your business depends on managing properties and creating monthly reports for your holding companies. Customize and memorize reports to analyze each property's income and expenses for the holding company.

There are four important reports you should customize and memorize for each property owner or holding company:

- The Profit & Loss Summary report summarizes the money received and spent for each property
- The Profit & Loss Detail report shows each transaction with detail of monies which were received and paid for each property
- The Security Deposit report shows each tenant deposit, paid or unpaid, for each property

Once you initially memorize the reports, you can review them monthly, as needed.

> **TIP**
> After you create the reports each month, print them to a PDF and save them for future reference. You can also email them to appropriate parties. Click **File** or **Print** and select Save as PDF to create a PDF file.

> **IMPORTANT**
> Save time and money by using an app that creates owners summary and detail reports to PDF in 5 minutes. Contact us for more resources.

Be sure to select the correct report and memorize it with a new name under the right group of the report. Customize and memorize reports for each property owner.

PROPERTY OWNER'S REPORT CUSTOMIZATION CHECKLIST

	Report Name	Filters Tab		
		Filter		Select
☐	Filter tab	Class	=	Property
☐	Header/Footer tab	Name	=	Add Property in front of the title

Checklist 7 Property Owner's Report Customization

CUSTOM REPORTING

Save time by using an app that creates owners report in few seconds.

Skip customizing reports for the owner and their properties. Contact your consultant or us, to learn about apps to save time and money.

PROPERTY OWNERS

CUSTOMIZE PROFIT & LOSS REPORT

Select the template and then customize it further under the Memorized Reports

To customize the Profit & Loss report:

- Click **Reports** on the Icon Bar
- Select Memorized Reports
- Scroll down to Property Owners group
- Click **Profit & Loss Summary** (for summary report) or
- Click **Profit & Loss Detail** (for detail report)
- Click **Customize Report**
- Click **Filters** tab

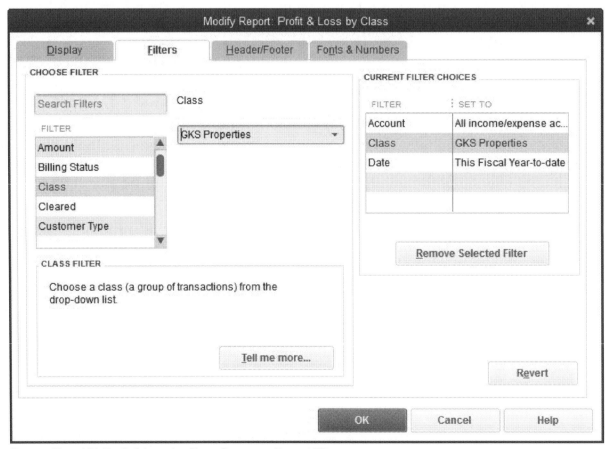

Screen Shot 116 Profit & Loss by Class Summary Report Filters

PROPERTY OWNERS

- Complete the fields as follows:

Field	Data
Choose Filter	Type in search terms for easy selection
Current Filter Choices (box on the far right)	
Click **Date** (in the middle of the screen)	Select the date of the report
Current Filter Choices (box on the far right)	
Click **Class** (in the middle of the screen)	Property Owner or Holding Company Name (not the Property Name unless you want to memorize reports for each Property) **TIP:** Copy the name, exactly as you have typed it, to paste on the next screen under Report Title.
Click **Header/Footer** tab	

Table 16 Profit & Loss Summary Report Filters

Header/Footer

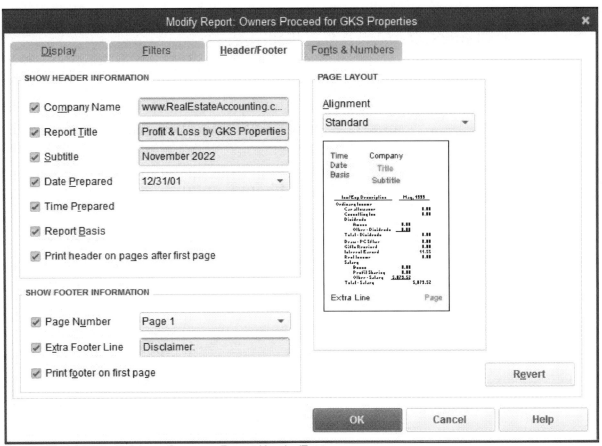

Screen Shot 117 Profit & Loss Summary Report Header/Footer

- Complete the fields as follows:

Field	Data
Show Header Information	
Company Name	Prefills
Report Title	Paste the name of the Property Owner from the Class field above to add the owner's name to the title
Subtitle	Prefills
Date Prepared	
Time Prepared	
Report Basis	
Print header on pages after the first page	
Show Footer Information	
Page Number	Prefills
Extra Footer Line	As needed
Print footer on the first page	
Page Layout	
Alignment	As needed
Click **OK**	

Table 17 Profit & Loss Summary Report Header/Footer

Review the Profit & Loss Summary report to check your work and then memorize the report so you can automatically produce it in the future.

PROPERTY OWNERS

Memorize the Report

To memorize the Profit & Loss Detail report:

- Click **Memorize** on the top of the report screen

Screen Shot 118 Memorize Profit & Loss Summary Report

- Complete the fields as follows:

Field	Data
Name	Title of report
Save in Memorized Report Group	Select the group
Share this report template with others	Do **NOT** check this box unless you wish to share the template with all QuickBooks users
Click **OK**	

Table 18 Memorize Profit & Loss Summary Report

REPORT: PROFIT & LOSS SUMMARY

To view the Profit & Loss Summary report:

- Click **MemRpts** on the Icon Bar
- Double-click the report you customized under the Property Owner's group

www.RealEstateAccounting.com
Profit & Loss by GKS Properties
November 2022

	Fun Road 142 (GKS Properties)	Swamp Road (GKS Properties)	Total GKS Properties
Ordinary Income/Expe...			
▼ Income			
▼ Total Rent			
Rental	5,000.00	2,500.00	7,500.00
Total Total Rent	5,000.00	2,500.00	7,500.00
Total Income	5,000.00	2,500.00	7,500.00
▼ Cost of Goods So...			
Property Repa...	1,598.00	2,750.00	4,348.00
Total COGS	1,598.00	2,750.00	4,348.00
Gross Profit	3,402.00	-250.00	3,152.00
Net Ordinary Income	3,402.00	-250.00	3,152.00
Net Income	3,402.00	-250.00	3,152.00

Report 4 Profit & Loss Summary

REPORT: PROFIT & LOSS DETAIL

To view the Profit & Loss Detail report:

- Click **MemRpts** on the Icon Bar
- Double-click report you customized under the Property Owner's group

www.RealEstateAccounting.com
Profit & Loss Detail by GKS Properties
November 2022

Type	Date	Num	Source Name	Memo	Paid Amount
Ordinary Income/Expense					
Income					
Total Rent					
Rental					
Invoice	11/03/2022	7	GKS Properties:Fun Road...	Rent for the...	5,000.00
Invoice	11/03/2022	9	GKS Properties:Swamp R...	Rent for the...	2,500.00
Total Rental					7,500.00
Total Total Rent					7,500.00
Total Income					7,500.00
Cost of Goods Sold					
Property Repairs					
Check	11/03/2022	819		-MULTIPLE-	4,348.00
Total Property Repairs					4,348.00
Total COGS					4,348.00
Gross Profit					3,152.00
Net Ordinary Income					3,152.00
Net Income					**3,152.00**

Report 5 Profit & Loss Detail

CHAPTER 24 PROPERTIES

Entering each property as a Subclass and a Job allows you to view reports with totals and subtotals for each:

- Property (as a Job) and Property Owner or Holding Company (as a Customer)
- Property (as a Subclass) and Property Owner (as a Class) (optional)

> **TIP**
>
> **Be consistent when entering property names,** using the street name followed by the number. For example, Fun Road 142 or Fun Rd W 142.
>
> Be sure the name is entered in the same format for both Customer:Job and Class.

Objectives

Upon completion of this chapter, you will be able to:

- Review our Checklist
- Enter Properties
- Group Properties
- Memorize Reports
- View Reports

PROPERTIES

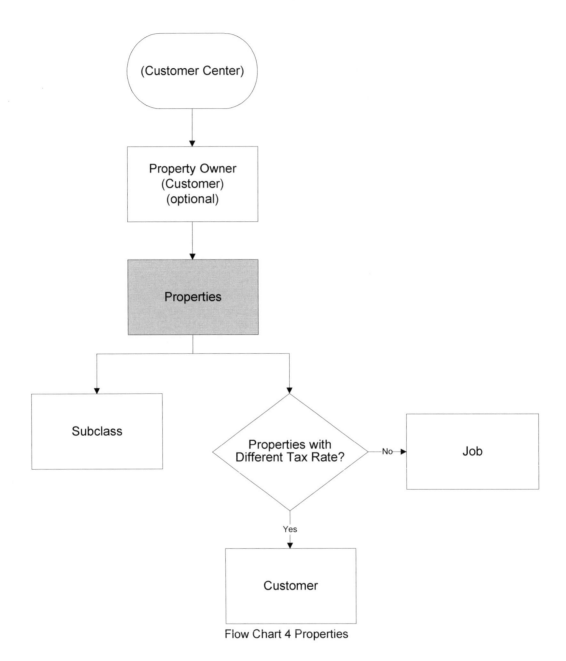

Flow Chart 4 Properties

PROPERTY CHECKLIST

Property
☐ Property Address
☐ What is rentable in the Property or each Unit (door)?
☐ Sales Tax Rate
☐ Contracts, Licenses, Inspections, and Permits
☐ List of Contractors and Vendors, including Contact Information
☐ Deposits with Contractors and Utility Companies
☐ Insurance and Policies
☐ Open Work Orders
☐ Details of Unpaid Bills
☐ Inventory of Each Item in the Property or Unit
☐ Location of Additional Items Stored
☐
☐
☐
☐

Checklist 8 Property

Decide How to Enter a Property

When entering a property, you should add it as a Subclass, and then either as a Customer or Job, depending on the tax rates.

Properties with Same Sales Tax Rates

If the properties have the same tax rate, enter them as a Jobs under the property owner or holding company.

Refer to the section on Property as a Job in this chapter.

Properties with Different Sales Tax Rates

When you manage multiple properties under one property owner or holding company and the properties, have different tax rates, enter the properties as Customers. Enter the property name followed by the property owner or holding company's name.

Refer to the section on Property as a Customer in this chapter.

PROPERTIES

Property as a Subclass

To enter a property as a Subclass:

- Click **Lists** on the Menu Bar
- Select Class List
- Right-click on the Property Owner
- Select New

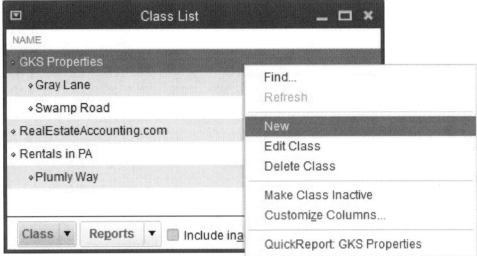

Screen Shot 119 New Subclass

Commercial Property Management for Managers: QuickBooks Desktop

The New Class window appears.

Screen Shot 120 Property as a Subclass

- Complete the fields as follows:

Field	Data
Class Name	Street name and number
Subclass of	Check the box and select the Property Owner's name from the drop down menu
Click **OK** or **Next** to enter another property	

Table 19 Property as a Subclass

To view the Property List by class, view the Class List (no reports).

PROPERTIES

Property as a Job

IMPORTANT
Enter the property as a Job to relate the property to the holding company ONLY if the tax rate for the property is the same as that of the holding company/owner.

To enter a property as a Job:

- Click **Tenants** on the Icon Bar
- Right-click the Property Owner
- Select Add Job

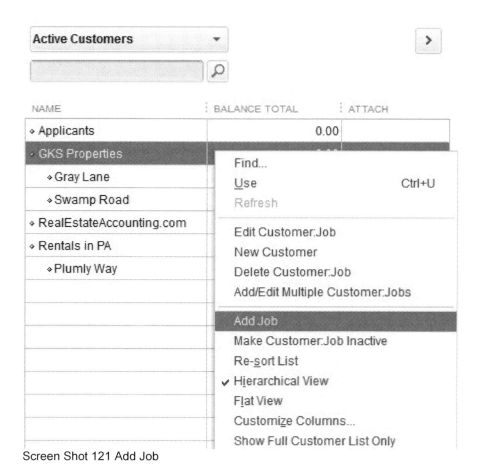

Screen Shot 121 Add Job

Commercial Property Management for Managers: QuickBooks Desktop   191

PROPERTIES

The New Job window appears.

Address Info

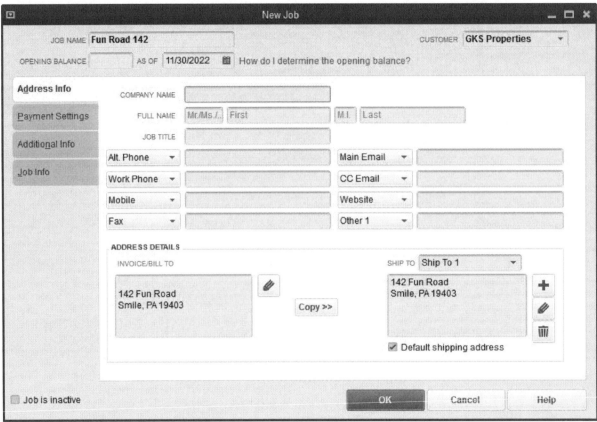

Screen Shot 122 Property Address Info

PROPERTIES

- Complete the fields as follows:

Field	Data
Job Name	Property Name
Customer	Prefills, change as needed
Opening Balance	Leave blank
as of	Leave as is
Remove prefilled data under all fields	
Ship To	
If you want the location of the Property to show on invoices and sale receipts, add the Ship To address of the Property or Unit. If you select the Job when entering the invoice or sales receipt and check the Default Shipping Address option, the Ship To address appears. Click the ➕ to Add the Rental Property Address. The Address you enter populates on invoices and sales receipts to show the location of the rental. This field is used only for short-term rentals.  Screen Shot 123 Add Shipping Address	
Click **Payments Settings** tab	

Table 20 Property Address Info

Commercial Property Management for Managers: QuickBooks Desktop   193

PROPERTIES

Payments Settings

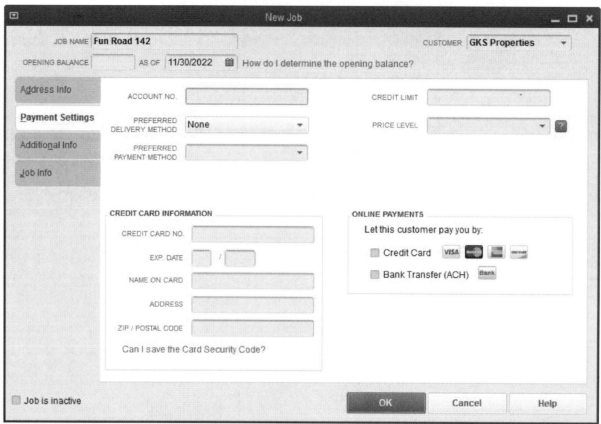

Screen Shot 124 Property Payment Settings

- Complete the fields as follows:

Field	Data
Account No.	Property Street Address
Price Level	As needed
All other fields	As needed
Click **Additional Info** tab	

Table 21 Property Payment Settings

Commercial Property Management for Managers: QuickBooks Desktop

PROPERTIES

Additional Info

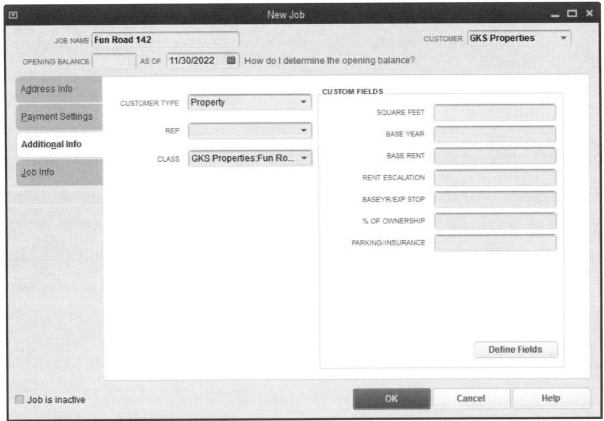

Screen Shot 125 Property Additional Info

- Complete the fields as follows:

Field	Data
Customer Type	Property
Rep	As needed
Class	Select Property Name (only in Enterprise version)
Custom Fields	As needed
Click **Job Info** tab	

Table 22 Property Additional Info

Class: Only available in Enterprise version. When you enter a transaction selecting a property (Job) name, the property name (Class) will prefill.

Custom Fields: There are 12 custom fields available in the Enterprise version and the type of data you can enter by amount, date, numbers, text and multi-choice which makes it easy to filter and report.

Commercial Property Management for Managers: QuickBooks Desktop

Job Info

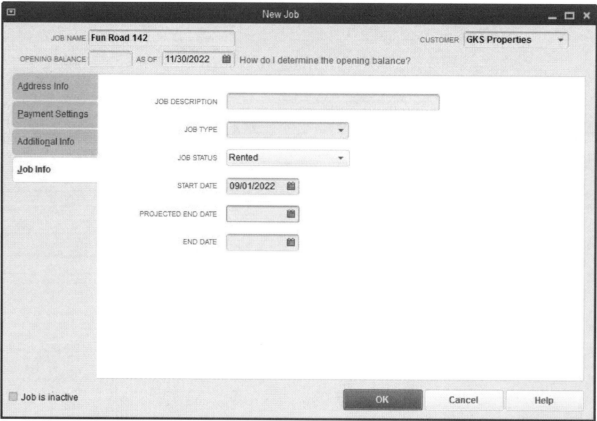

Screen Shot 126 Property Job Info

- Complete the fields as follows:

Field	Data
Job Description	Property details (how many bedrooms, bathrooms, etc.)
Job Type	Leave blank
Job Status	Rented
Start Date	Agreement Signed
Projected End Date	Property to be rented
End Date	Agreement ended
Click **OK**	

Table 23 Property Job Info

Property as a Customer

To enter a property as a Customer, follow the same steps as you did to enter the property as a Job, except that you should right-click and select New Customer. Enter the property with the owner's name at the end.

The image below displays how properties should look in QuickBooks. In this example, the Property name is Fun Road 142 – GKS Properties.

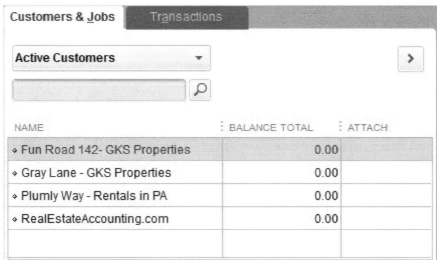

Screen Shot 127 Properties as Customers

PROPERTIES

REPORT: PROPERTY LIST

The Property List report displays the location of each Property (Ship to Address).

To view the Property List report:

- Click **MemRpts** on the Icon Bar
- Double-click Property List under Lists

www.RealEstateAccounting.com
Property List

Customer	Bill to 2	City	State	Zip
GKS Properties:Fun Road 142	142 Fun Road	Smile	PA	19403
GKS Properties:Gray Lane	42 Gray Lane	Purpling	PA	18976
GKS Properties:Swamp Road	578 Swamp Road	Property Land	PA	19047
Rentals in PA:Plumly Way	32 Plumly Way	Elden	PA	19874

Report 6 Property List

PROPERTIES

ADD PROPERTY GROUPS

Add a group for each property in the Memorized Transaction List to organize transactions associated with each property. Refer to the chapter on Recurring Transactions.

The image below displays how the Memorized Transaction List should look in QuickBooks.

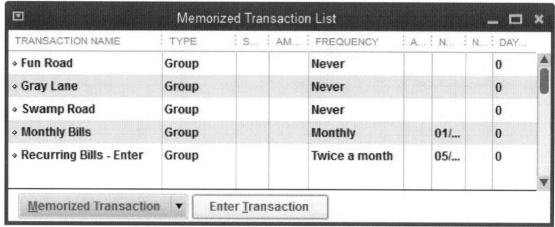
Screen Shot 128 Memorized Transaction List

MEMORIZE PROPERTY REPORTS

Memorize the Profit & Loss Summary report for each property. Refer to the chapter on Property Owners.

If you have already created the Profit & Loss Summary reports by Property Owner, filter by Class (Property) and rename the reports.

The image below displays how the Memorized Report List should look in QuickBooks.

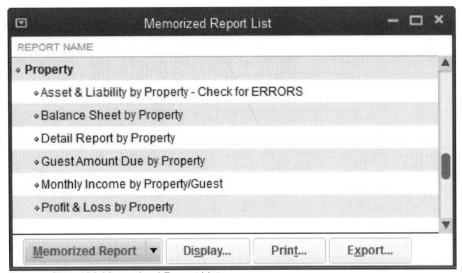
Screen Shot 129 Memorized Report List

CHAPTER 25 CAM AND NON-CAM

Tracking expenses are crucial in calculating at the end of the year. Review expenses incurred for each property and if they should be included in the expense recovery process.

Objectives

Upon completion of this chapter, you will be able to:

- Enter CAM and Non-CAM
- View Reports

CAM AND NON-CAM AS A JOB

Enter the CAM and Non-CAM as a Job for each property. Just follow the same procedure as you entered the Property.

The image below displays how CAM and Non-CAM (as Jobs of the Property) should look in QuickBooks. Remember to change the Customer Type as CAM and Non-CAM respectively.

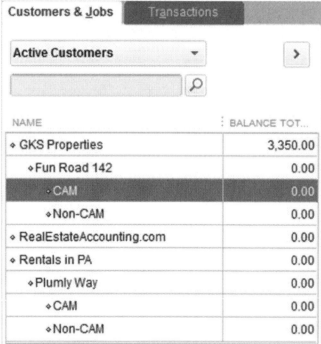
Screen Shot 130 Unit as a Job of Property

CUSTOMIZE REPORTS

Customize reports for each property for CAM and Non-CAM Jobs. Refer to chapter Expense Recovery.

CHAPTER 26 UNITS

Entering units as Jobs allows you to view reports with subtotals and totals for each unit and its associated tenants.

IMPORTANT
STOP – Enter units only if you want to track income and expenses by unit and tenants for each unit. If the property is a single rental unit, skip this chapter. Do not create a subclass for each unit.

Objectives

Upon completion of this chapter, you will be able to:

- Enter Units
- View Reports

UNITS

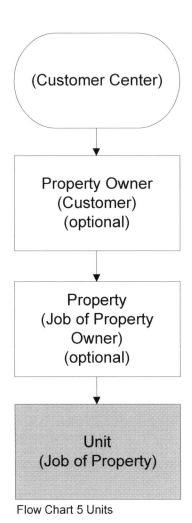

Flow Chart 5 Units

UNIT AS A JOB

Enter the unit as a Job to relate it to the property, list tenant details, track tenant expenses, and report vacancies for each unit.

The image below displays how units (as Jobs of the Property) should look in QuickBooks.

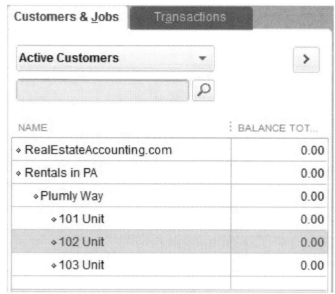

Screen Shot 131 Unit as a Job of Property

Reports will display subtotals and totals for each:

- Property Owner (as a Customer)
- Property (as a Job) of a Property Owner (as a Customer) (optional)
- Unit (as a Job) of a Property (as a Job) (optional)

TIP
Create a unique name for each unit and tenant. If the Customer:Job name is duplicated, your data will be corrupted.

> **IMPORTANT**
> For multi-unit properties such as single apartment buildings, all units for the property must have the same number of digits. Use leading zeros when necessary. For example:
>
> - If your Property has less than 10 Units, Unit number 1 would be 1
> - If your Property has 10 to 99 Units, Unit number 1 would be 01
> - If your Property has 100 to 999 Units, Unit number 1 would be 001
>
> Label units by unit number, street name, and address number. Abbreviate the property address. For example, Unit 1 at 142 Fun Road can be entered as 01 Fun 142.

To enter a unit as a Job:

- Click **Tenants** on the Icon Bar
- Right-click on the Property
- Select Add Job

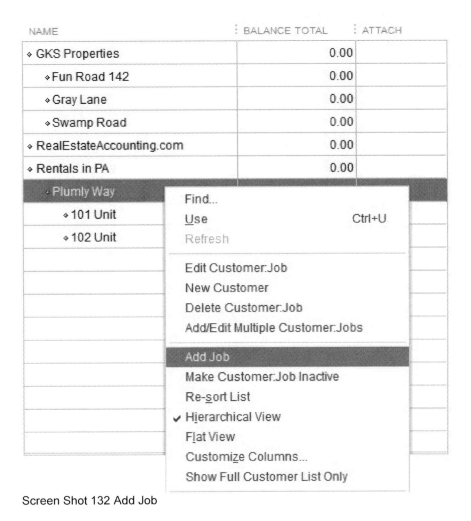

Screen Shot 132 Add Job

Address Info

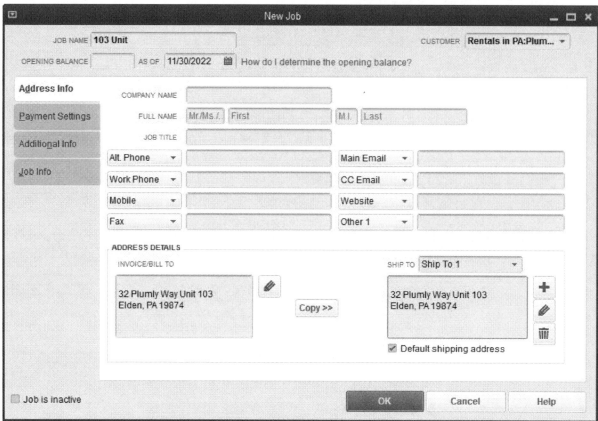

Screen Shot 133 Unit Address Info

UNITS

- Complete the fields as follows:

Field	Data
Job Name	Unit Number
Customer	Property Name
Opening Balance	Leave blank
as of	Leave as is
Remove prefilled data under all fields	
Ship To	

Click on the ➕ to add the Address Name and details of the Unit. Select the check marks to show the window again in case of an incomplete address and to define the default shipping address.

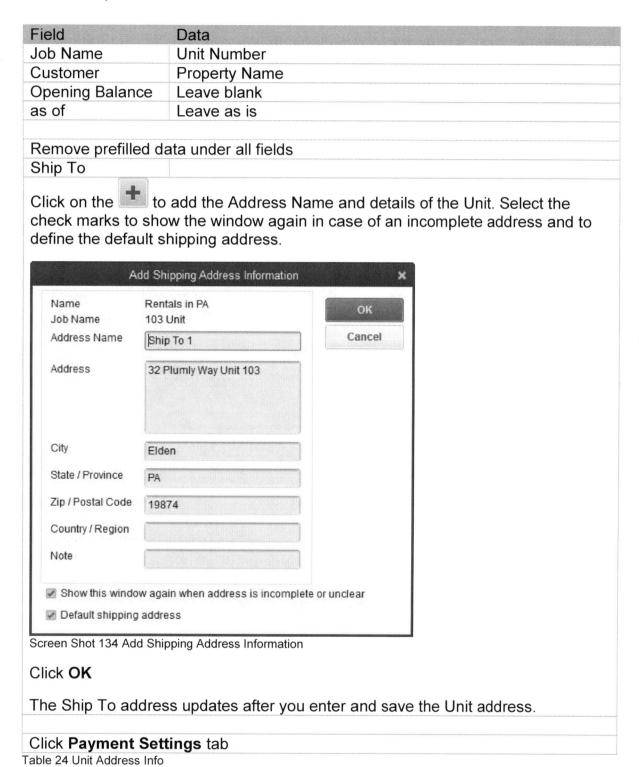

Screen Shot 134 Add Shipping Address Information

Click **OK**

The Ship To address updates after you enter and save the Unit address.

Click **Payment Settings** tab

Table 24 Unit Address Info

Payment Settings

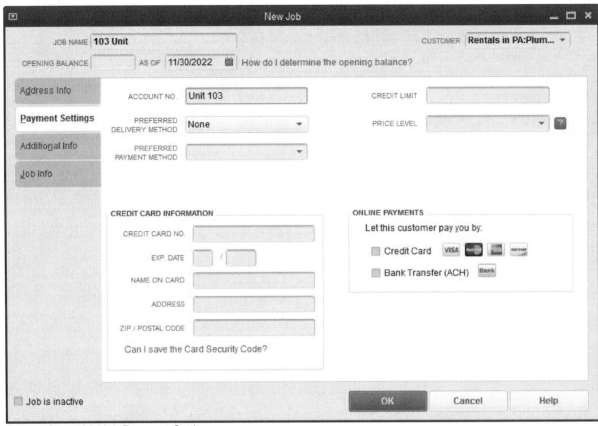

Screen Shot 135 Unit Payment Settings

- Complete the fields as follows:

Field	Data
Account No.	Property Street Address
Price Level	As needed (if you track rental prices in QuickBooks)
All other fields	As needed
Click **Additional Info** tab	

Table 25 Unit Payment Settings

UNITS

Additional Info

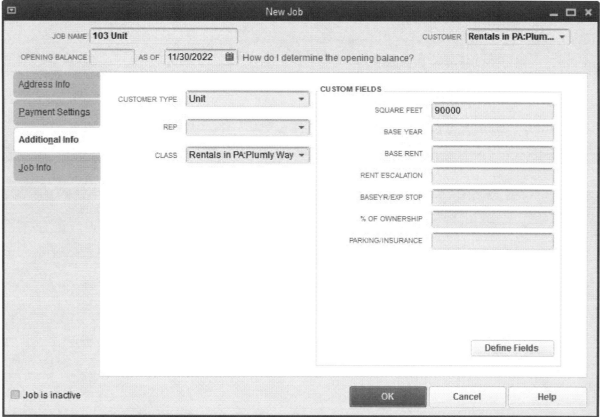

Screen Shot 136 Unit Additional Info

- Complete the fields as follows:

Field	Data
Customer Type	Unit
Rep	As needed
Class	Select Property name (only in Enterprise version)
Custom Fields	As needed
Click **OK** (Skip the Job Info tab)	

Table 26 Unit Additional Info

Class: Only available in Enterprise version. When you enter a transaction selecting a unit (Job) name, the property name (Class) will prefill.

Custom Fields: There are 12 custom fields available in the Enterprise version and the type of data you can enter by amount, date, numbers, text and multi-choice which makes it easy to filter and report.

Commercial Property Management for Managers: QuickBooks Desktop   211

REPORT: UNIT LIST

To view the Unit List report:

- Click **MemRpts** on the Icon Bar
- Double-click Unit List under Lists

www.RealEstateAccounting.com
Unit List

Customer	Bill to 2	City	State	Zip
Rentals in PA:Plumly Way:101 Unit	32 Plumly Way 101 Unit	Elden	PA	19874
Rentals in PA:Plumly Way:102 Unit	32 Plumly Way 102 Unit	Elden	PA	19874
Rentals in PA:Plumly Way:103 Unit	32 Plumly Way Unit 103	Elden	PA	19874

Report 7 Unit List

CHAPTER 27 TENANTS

A tenant rents a property or unit. Entering tenants as a Job will allow you to track each tenant's rent, reimbursed expenses, security deposits, repair orders, and any other information needed to manage the units efficiently.

> **IMPORTANT**
> STOP – If you have another system outside of QuickBooks for tracking tenant balances and details, skip this chapter.

QuickBooks Pro and Premier can handle 14,500 names. The Enterprise version can hold 100,000 names and is now available for one licensed user. If you purchased the Enterprise version of QuickBooks, contact the author to receive a refund equal to the cost of this book.

Objectives

Upon completion of this chapter, you will be able to:

- Enter Tenant Names
- View Tenant Information
- View Reports

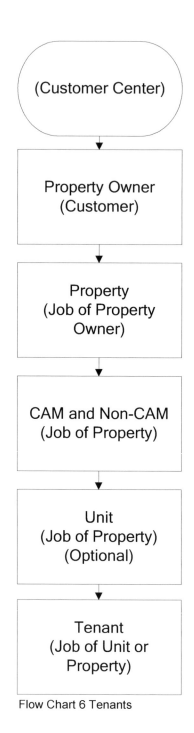

Flow Chart 6 Tenants

SINGLE TENANT

We are modifying Customer:Job to track the balance owed by each tenant in the following way:

- Property Owner as a Customer
- Property as a Job of a Property Owner (Customer) (optional)
- Unit as a Job of a Property (Job) (optional)
- Tenant as a Job of a Property or Unit (Job) (optional)

If a property does not have any units, add the tenant as a Job of the Property.

> **NOTE**
> If you enter the contact details for each tenant (physical address, name, phone, and email), you will be able to produce agreements and invoices from within QuickBooks.

SUBLEASE

A sublease is when the original tenant leases the unit to another tenant. It is also known as a "sandwich lease." Right-click on the Tenant and Add Job. Follow the same steps to add a tenant. In the Additional Info tab, select Sublet as the Customer Type.

To view a report of sublease tenants:

- Click **MemRpts** on the Icon Bar
- Double-click Sublease Tenants List under Lists

TENANTS

The image below displays how the tenants (as Jobs of a Properties or Units) should look in QuickBooks.

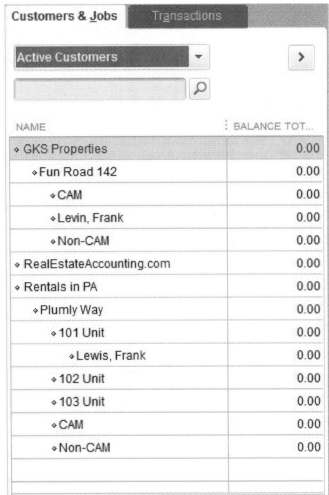

Screen Shot 137 Tenant Center

To enter a tenant as a Job (Customer:Job):

- Click **Tenants** on the Icon Bar
- Right-click the Unit name
- Select Add Job

Address Info

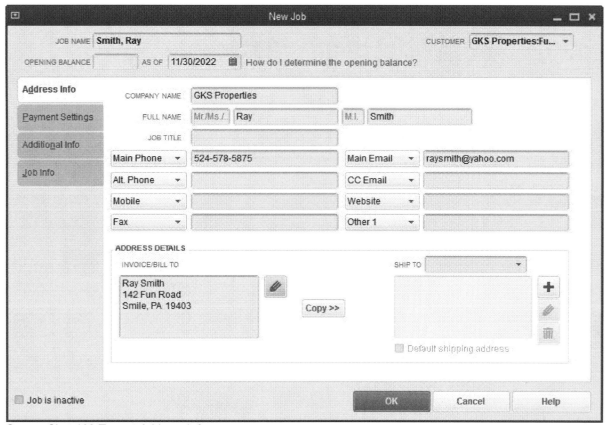

Screen Shot 138 Tenant Address Info

- Complete the fields as follows:

Field	Data
Job Name	Tenant Name
Customer	Leave as is (select property name)
Contact details	As needed
Address Details	
Invoice/Bill To	Tenant's invoice is mailed
Ship to	Click **Copy** and change the address to the physical location address
Click **Payment Settings** tab	

Table 27 Tenant Address Info

TENANTS

Payment Settings

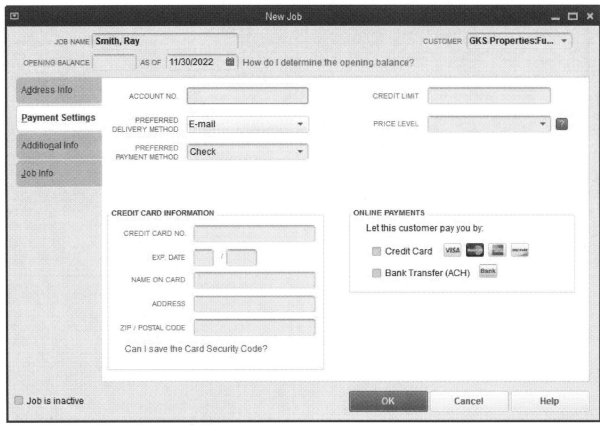

Screen Shot 139 Tenant Payment Settings

- Complete the fields as follows:

Field	Data
Account No.	Prefills
Credit Limit	Optional
Preferred Delivery Method	Select a method for contacting the Tenant
Price Level	As needed
Preferred Payment Method	Select a method of payment
Credit Card Information	As needed
Click **Additional Info** tab	

Table 28 Tenant Payment Settings

TENANTS

Additional Info

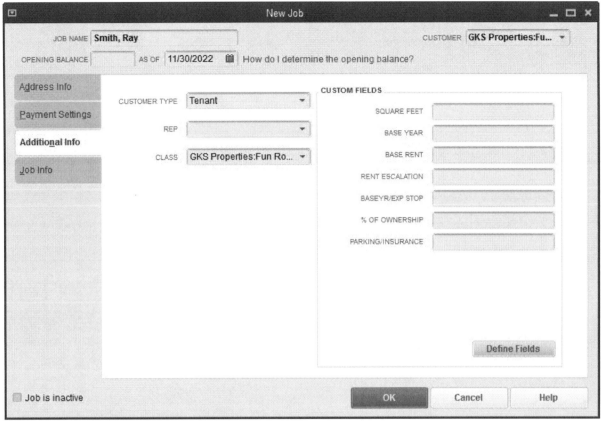

Screen Shot 140 Tenant Additional Info

- Complete the fields as follows:

Field	Data
Customer Type	Tenant
Rep	As needed
Class	Property name (only in Enterprise version)
Custom Fields	As needed
Click **Job Info**	

Table 29 Tenant Additional Info

Class: Only available in Enterprise version. When you enter a transaction selecting a tenant (Job) name, the property name (Class) will prefill.

Custom Fields: There are 12 custom fields available in the Enterprise version and the type of data you can enter by amount, date, numbers, text and multi-choice which makes it easy to filter and report.

Job Info

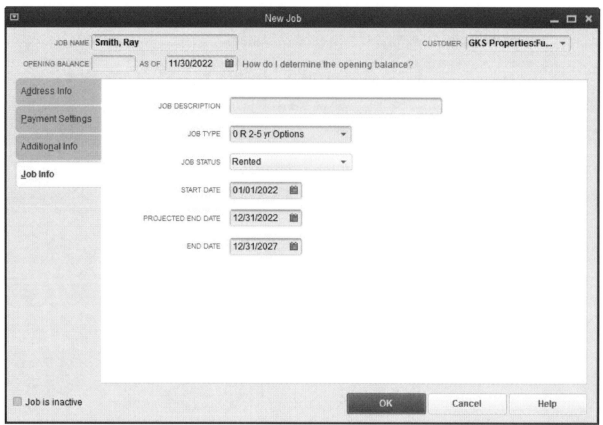

Screen Shot 141 Tenant Job Info

- Complete the fields as follows:

Field	Data
Job Status	Rented
Start Date	Date lease started
Projected End	Rent increase date
End Date	Lease expiration (option) date
Job Description	As needed
Job Type	Renewal Option in years (i.e., 1-year, 2-year, 3-year)
Click **OK** to save or **Next** to enter another tenant	

Table 30 Tenant Job Info

IMPORTANT
If we use 0 R 2-5 yr Options as Job Type: 0 is used for the start of the lease (Original Lease) R is used for renewal 2 is used for how many times they can exercise the option 5 yr is the length of the option Using this example, if a tenant exercised their option to renew for the first of the 5-year terms, you would update Job Type to 1 R 2-5 yr Options.

TENANTS

Change Tenant Status

Update the Tenant Job Info status when there are changes to the lease.

To update Tenant status:

- Click **Tenants** on the Icon Bar
- Double-click the Tenant
- Select the Job Info tab
    - Change Job Type to number of option exercised
    - Change Job Status as needed
    - Change Projected End date to the next lease increase
    - Change the End date to Lease Expiration, Evicted, or Moved date

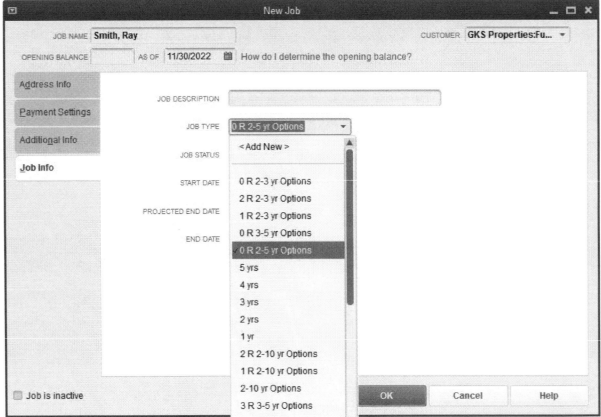
Screen Shot 142 Change Expiration Date

Commercial Property Management for Managers: QuickBooks Desktop

TENANT INFORMATION

To view a tenant's information, click **Tenant Name**:

Screen Shot 143 Tenant Information

REPORT: TENANT LIST

To view the Tenant List report:

- Click **MemRpts** on the Icon Bar
- Double-click Tenant List under Lists

www.RealEstateAccounting.com
Tenant List

Customer	Main Phone	Start Date	Projected End	Job Type
GKS Properties:Fun Road 142:Smith, Ray	524-578-5875	09/01/2022	08/31/2023	Yearly
GKS Properties:Swamp Road:Flippet, Groue		04/01/2022	03/31/2023	Yearly
Rentals in PA:Plumly Way:101 Unit:Lewis, Frank		11/01/2022	10/31/2023	Yearly

Report 8 Tenant List

REPORT: LEASE EXPIRATION

To view the Lease Expiration report:

- Click **MemRpts** on the Icon Bar
- Double-click Lease Expiration under Lease Expiration

www.RealEstateAccounting.com
Lease Expiration

Company	First Name	Last Name	Main Phone	Ship to 3	End Date	Job Type
Wawa	Ray	Smith	524-578-5875	142 Fun Road	12/31/2027	0 R 2-5 yr Options
Delicious Pizza	Robin	Cruso	215-545-5677	32 Plumly Way	06/30/2023	2 R 3-5 yr Options
Dunkin Donut			718-972-5791	578 Swamp Ro...	01/31/2021	2 R 3-5 yr Options

Report 9 Lease Expiration

The above is an example of a comprehensive report – there are several parameters to choose from depending on your specific needs.

The following reports can also be viewed for Lease Expiration:

- Lease Expiration
- Lease Expiration – Last Month
- Lease Expiration – Next Month
- Lease Expiration – Next Quarter
- Lease Expiration – Next Year

REPORT: RENT ESCALATION DATE

To view the Rent Escalation Date report:

- Click **MemRpts** on the Icon Bar
- Double-click Rent Escalation Date under Tenant

www.RealEstateAccounting.com
Rent Escalation Date Report

First Name	Last Name	Main Phone	Ship to 3	Projected End	Job Type
Robin	Cruso	215-545-5677	32 Plumly Way	07/01/2020	2 R 3-5 yr Options
Ray	Smith	524-578-5875	142 Fun Road	12/31/2022	0 R 2-5 yr Options
		718-972-5791	578 Swamp Road...	01/31/2031	2 R 3-5 yr Options

Report 10 Rent Escalation Date

CHAPTER 28 MULTI-UNIT TENANTS

A multi-unit tenant is a tenant who occupies more than one unit.

Objectives

Upon completion of this chapter, you will be able to:

- Understanding Single-Unit vs. Multi-Unit Tenants
- Sending Invoices
- View Reports

ENTER A MULTI-UNIT TENANT

Under some circumstances, a tenant may occupy multiple units.

The situation below illustrates how entering a multi-unit tenant differs from entering a single-unit tenant. To enter Jobs, refer to chapter Tenants.

Auntie Anne's is currently only leasing Store 101. You would enter Auntie Anne's as a Job of Store 101.

Auntie Anne's decides to lease an additional unit, Kiosk 220. In this situation, Store 101 and Kiosk 220 would become Jobs of Auntie Anne's. Create a new Job for each unit. Select Multi-Unit Tenant as the Customer Type.

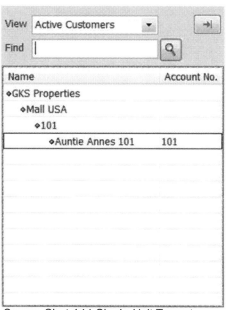

Screen Shot 144 Single-Unit Tenant

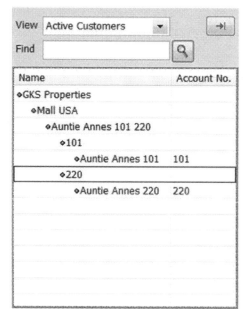

Screen Shot 145 Multi-Unit Tenant

INVOICE

You have two options:

- Create one invoice for one tenant, Auntie Annes 101 220, entering unit details under the description. One invoice for both the unit. The disadvantage to invoicing the tenant is that you will not be able to track revenue by the unit. Refer to chapter Invoices.
- Alternatively, create an invoice for each unit, Auntie Annes 101 and Auntie Annes 202.

STATEMENTS

To send the tenant one invoice for both units, create a statement using the Multi-Unit Tenant Template and select Create One Statement per Customer. Refer to chapter Statements. You can always send the tenant an invoice for each unit individually.

REPORTS

Customize your multi-unit tenant reports as per your needs. We recommend selecting the tenant's name under the unit, not the unit itself. From the example above, select Auntie Annes 101 and Auntie Annes 220, not 101 and 220, to display accurate reports.

TERMINATION OF LEASE

When the tenant vacates, drag the unit to its original position. The tenant's name, Auntie Annes 101, will move underneath the unit number. Inactivate the tenant's name under the unit.

If Auntie Annes only vacate unit 101, drag both the units back under the property name. Inactivate Auntie Annes 101 and Auntie Annes 101 220.

CHAPTER 29 VENDORS

A vendor is a person or company that you pay. Examples include subcontractors, credit card companies, tax authorities, and other parties. Although you will soon learn how to make payments, this chapter focuses on how to set up a vendor.

Once vendors are set up, you will be able to recognize them as payees when it is time to write checks, enter credit card charges, or enter and pay bills. You will also be able to track bills you owe, vendors whom you owe, and amounts paid to vendors.

Objectives

Upon completion of this chapter, you will be able to:

- Enter Vendors including Travel Agents
- Track Vendors with Single or Multiple Accounts
- Capture 1099 Information

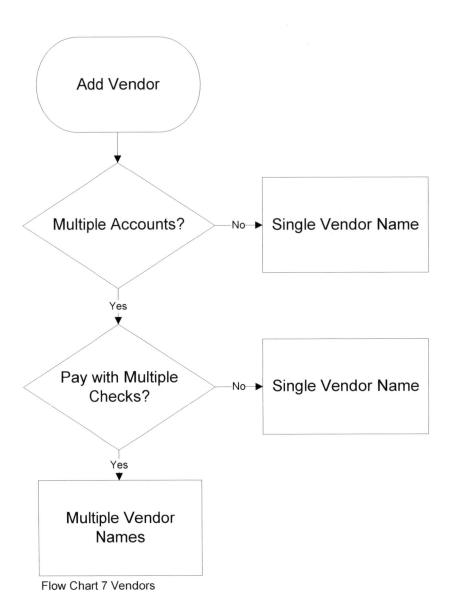

Flow Chart 7 Vendors

DECIDE HOW TO ENTER A VENDOR

Before adding a vendor, determine if the vendor should be entered once or with multiple accounts. A vendor requires a single account if you have one account number and will write one check. For example, the telephone company providing business phone lines for which you pay a monthly bill.

A vendor requires multiple accounts if you pay more than one account to them. For example, the water company provides services to each unit, with each bill having a different account number. You write many checks, paying each bill separately.

Vendor with Single Account

When a vendor requires one check, whether it is for a single account or multiple accounts, simply enter the Vendor Name without an account number.

Vendor with Multiple Account Numbers

When you pay one vendor with separate checks, each reflecting a different account, enter the vendor name, last four digits of the account number, and the property or unit.

With the example of separate water bills for each unit, create a separate vendor for each water account, as shown below:

Water Revenue
Water Revenue 5873 Plumly Way Unit A
Wells Fargo 8745 Fun Road

Screen Shot 146 Multiple Vendor Name

VENDORS

GITA'S NAMING RULES

Be consistent with list names to keep your file and reports clean and organized.

To name vendors, use the following format:

- Shortened Vendor name
- Last four digits of account number (if applicable)
- Payment method (if applicable). For example, enter Auto if you make automatic payments
- Property (if applicable)

For example, Expert Cleaners should be named Expert Cleaners 7856, PECO Electric Company, PECO Electric Auto, and Water Revenue Bureau, Water Revenue 5213 Plumly.

REPORT: VENDOR CONTACT LIST

As you enter vendors, review the Vendor Contact List to check your work.

To view the Vendor Contact List report:

- Click **MemRpts** on the Icon Bar
- Double-click Vendor Contact List under Vendors

www.RealEstateAccounting.com
Vendor Contact List

Vendor	Account No.	Bill from	Main Phone	Balance Total
Ala Zachery		Ala Zachery		250.00
Allen Pools & Spa		Allen Pools & Spa 842 Main Street Richboro, PA 18940		0.00
Allstate Insurance		Allstate Insurance		0.00
GMAC 4561 Swamp Rd		GMAC 4561 Swamp Rd		0.00
Home Depot		Home Depot		0.00
RealEstateAccounting.com - V		RealEstateAccounting.com - V		0.00
Staples		Staples		0.00
TD Bank		TD Bank		0.00
Verizon Wireless		Verizon Wireless		968.16
Water Revenue 5873 Unit 01	5215465873	Water Revenue Bureau 876 River Road Langhorne, PA 19047	215-765-5432	0.00
Wells Fargo 5789 AUTO Fun Road		Wells Fargo 5789 AUTO Fun Road 345 Money Lane Goldtown, PA 18956		0.00

Report 11 Vendor Contact List

VENDORS

To enter a vendor:

- Click **Vendors** on the Icon Bar

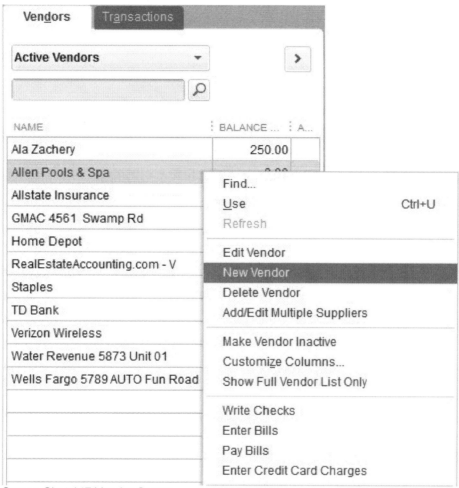

Screen Shot 147 Vendor Center

- Right-click on a Vendor name
- Select New Vendor

Address Info

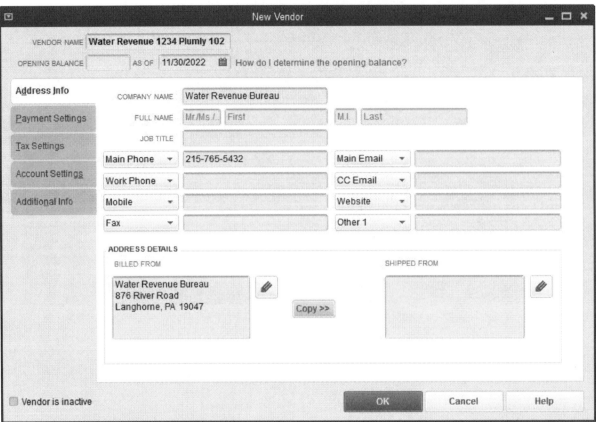

Screen Shot 148 Vendor Address Info

VENDORS

- Complete the fields as follows:

Field	Data
Vendor Name	Shortened Vendor Name as shown (add last four digits of the account number and the Property name if you want to track payments by each vendor account) Water Revenue 5873 Plumly Way Unit A Wells Fargo 8745 Fun Road Screen Shot 149 Multiple Vendor Name
Opening Balance	Leave blank
as of	Leave as is
Address Info	
Company Name	Company name
Full Name	
Mr./Ms./…	Leave blank
First	First name (optional)
M.I.	Middle initial (optional)
Last	Last name (optional)
Job Title	Title
Main Phone	
Main E-mail	
Work Phone	
CC Email	As needed
Mobile	
Website	
Fax	
Other 1	
Address Details	
Billed From	Name prefills (On the next line, enter the mailing address to which the check should be mailed)
Shipped From	As needed
Click **Payment Settings** tab	

Table 31 Vendor Address Info

Payment Settings

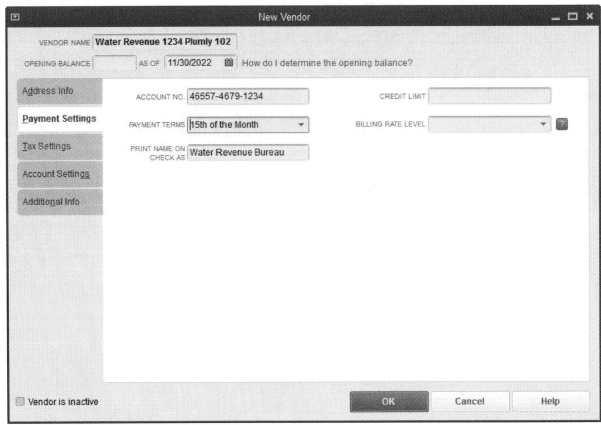

Screen Shot 150 Vendor Payment Settings

- Complete the fields as follows:

Field	Data
Account No.	Enter Account Number or leave blank if you pay multiple accounts with one check
Credit Limit	Optional
Payment Terms	Select payment terms, if applicable
Billing Rate Level	As needed
Print Name on Check As	Change the name to check recipient
Click **Tax Settings** tab	

Table 32 Vendor Payment Settings

Tax Settings

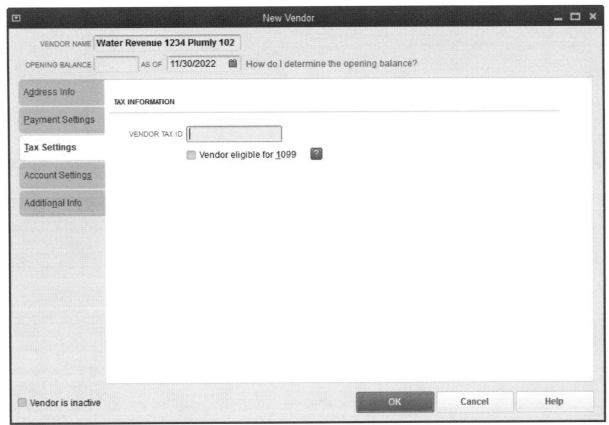

Screen Shot 151 Vendor Tax Settings

- Complete the fields as follows:

Field	Data
Vendor Tax ID	Social Security number or EIN of the vendor (if you do not have the number, add a dummy number, which acts as a reminder for you at the end of the year)
Vendor eligible for 1099	Check box if vendor is eligible to receive 1099
Click **Account Settings** tab	

Table 33 Vendor Tax Settings

VENDORS

Account Settings

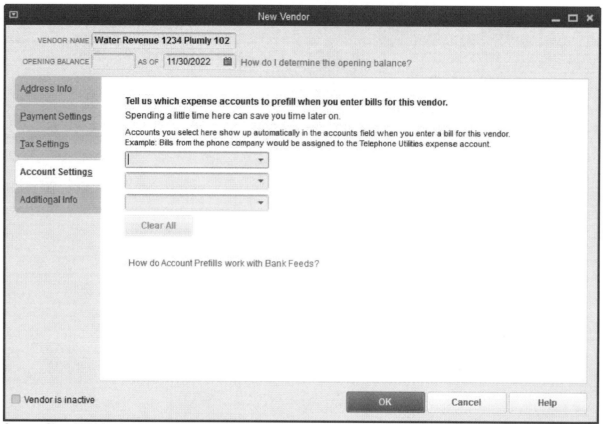

Screen Shot 152 Vendor Account Settings

IMPORTANT
Only select accounts to prefill transactions if the expenses are related to the Overhead class. Do not use the Account Prefill feature for a property's expenses.

- Complete the fields as follows:

Field	Data
Select accounts to prefill transactions	Type account name or select accounts from the drop down menu
Click **Additional Info** tab	

Table 34 Vendor Account Settings

Commercial Property Management for Managers: QuickBooks Desktop   240

Additional Info

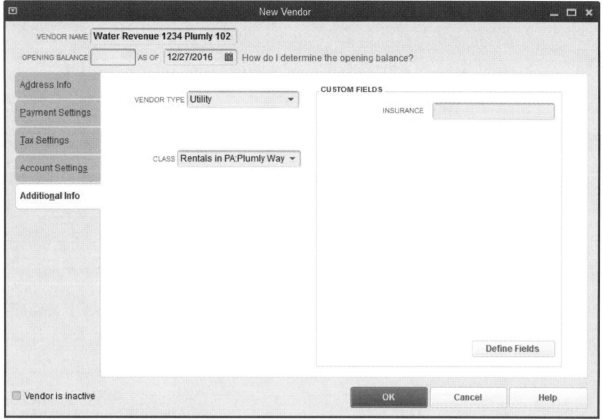

Screen Shot 153 Vendor Additional Info

- Complete the fields as follows:

Field	Data
Vendor Type	Select from drop down menu
Class	Select property name (only in Enterprise version)
Custom Fields	As needed
Click **OK**	

Table 35 Vendor Additional Info

Class: Only available in Enterprise version. When you enter a transaction selecting a Vendor name, the property name (Class) will prefill.

Custom Fields: There are 12 custom fields available in the Enterprise version and the type of data you can enter by amount, date, numbers, text and multi-choice which makes it easy to filter and report.

REPORT: VENDOR LIST

To view related reports:

- Click **MemRpts** on the Icon Bar
- Select by double-clicking the following under Lists:
    - Property Owner Vendor List
    - Vendor List
    - Vendor 1099 List

SECTION 5

BALANCES

Entering balances is the first step to starting a new file or making adjustments to an existing file, giving you access to accurate financials in QuickBooks. Review your financial information on demand, rather than guessing or attempting to combine multiple Excel sheets and paper reports, additionally, tracking a budget and forecast for each property and your Company is crucial to the growth of your business.

Before you begin entering opening balances, compile the information about your business operations and properties in one place.

When you begin with a new file, it is very important that you enter all the opening balances the day before your start date. For example, if you are going to start entering data from July 14th, then your balances should be recorded as of July 13th.

It is vital you follow the steps in order.

BALANCES

BALANCE CHECKLIST

	Your Company Financials
☐	Budget
☐	Trial Balance Year-To-Date and Prior Year
☐	Last Month's Bank Statements
☐	Petty Cash Balance
☐	Uncleared Deposits
☐	Uncleared Vendor Bills
☐	Open Invoices and Credit Memos
☐	Unpaid Bills and Credits
☐	Escrow, Earnest Deposit, and Settlement Check
☐	Loans and Investments

Checklist 9 Your Company Financials

CHAPTER 30 OPENING BALANCES

Whether you are starting a new company or are updating an existing file, you will need to enter or verify the balances.

Follow the steps outlined in this chapter, in the order; they are listed, enter the opening balances for properties, vendors, assets, liabilities, and equity.

> **IMPORTANT**
> Be sure you have completed the section Manage Names before entering opening balances.

Objectives

Upon completion of this chapter, you will be able to:

- Enter Opening Balances
- Update an Existing File
- View Reports

Security Deposits & Reserve Funds

- Enter each tenant money received in full or partial as an invoice with the original invoice number, date, and amount. Refer to the chapter on Invoices.
- Enter each payment with an original reference number, date, and memo using Receive Payment. Refer to the chapter on Payments and Deposits.
- Make the deposit to Petty Cash bank account by selecting all the payments received and date the deposit. Refer to chapter Payments and Deposits.
- Double-check your work, by referring to the Security Deposit and Reserve Funds report.
- Review the bank and liability account on the Balance Sheet report.

Outstanding Customer Invoices, Payments, and Credits

- Enter each open invoice including original invoice number, date, and items using Invoices. Refer to chapter Invoices.
- Enter each credit and overpayment with an original reference number, date, and items using Credit Memo. Refer to chapter Credit or Write off.
- Make a deposit in the Opening Balance account.
- Double-check your work, by referring to the Open Invoices report.
- Review the Accounts Receivable account on the Balance Sheet report.

Tax Owed

Enter the tax owed for each authority. Refer to the chapter on Entering Bills.

Credit Card Balance

- Enter a bill for the amount due, per your last statement. Refer to the chapter on Entering Bills.
- Match the balance from the previous statement on the Accounts Payable report.
- Enter credit card charges since the statement date. Refer to the chapter on Entering Bills.
- Review the credit card balance on the Balance Sheet report.

Outstanding Vendor Bills and Credits

- Enter each open bill with the original bill number, date, expense, and items using Bills. Refer to the chapter on Entering Bills.
- Enter each bill credit with original credit number, date, and items using Bills. Refer to the chapter on Entering Bills.
- Double-check your work by referring to the Vendor Unpaid Bills report.
- Review the Accounts Payable account on the Balance Sheet report.

BANK BALANCES

- Enter the ending bank balance from the last bank statement. Make a deposit, refer to the chapter on Payments and Deposits.
- Check bank balances on the Balance Sheet report.

UNCLEARED CHECKS AND DEPOSITS

- Enter uncleared deposits into the Opening Balance account. Make a deposit using the original dates, refer to chapter on Payments and Deposits.
- Enter uncleared checks into the Opening Balance account. Write checks using the original dates, refer to chapter on Writing Checks.

PETTY CASH BALANCE

- Transfer any balance to Opening Balance Account. Balance should be zero.
- Enter the balance on hand. Make a deposit, refer to the chapter on Payments and Deposits. Balance should be the amount you have on hand.
- Check balances on the Balance Sheet report.

OPENING BALANCE ACCOUNT

Transfer all the money from the opening balance account to Equity Account or Loan account.

ASSET AND LIABILITY BALANCES

- **DO NOT** enter balances for the property, Accounts Receivable, and Accounts Payable because you already did with following the steps in this chapter.
- For your business, create a journal entry by debiting assets and crediting liabilities for your Company (Class). Refer to the chapter on Navigating QuickBooks.
- Check balances on the Balance Sheet report.

UPDATE EXISTING QUICKBOOKS FILE

I firmly suggest that you start a new QuickBooks file using our template to enter the data. However, if you choose to modify the transactions in your existing file, use the template file as a guide, add the appropriate accounts and items, and customize the reports.

First, check the current Balance Sheet and Profit & Loss by Property reports for accuracy. If the balances are not accurate, modify or enter the transactions, as per the previous instructions in this chapter.

Check the following to ensure that the balances are reflected accurately:

- Properties
- Lenders
- Equity Holders
- Vendor Names
- Chart Accounts

You can recreate the reports in your existing file. Look at the reports in the file and refer to the chapter on Customize Your Reports and Customized Reports for You.

INCOME & EXPENSES

- If you entered all the transactions as mentioned above, your Profit & Loss report should not show any transactions.

REPORTS FOR OPENING BALANCES

To view related reports:

- Click **MemRpts** on the Icon Bar
- Select by double-clicking the following:
    - Property List
    - Vendor Contact List
    - Open Invoices
    - Open Vendor Bills
    - Profit & Loss by Property
    - Balance Sheet

CHAPTER 31 BUDGETS AND FORECASTS

Creating a budget is an excellent way to determine if your business idea is viable. It also helps you to track expenses, analyze income, and anticipate future financial needs. A business forecast, on the other hand, is a prediction of the amounts a company will incur and earn.

What's the difference? The budget plans for how the business *should* be while the forecast predicts how the business *will* be. Create both for your Company and for each property.

> **IMPORTANT**
> You cannot enter a Budget or Forecast if the account is not listed in the Chart of Accounts. The following screen shots are for setting up a budget. The process to set up a forecast is similar.

Objectives

Upon completion of this chapter, you will be able to:

- View Reports
- Create a Profit and Loss Budget or Forecast

> **NOTE**
> - Budgets and Cash Flow Projections are available in all versions of QuickBooks Desktop.
> - Forecast and Business Plan tool are available in QuickBooks Accountant and Enterprise versions.

REPORTS FOR BUDGETS AND FORECASTS

To view related reports:

- Click **MemRpts** on the Icon Bar
- Select by double-clicking the following under Budgets & Forecasts:
    - Budget Overview
    - Budget vs. Actual
    - Profit & Loss Budget Performance
    - Budget vs. Actual Graph
    - Forecast Overview
    - Forecast vs. Actual

BUDGETS

To create a budget or forecast:

- Click **Company** on the Menu Bar
- Select Planning & Budgeting
- Click **Set Up Budgets** or **Set Up Forecast**

BUDGETS AND FORECASTS

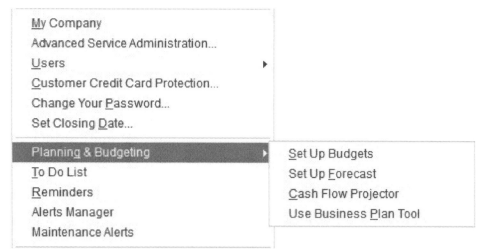
Screen Shot 154 Set Up Budgets or Set Up Forecasts

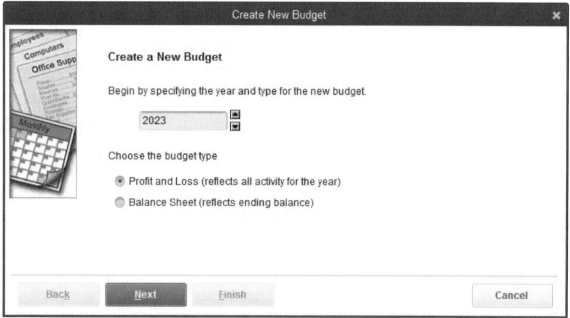
Screen Shot 155 Create a New Budget

- Select the year
- Select Profit and Loss or Balance Sheet
- Click **Next**

BUDGETS AND FORECASTS

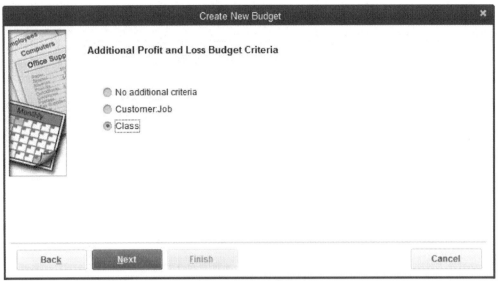

Screen Shot 156 Additional Profit and Loss Budget Criteria

- Select No additional criteria, Customer:Job, or Class
- Click **Next**

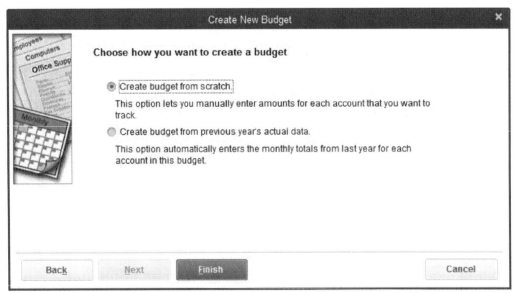

Screen Shot 157 Choose How You Want to Create a Budget

- Select Create budget from scratch or Create budget from previous year's actual data.
- Click **Finish**

Select the appropriate Class to create a budget for each property.

Same Amount Each Month

If the budgeted amount for an account is the same each month:

- Enter the amount in the month column
- Click **Copy Across** on lower left

This results in the same amount will prefill automatically each month.

Adjust Row Amounts

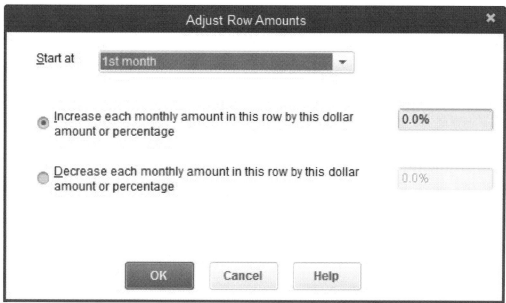

Screen Shot 158 Adjust Row Amounts

You can adjust the monthly amount by dollar amount or percentage and start at the 1st month or select the current month. Click **OK**.

BUDGETS AND FORECASTS

Different Amount Each Month

If the budgeted amount for an account is not the same each month, enter the appropriate amount in each column.

If an account or a month within an account has no budgeted amount, leave the column blank.

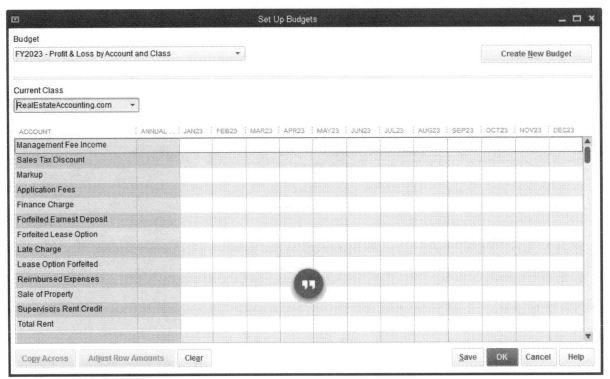
Screen Shot 159 Set Up Budgets

- Click **Save**
- Click **OK** to close the window

Commercial Property Management for Managers: QuickBooks Desktop

CHAPTER 32 ADDING PRIOR RENTS AND CAM EXPENSES

This chapter is optional. However, we strongly recommend that you enter the previous budgets and year's summary by the property. You will need the data from earlier years for rent escalation and recovery expenses.

Objectives

Upon completion of this chapter, you will be able to:

- Add Prior Rent Charges
- Add Prior CAM Expenses

Adding Prior Rents and CAM Expenses

To add CAM expenses and rent from prior years:

- Click **MemTx** on Icon Bar
- Double-click Tenant under CAM & Rent Prior Year

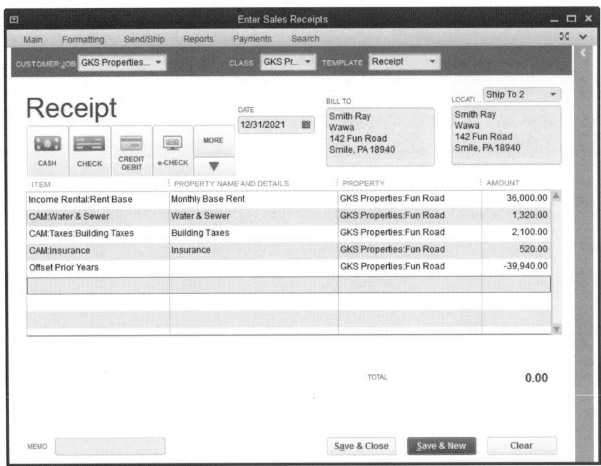

Screen Shot 160 Prior Rent and CAM Expenses

Adding Prior Rents and CAM Expenses

- Complete the fields as follows:

Field	Data		
Customer:Job	Tenant		
Class	Property		
Template	Receipt		
Date	Last day of rent escalation period		
Bill To	Prefills		
Ship To	Prefills		
Terms	Due on receipt		
	Item	Description	Amount
Line 1	Rent	As needed	Amount
Line 2	CAM Expenses, etc.	As needed	Amount
As per the lease, add line items if the tenant is responsible for reimbursing additional expenses.			
Line 3	CAM: Offset Prior Years	As needed	Total amount (negative)
Property	Property		
Total	Should equal ZERO		
Do NOT click **Save & Close**			

Table 36 Add Prior Year's Rent and CAM Expenses

To easily enter additional years, memorize the transaction for each tenant. When entering additional years, change the date and amounts.

Adding Prior Rents and CAM Expenses

- To memorize the transaction:

Right-click the sales receipt and select Memorize Sales Receipt

Screen Shot 161 Memorize Transaction

Field	Data
Name	Tenant
Add to Group	
Group Name	CAM & Rent Prior Year
Click **OK**	

Table 37 Memorize Transaction

- Click Save & Close

After entering the all prior year summaries, delete the memorized transaction. Refer to chapter Recurring (Memorizing) Transactions.

SECTION 6

MANAGE LEASES AND TENANTS

Leases are the cornerstone of property management as they outline the relationship between the Your Company and the tenant. It is important to track lease information as well as changes to the lease to maintain good financial records.

Where would your rental business be without tenants? Be sure they keep coming back by giving them the best possible experience. Depending on how your Company handles the tracking of tenant balances, you will learn how to stay organized, prepare and manage tenants.

In the following chapters, we will cover everything from how to manage your tenants from application to renewals to eviction. Record funds received from tenants such as security deposits, rent payments, and late fees. Communicate with tenants by creating invoices, eviction letters, and tenant statements.

CUSTOMERS CENTER

Customers Menu

To enter transactions:

- Click **Customers** on the Menu Bar
- Select one to enter

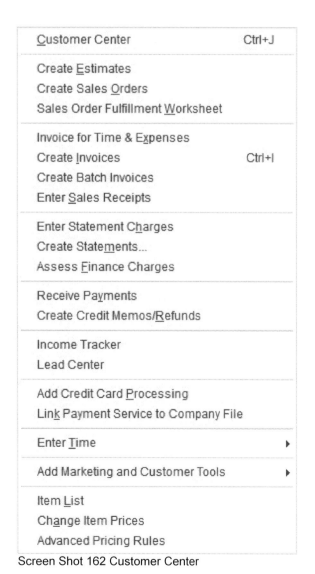

Screen Shot 162 Customer Center

Customers & Receivable Reports

To view reports:

- Click **Reports** on the Menu Bar
- Select Report Center
- Click on **Customers & Receivables** under Standard tab
- Select one of the reports

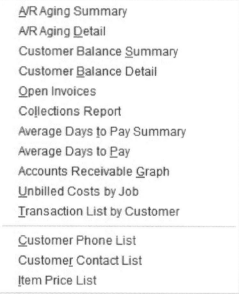

Screen Shot 163 Report List

Additional reports can be found in the file provided by me, and a list can be found in chapter Customized Reports For You.

CHAPTER 33 APPLICATION FEES

An application fee is charged to prospective tenants to check their credit history, run background checks, and process the applications.

Objectives

Upon completion of this chapter, you will be able to:

- Enter Application Fees
- View Reports

APPLICATION FEES

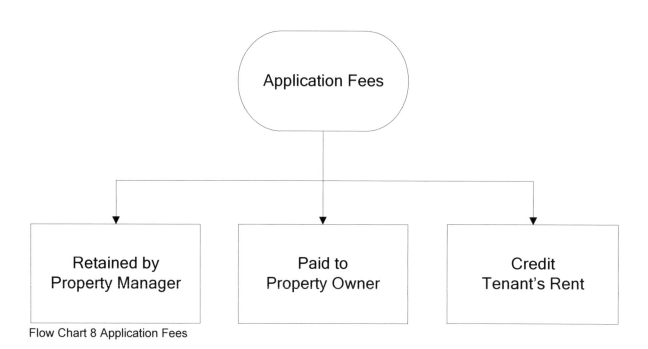

Flow Chart 8 Application Fees

APPLICATION FEES

Depending upon the agreement between the Property Manager and the Property Owner, the application fee may be retained by the Property Manager, paid to the Owner, or credited towards the Tenant's rent.

If the applicant pays the fee, when submitting the application, create a Sales Receipt. If the applicant plans to pay at a later date, create an invoice.

Retained by Property Manager

If the Property Manager retains the application fee, create a Sales Receipt using Your Company as Class. The application fee will be reflected on your Profit & Loss Your Company Report.

Paid to Property Owner

If you are going to reimburse the application fee to the Owner, create a Sales Receipt using Property as Class. The application fee will be reflected on the Profit & Loss by Class (Property) Report.

Credit Tenant's Rent

If the application fee is to be credited to the Tenant's rent, create an Invoice using either Your Company or Property Name as Class and Receive Payment.

Create a Credit Memo using the same Class you used for the Invoice and apply the credit to the rent invoice.

Refer to chapter Credit or Write off to create a credit memo and apply to the open invoice.

CREATE A SALES RECEIPT

To create a Sales Receipt for the application fee:

- Click **Customers** on Menu Bar
- Click **Enter Sales Receipts**

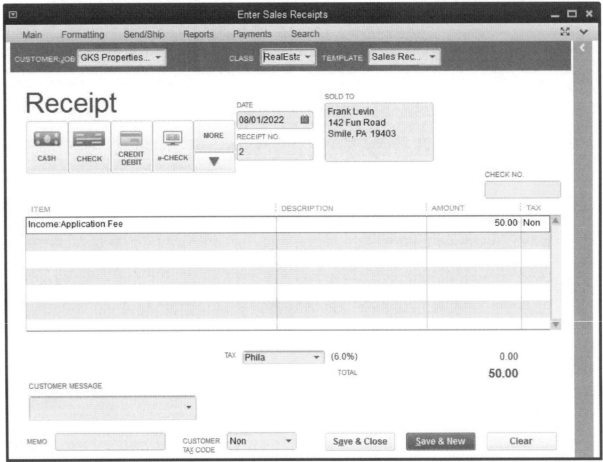

Screen Shot 164 Enter Sales Receipts

APPLICATION FEES

- Complete the fields as follows:

Field	Data
Customer:Job	Type in "Applicants:" or Tenant Name
Class	Your Company or Property
Date	Prefills to current date
Item	Application Fee
Description	Applicant's Name
Class	Your Company or Property
Amount	Amount to be charged
Memo	As needed
Click **Save & Close**	

Table 38 Enter Sales Receipts

REPORT: APPLICATION FEES

To view the Application Fees report:

- Click **MemRpts** on the Icon Bar
- Double-click Application Fees under Application Fees

www.RealEstateAccounting.com
Application Fees
July 1 through August 30, 2022

Date	Num	Amount
GKS Properties		
Fun Road 142		
Levin, Frank		
08/01/2022	2	50.00
Total Levin, Frank		50.00
Total Fun Road 142		50.00
Total GKS Properties		50.00
Rentals in PA		
Plumly Way		
101 Unit		
Lewis, Theresa		
07/20/2022	3	50.00
Total Lewis, Theresa		50.00
Total 101 Unit		50.00
Total Plumly Way		50.00
Total Rentals in PA		50.00
TOTAL		**100.00**

Report 12 Application Fees

CHAPTER 34 LEASES

A lease is a contractual agreement between a Tenant and the Landlord or Management Company for a rental. Upon expiration of the lease, the Tenant decides whether to renew the lease for another term or move out.

Print the lease right from merge Microsoft Word with QuickBooks. Refer to chapter on Letters and Envelopes.

We have provided checklists for each scenario. Remember to view reports making sure your information is entered correctly.

Objectives

Upon completion of this chapter, you will be able to:

- Add a New Lease
- Renew a Lease
- Update Rent Escalation
- Exercise the Option
- Terminate Lease

LEASES

NEW LEASE

NEW LEASE CHECKLIST

If you are setting up your QuickBooks file, enter all existing leases as you would a new lease. When a new tenant leases the unit, enter the tenant information and perform the tasks below.

	Task	Refer to Chapter
☑	Enter a Tenant	Tenants
☑	Enter To Do Reminder (optional)	Notes, To Do List & Reminders
☑	Enter Security Deposit, Last Month Rent and Pet Deposit	Security Deposit
☑	Create Rent Roll	Rent Roll
☑	Enter an Invoice	Invoices
☑	Memorize the Invoice	Recurring Transactions
☑	Add Tenant to Memorized Transactions	Recurring Transactions

Checklist 10 New Lease

IMPORTANT
Rent Escalation: Do you know the rent increase amount each year when you are entering the tenant? If so memorize the invoice for each year TODAY.

LEASES

LEASE RENEWAL

LEASE RENEWAL CHECKLIST

When a tenant renews the lease, the expiration date will change. If there is an increase in rent, the security deposit and rent amounts will need to be updated. Perform the tasks below.

	Task	Refer to Chapter
☑	Edit Tenant's Job Info	Tenants
☑	Change To Do Reminder (optional)	Notes, To Do List & Reminders
☑	Update Memorized Rent Invoice	Recurring Transactions
☑	Update Tenant in Property Transactions	Recurring Transactions
☑	Enter Security Deposit (if needed)	Security Deposit
☑	Update Rent Roll	Rent Roll

Checklist 11 Lease Renewal

> **IMPORTANT**
> Rent Escalation: Do you know the rent increase amount each year when you are entering the tenant? If so memorize the invoice for each year TODAY.

Commercial Property Management for Managers: QuickBooks Desktop

RENT ESCALATION

RENT ESCALATION CHECKLIST

At the time of the lease escalation date, the projected end date will change. If there is an increase in rent, rent amounts need to be updated. If the amount is known when entering the tenant, memorize each year's transaction. When escalating the rent amount, perform the tasks below.

	Task	Refer to Chapter
☑	Calculate Rent Escalation and CAM	Rent Escalation
☑	Update Lease Abstract	Lease Abstract
☑	Update Rent Roll	Rent Roll
☑	Update Memorized Rent Invoice	Recurring Transactions
☑	Update Tenant in Property Transactions	Recurring Transactions
☑	Change Projected End Date	Tenants

Checklist 12 Rent Escalation

IMPORTANT
Rent Escalation: Do you know the rent increase amount each year when you are entering the tenant? If so memorize the invoice for each year TODAY.

LEASES

EXERCISE THE OPTION

EXERCISE THE OPTION CHECKLIST

When a lease is signed for a given term, the tenant can exercise the option to extend the lease for additional terms. When the tenant exercises the option, perform the tasks below.

	Task	Refer to Chapter
☑	Calculate Rent Escalation and CAM	Rent Escalation
☑	Update Lease Abstract	Lease Abstract
☑	Update Rent Roll	Rent Roll
☑	Update Memorized Rent Invoice	Recurring Transactions
☑	Update Tenant in Property Transactions	Recurring Transactions
☑	Change End Date & Job Type for Option Period	Tenants

Checklist 13 Exercise the Option

IMPORTANT
Rent Escalation: Do you know the rent increase amount each year when you are entering the tenant? If so memorize the invoice for each year TODAY.

LEASE TERMINATED

LEASE TERMINATED CHECKLIST

Leases can be terminated in four ways: expiration of the lease, surrender, and acceptance, breach of conditions, or eviction. Surrender and acceptance are an agreement between the owner and tenant to terminate the lease. When the tenant or owner fails to uphold their responsibilities as outlined in the lease, it is a breach of conditions. A tenant is evicted when they do not follow terms of the contract. If any of these situations occur, perform the tasks below.

	Task	Refer to Chapter
☑	Delete Memorized Invoice	Recurring Transactions
☑	Remove Tenant from Property Transactions	Recurring Transactions
☑	Inactivate To Do Reminder (optional)	Notes, To Do & Reminders
☑	Change Rent Roll Template	Rent Roll
☑	Update Tenant's Job Info	Tenants
☑	Inactivate Tenant (if no outstanding balance)	Working with Lists
☑	Enter Vacancy Loss (optional)	Vacancy Rent Loss
☑	Credit Security Deposit	Security Deposit
☑	Transfer Funds	Security Deposit

Checklist 14 Lease Terminated

CHAPTER 35 LEASE ABSTRACT

An abstract of a commercial lease is a synopsis of the terms of the lease. The commercial lease abstract summarizes all the important information and makes it easy to access within QuickBooks.

The lease specifies the base rent, a fixed minimum amount due to the landlord. It is calculated from the base rate, the rental rate per square foot per year. The base rate is also used in escalating rent.

Sometimes it is as easy to create an excel sheet.

Chapter is optional.

Objectives

Upon completion of this chapter, you will be able to:

- Review and Update list
- Create Lease Abstract
- Update Lease Abstract Template
- View Reports

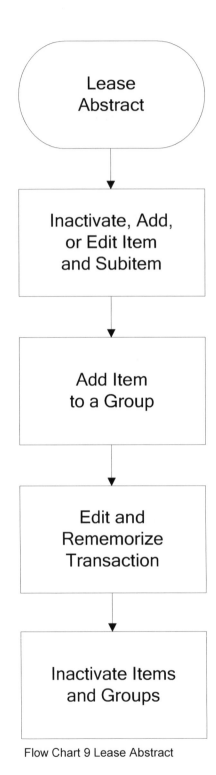

Flow Chart 9 Lease Abstract

LEASE ABSTRACT GROUP

All Items associated with the Lease Abstract are included in the Lease Abstract Group. After making additions and changes to the Item List, you MUST add it to the Group.

Creating a group will allow you to automatically enter multiple Items without typing in each and every line item.

We have included a distinctive list of basic items in the template file. These items are further grouped under several crucial categories as shown below.

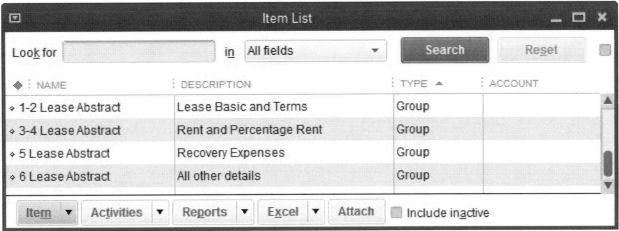
Screen Shot 165 Lease Abstract Groups

To add an item to a Lease Abstract Group:

- Click **Lists** on the Menu Bar
- Click **Item List**
- Check Include inactive box on the bottom right of the screen to view the complete Item List
- Activate the Group by clicking on the "X."
- Right-click and Select Edit Item
- Insert a line and add the Item to the Group
- Click **OK**

IMPORTANT
Add the Groups to the Memorized Lease Abstract.

LEASE ABSTRACT

LEASE ABSTRACT ITEMS

Entering an Estimate does not post any amount to your financials.

To view all the lease abstract items:

- Click **Lists** on the Menu Bar
- Click **Item List**
- Check Include inactive box on the bottom right of the screen to view the complete Item List

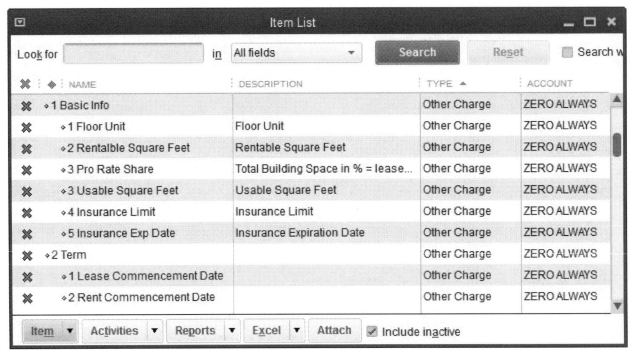
Screen Shot 166 Lease Abstract Item List

> **IMPORTANT**
> When adding or editing a lease abstract item to the Item List or a Group:
>
> - It MUST always be a subitem of a numbered item
> - Use ZERO ALWAYS as the Account
> - It must be an Active Item
> - Add it to the Group
> - Inactivate the Item

Commercial Property Management for Managers: QuickBooks Desktop

ADD OR EDIT LEASE ABSTRACT ITEM

To add or edit the lease abstract item:

- Click **Lists** on the Menu Bar
- Click **Item List**
- Check Include inactive box on the bottom right of the screen to view the complete Item List
- Activate the Item or the Subitem by clicking on the "X" (this is the only way to make changes)
- Right-click and select New Item or Edit Item
- Make the necessary changes
- Click **OK** to save

IMPORTANT
Add the Item to the Lease Abstract Group.

UPDATING MEMORIZED LEASE ABSTRACT

To update a Group in the Memorized Lease Abstract:

- Click **MemTx** on the Icon Bar
- Double-click Abstract under Lease Abstract
- Right-click and select Insert Line
- Delete the updated group
- Reenter the group
- Rememorize the lease abstract
- Inactivate the item, subitem, and group on the Item List

CREATE LEASE ABSTRACT

Enter a lease abstract for each tenant. When a tenant renews, exercises an option, rent escalates or changes the lease agreement you HAVE to change the lease abstract.

To create a Lease Abstract:

- Click **MemTx** on the Icon Bar
- Double-click Abstract under Lease Abstract
- (partial screen)

ITEM	DESCRIPTION	TOTAL
1-2 Lease Abstract		
1 Basic Info		0.00
1 Basic Info:1 Floor Unit	Floor Unit C	0.00
1 Basic Info:2 Rentable Square Feet	Rentable Square Feet 19547	19,487.00
1 Basic Info:3 Pro Rate Share	Total Building Space in % = leased space X 100 / total bldg sq ft	0.00
1 Basic Info:4 Insurance Limit	Limit and Expiration Date 100,000 12/31/2023	0.00
2 Term		0.00
2 Term:1 Lease Commencement Date	01/01/21	0.00
2 Term:2 Rent Commencement Date	01/01/21	0.00
2 Term:3 Lease Expiration	12/31/31	0.00
2 Term:4 Lease Term	Lease Term	5.00
2 Term:5 Lease Options	5_ year lease option	5.00
2 Term:6 Holdover		0.00
2 Term:7 Days Notice	60__ Days prior to Lease End Date	60.00
2 Term:8 When CAM is charged	Monthly - Reconcile in March	0.00
2 Term:9 CPI Increase	Cost of Living Increase not less 2% or more than 5% - paid monthly	0.00

Screen Shot 167 Enter Lease Abstract

NOTE
Start the Estimate number with LA to differentiate Lease Abstracts.

LEASE ABSTRACT

- Complete the fields as follows:

Field	Data
Customer:Job	Tenant
Class	Property
Template	Lease Abstract
Date	Lease start date
No.	LA and add number
Bill To	Prefills
Location	Property address should prefill
Terms	Due on receipt
Item	Delete any lines that are not applicable to the tenant lease
Description	The prefilled description clarifies what should be entered in the column. Replace the text as you enter the details.
Total	Anything that involves an amount, percentage, or square feet will be entered in this column. QuickBooks allows up to 5 decimal places in the total column.
To be e-mailed	Leave blank
Memo	As needed
Click **Save & Close**	

Table 39 Enter Lease Abstract

UPDATE LEASE ABSTRACT

When a tenant vacates the unit, you no longer need the lease abstract. Change the lease abstract template to produce accurate reports. To update the lease abstract:

- Click **Tenants** on the Icon Bar
- Highlight the Tenant who has vacated the unit
- Select Estimates from the Show drop-down menu
- Double-click the Lease Abstract

> **NOTE**
> Start the Estimate number with LA to differentiate Lease Abstracts.

- Right-click Lease Abstract and select Duplicate Estimate
- Change the date and record the other changes to the lease abstract
- Delete all information that does not change
- Click **Save & Close**
- Open the original lease abstract
- Change the Template to Lease Summary: Former Tenant from the drop down menu
- Click **Yes** to record the change
- Click **Save & Close**

REPORT: LEASE ABSTRACT

> **IMPORTANT**
> When viewing reports for the lease summary and abstract, keep in mind that QuickBooks recognizes amounts as dollar values and adds two decimal places. Read the row headings carefully.

QuickBooks allows up to 5 decimal places. Reports can also be customized by the property.

To view the report Click **MemRpts** on the Icon Bar and Double-click Lease Abstract under Lease Summary

CHAPTER 36 DEPOSIT AND LAST MONTH RENT

A security deposit is placed in escrow to provide insurance to a landlord for damage to the rented premises or unpaid tenant balance.

You **must** create an invoice for all money owed by tenants such as rent, reimbursed utilities, expenses, security deposit, late fees, and damages. You cannot receive payments without first creating an invoice.

After the tenant moves out, you would forfeit or refund the security deposit in full. If the tenant owes any amount, apply the security deposit and refund any partial amount remaining. The same concept applies to last month's rent payment.

Objectives

Upon completion of this chapter, you will be able to:

- Deposit to Owner
- Enter Deposits
- Refund Deposits With or Without Deductions
- Forfeit Deposits
- Apply Last Month Rent
- Transfer Money between Bank Accounts
- View Reports

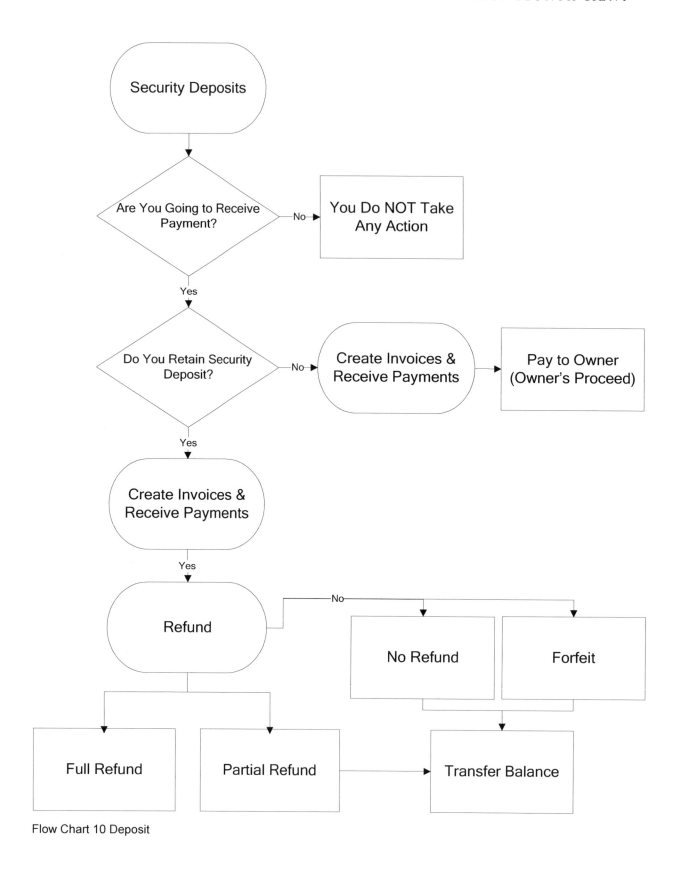

Flow Chart 10 Deposit

DEPOSIT AND LAST MONTH RENT

WAY YOU MAY HANDLE

There are several ways of handling deposits and last month payment on your agreement with the owner.

The owner may collect the deposit and retain it: In this situation, you do not take any action in your QuickBooks file as you did not receive the money and was not deposited in your bank accounts.

You may collect the deposit and make a deposit into your bank account and:

- You may give the money to the owner to be held. In this case, you will pay to consider this amount to be reimbursed to the owner at the time you calculate owners proceed; or
- Retain it for the full term of the tenant's lease; or

The same concept will apply to last month rent and pet deposit.

Screen Shot 168 Deposit Items and Accounts

Deposit to Owner

When you collect the deposit and pass it along to the owner, create an invoice and use Security Deposits to Owner item name. This will reflect as income on the owners proceed report.

Just make sure this is stated in your agreement with the Owner, and it is signed.

Commercial Property Management for Managers: QuickBooks Desktop

Enter Deposit & Last Month Rent

Create separate invoices for rent, last month's rent, and deposits.

It is very important to enter invoices for all monies owed by the tenant when they are evicted or move out. Confirm the correct amount of security deposit to be returned to the tenant by viewing the Security Deposits report.

To create an invoice for deposit:

- Click **Deposit & Rent** on the Icon Bar

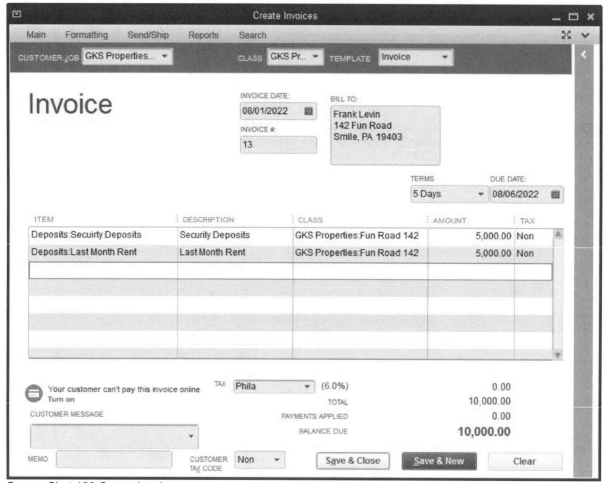

Screen Shot 169 Create Invoice s

DEPOSIT AND LAST MONTH RENT

- Complete the fields as follows:

Field	Data
Customer:Job	Tenant Name
Class	Property Name
Template	Invoice
Invoice Date	Date
Invoice #	Prefills
Bill To	As needed
Terms	Select from dropdown
Due Date	Prefills
Item	Select from dropdown
Description	As needed
Property Name	Property Name
Amount	Amount
Tax	Non
Online Pay	As needed
Tax	Non
Customer Message	As needed
Memo	
Customer Tax Code	Non
Click **Save & Close** or **Save & New** to enter another invoice	

Table 40 Create Invoices

RECEIVE SECURITY DEPOSIT

After you receive payment, make a deposit. Refer to Payment & Deposit. To receive payments:

- Click **Payment** on the Icon Bar

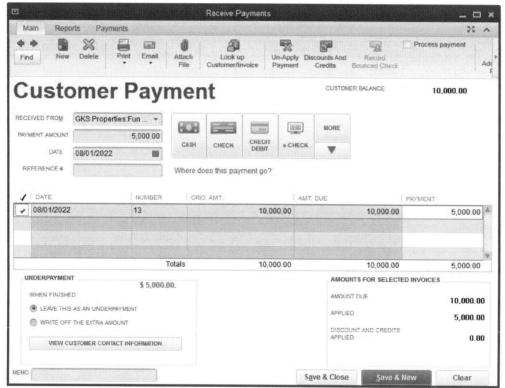
Screen Shot 170 Receive Payments

- Complete the fields as follows:

Field	Data
Received From	Tenant
Amount	Amount of check
Date	Enter the date the check was received
Pmt. Method	Select payment method from the drop-down menu
Check #	As needed
Memo	As needed

Click **Save & Close** or **Save & New**

Table 41 Receive Payments

Full Refund

When a tenant moves out and has no outstanding balance, the security deposit received will be refunded to the tenant.

Issuing a refund check will reduce the bank balance and create a zero balance in the security deposit liability account.

Create a credit memo using the security deposit as an item and issue a check refer to chapter Credit or Write off. Then transfer the deposit from the security deposit bank account to the checking account.

Partial Refund

Create invoice for any expenses the tenant is liable for.

When a tenant has an outstanding balance, the security deposit will be applied to those open invoices and any balance will be refunded to the tenant.

The full amount of the security deposit needs to be credited and applied to open invoices regardless of whether or not the tenant has paid the deposit in full. Apply the credit towards any unpaid security deposit invoice first and then to any other open invoices.

Doing this will reduce the balance of open invoices in the tenant's register and create a zero balance in the security deposit liability account, and the balance will be refunded to the tenant.

Create a credit memo using the security deposit item and total amount, apply to invoices, and issue a check refer to chapter Credit or Write off. Then transfer the deposit from the security deposit bank account to the checking account.

NO REFUND

When a tenant has an outstanding balance, the security deposit will be applied to those open invoices and not refunded to the tenant. Occasionally there may be a balance to be forfeited. Create an invoice using the item Forfeited Security Deposit for the balance of the amount.

The full amount of the security deposit needs to be credited whether or not the tenant paid the amount in full. Apply the credit towards any unpaid security deposit invoice first and then to any other open invoices.

Doing this will reduce the balance of open invoices in the tenant's register and create a zero balance in the security deposit liability account.

Create a credit memo using the security deposit item and total amount, apply to invoices, refer to chapter Credit or Write off. Then transfer the deposit from the security deposit bank account to the checking account.

FORFEIT DEPOSIT & LAST MONTH RENT

When a tenant breaks the lease agreement, the deposit is not refunded to the tenant nor does the tenant have an open balance.

Doing this will create a zero balance in the deposit liability account and show forfeited amount as income.

Create a credit memo for the tenant and use a Deposit account as the first line item (positive item) and use Forfeit Deposit as the second line item (negative item). Change the Tax and Customer Tax Code to Non (Remember not to save the tax codes to appear next time). Refer to chapter Credit or Write off.

ITEM	DESCRIPTION	AMOUNT	TAX
Deposits:Secuirty Deposits	Security Deposits	5,000.00	Non
Deposits:Forfeited Security Deposit		-5,000.00	Non

Screen Shot 171 Create Credit Memo to Forfeit Deposit

Apply Last Month Rent to Rent

Apply the last month rent to the outstanding rent amount.

Create a credit memo using the item Last Month Rent and apply it to the outstanding invoice. Refer to chapter Credit or Write off

Transfer Funds

To transfer funds from the Deposit bank account to the Operating bank account:

- Make an online transfer through your financial institution's website
- Print out the transfer, noting the tenant and property name, and file the paperwork for your records
- Record the transfer in QuickBooks by writing a check from the Deposit bank account to the Operating bank account

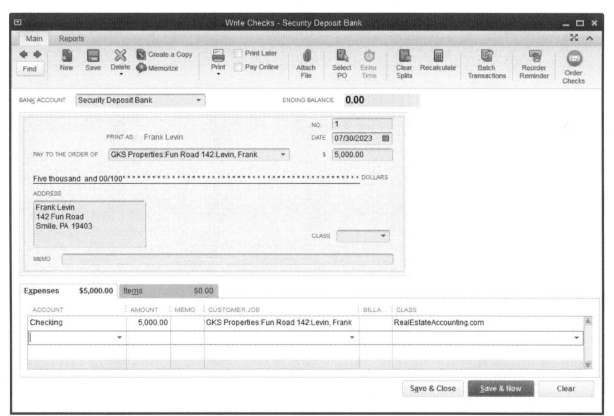

Screen Shot 172 Write Checks

REPORT: DEPOSIT

To view the deposit report:

- Click **MemRpts** on the Icon Bar
- Double-click Deposit – Last Month Rent under Security Deposit

www.RealEstateAccounting.com
Deposit - Last Month Rent
All Transactions

Type	Date	Num	Item	Paid	Open Balance	Amount
GKS Properties						
Fun Road 142						
Cruso, Robin						
Invoice	08/01/2022	13	Deposits:Secuirty Deposits	Paid		5,000.00
Invoice	08/01/2022	13	Deposits:Last Month Rent	Paid		5,000.00
Total Cruso, Robin					0.00	10,000.00
Total Fun Road 142					0.00	10,000.00
Gray Lane						
Fox, Sebrina HUD & T						
Fox, Sabrina Tenant						
Invoice	07/01/2022	29	Deposits:Secuirty Deposits	Unpaid	100.00	200.00
Total Fox, Sabrina Tenant					100.00	200.00
Total Fox, Sebrina HUD & T					100.00	200.00
Total Gray Lane					100.00	200.00
Swamp Road						
Flippet, Groue						
Invoice	04/01/2022	28	Deposits:Secuirty Deposits	Paid		2,500.00
Invoice	04/01/2022	28	Deposits:Last Month Rent	Paid		2,500.00
Total Flippet, Groue					0.00	5,000.00
Total Swamp Road					0.00	5,000.00
Total GKS Properties					100.00	15,200.00
TOTAL					100.00	15,200.00

Report 13 Deposit – Last Month Rent

CHAPTER 37 LEASE COMMISSION

Lease commission is charged when a unit is rented on behalf of the owner. The management company bills the owner commission based on their contractual agreement.

Objectives

Upon completion of this chapter, you will be able to:

- Enter Lease Commissions
- Transfer Funds
- View Report

LEASE COMMISSION

You may have two bank account, one for the escrow and another for the company's overhead income and expenses or you may just have one bank account.

ONE BANK ACCOUNT

When the commission remains in the same bank account, create a sales receipt to record the income to the management company and expense to the owner all in one transaction. Each and every lease commission charge should be entered in its new transaction.

To enter a lease commission:

- Click **Customers** on the Menu Bar
- Select Enter Sales Receipts

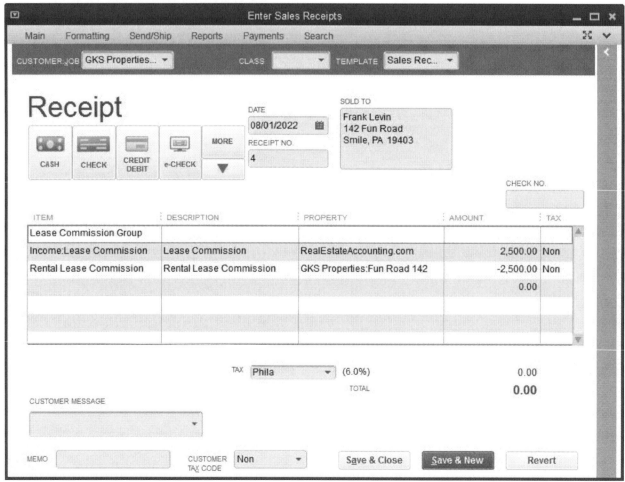

Screen Shot 173 Enter Lease Commission

LEASE COMMISSION

- Complete the fields as follows:

Field	Data		
Customer:Job	Tenant		
Class	Leave blank		
Template	Sales Receipt		
Date	Date		
Bill To	Prefills		
Terms	Select from the drop down menu		
Due Date	Leave as is		
Split Lines	Item	Property	Amount
Line 1	Lease Commission Group		
Line 2	Lease Commission	Your Company	Positive amount
Line 3	Unit Lease Commission	Property	Negative balance
Customer Message	As needed		
To be printed	As needed		
To be e-mailed	As needed		
Memo	As needed		
Click **Save & Close**			

Table 42 Enter Lease Commission

ANOTHER BANK ACCOUNT

When you have two different bank accounts it is a two step process. First you have to record the expense and then record the income.

- Write a check to enter the owner's expense using the Lease Commission item and Property as a Class; and
- Enter a Sales Receipts to record the income using the Lease Commission Income and Your Company as a Class

REPORT: LEASE COMMISSIONS

To view the Lease Commissions report:

- Click **MemRpts** on the Icon Bar
- Double-click Lease Commissions under Lease Commissions

www.RealEstateAccounting.com
Profit & Loss by Class
August 1, 2022
Fun Road 142

	(GKS Properties)	RealEstateAccounting.com	TOTAL
Ordinary Income/Expense			
▼ Income			
Lease Commission	0.00	2,500.00	2,500.00
Total Income	0.00	2,500.00	2,500.00
▼ Cost of Goods Sold			
Lease Commissions	2,500.00	0.00	2,500.00
Total COGS	2,500.00	0.00	2,500.00
Gross Profit	-2,500.00	2,500.00	0.00
Net Ordinary Income	-2,500.00	2,500.00	0.00
Net Income	-2,500.00	2,500.00	0.00

Report 14 Profit & Loss by Class

CHAPTER 38 RENT ROLL

Rent roll is a record of anticipated monthly rent for a tenant or a vacant unit.

Objectives

Upon completion of this chapter, you will be able to:

- Enter Rent Roll for Tenant
- Update Rent Roll
- View Reports

RENT ROLL FOR TENANT

On the rent roll estimate, include the rent, charges, and any additional amount.

To create a rent roll for each tenant:

- Click **Customers** on the Menu Bar
- Select Create Estimates

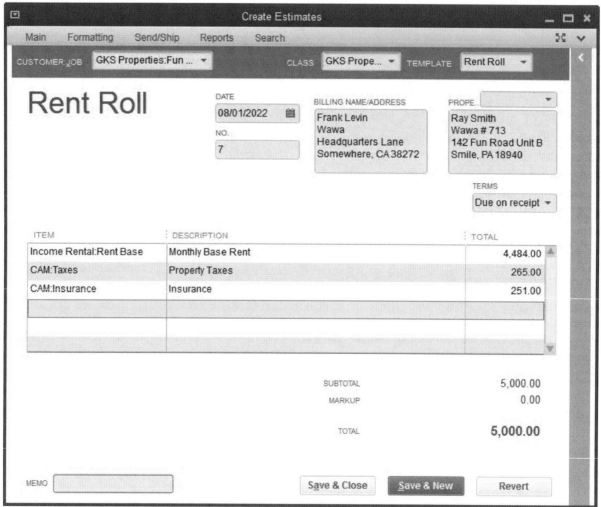

Screen Shot 174 Rent Roll

RENT ROLL

- Complete the fields as follows:

Field	Data		
Customer:Job	Tenant		
Estimate Active	Leave as is		
Class	Property		
Template	Rent Roll		
Date	Prefills to current date		
No.	RR and number prefills		
Bill To	Prefills		
Property Location (Ship To)	Prefills		
Terms	Due on receipt		
Split Lines	Item	Description	Amount
Line 1	Rent	As needed	Amount
Add Lines	CAM	As needed	Amount
Description	Prefills – add additional details as needed		
Total	Amount to be charged		
To be e-mailed	As needed		
Memo	As needed		
Click **Save & Close**			

Table 43 Rent Roll

Commercial Property Management for Managers: QuickBooks Desktop

PARTIAL REPORT: RENT ROLL

To view the Tenants Rent Roll report:

- Click **MemRpts** on the Icon Bar
- Double-click Rent Roll under Rent Roll

www.RealEstateAccounting.com
Rent Roll
August 1, 2022

Date	Item	Amount
GKS Properties		
Fun Road 142		
Levin, Frank		
08/01/2022	Income Rental:Rent Base	-4,484.00
08/01/2022	CAM:Taxes	-265.00
08/01/2022	CAM:Insurance	-251.00
Total Levin, Frank		-5,000.00
Total Fun Road 142		-5,000.00
Total GKS Properties		-5,000.00
TOTAL		-5,000.00

Report 15 Rent Roll

RENT ROLL

CHANGE RENT ROLL TEMPLATE

When a tenant vacates a unit, change the rent roll template to produce accurate reports.

To change the rent roll template:

- Click **Tenants** on the Icon Bar
- Highlight the Owner or Property who has vacated the unit
- Select Estimates from the Show drop-down menu

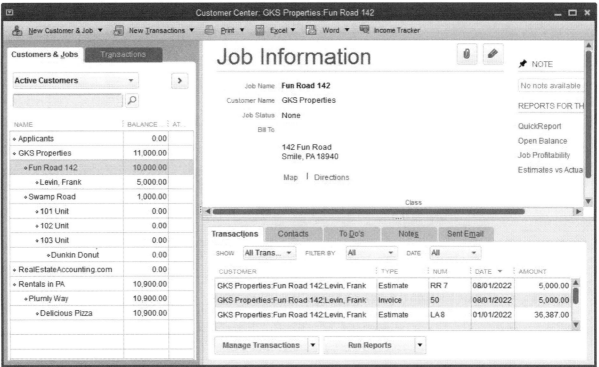
Screen Shot 175 Find Rent Roll

- Double-click the Rent Roll
- Change the Template to Rent Roll: Former Tenant from the drop down menu
- Click **Yes** to record the change
- Click **Save & Close**

Commercial Property Management for Managers: QuickBooks Desktop

REPORT: RENT ROLL

To view related reports:

- Click **MemRpts** on the Icon Bar
- Select by double-clicking the following under Rent Roll:
    - Rent Roll
    - Rent Roll for Former

CHAPTER 39 INVOICES

You **must** create an invoice for all money owed by tenants such as rent, reimbursed utilities, expenses, legal fees, security deposit, late fees, and damages. You cannot receive payment without first creating an invoice.

IMPORTANT
Create an a separate invoice for rent and security deposit and last month rent immaterial if the payment was made for the full amount listed on the lease. All partial payments will be applied proportionally to all items listed on the invoice.

IMPORTANT
Rent Escalation: Do you know the rent increase amount each year when you are entering the tenant? If so memorize the invoice for each year TODAY.

Objectives

Upon completion of this chapter, you will be able to:

- Record a Pro-Rated
- Record a Rent and CAM Invoice
- Record Rent Paid in Advance
- Memorize the Invoice
- View Report

PRO-RATED RENT

Pro-rated rent is based upon the number of days the unit is rented for the month by the tenant.

Follow the steps to create an invoice but do not memorize the invoice. Click **Save & Close**.

RENT PAID IN ADVANCE

Everything you do falls back on the agreement with the owner and state rules.

There are two options:

- Are you holding the rent received in advance till the invoice is due?
  - Next month before you run the owners proceed report review the open invoice report and apply the payment to the unpaid invoice. For, e.g., In Florida, Advanced rent cannot be disbursed to the owner until the rent is due.

- Alternatively, are you going to pay the money received the month it was received?
  - On the current month invoice: Increase the amount of the invoice by adding a line item Rent paid in advance Item with the overpaid amount and
  - In the next month invoice: Deduct the overpayment using Rent paid in advance item. See example below

ITEM	DESCRIPTION	PROPERTY	AMOUNT	TAX
Income:Rent	Rent for the Month	GKS Properties:Fun Road 142	2,500.00	Non
Income:Rent paid in advance		GKS Properties:Fun Road 142	-75.00	Non

Screen Shot 176 Rent Paid in Advance

Remember, we are "tweaking" QuickBooks' to be used as a Property and Financial Management Software.

Remember to charge a management fee on Rent paid in advance amount.

MONTHLY RENT INVOICE

Management and the tenant sign a lease agreeing to an amount to be paid monthly as rent, and any other charges. Follow the steps under Rent Invoice to create and memorize the invoice.

If you skip entering the rent roll, you will create an invoice by selecting Invoice and entering the details as shown below.

If you entered a rental roll create a rent invoice:

- Click **Rent & Sec Dep** on the Icon Bar

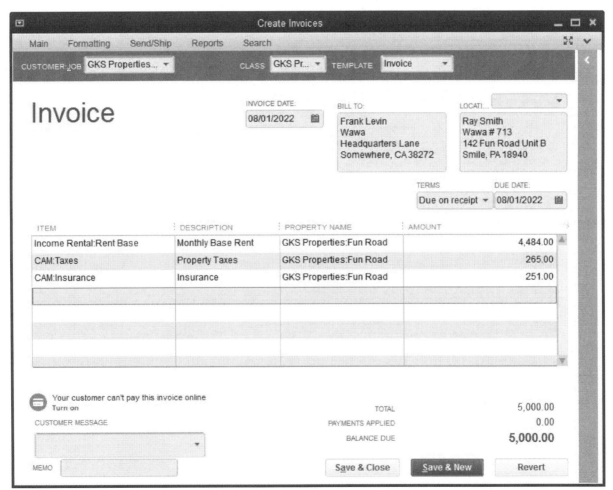

Screen Shot 177 Enter Invoices

- Select the tenant's name and press the Tab Key

INVOICES

The available Estimates (rent roll) screen will appear.

- Highlight the estimate
- Click **OK**

- Complete the fields as follows:

Field	Data
	Rent transactions will be prefilled from the estimate (rent roll) you already created. Change fields as required. If you did not enter the rent roll, enter all fields on the invoice.
DO NOT CLICK Save & Close	

Table 44 Enter Invoices

We are going to memorize a rent invoice and then click **Save & Close**. If you accidentally click **Save & Close** before memorizing the invoice, view the Tenant Center, highlight the tenant's name, and double-click on the invoice on the right.

Memorize the Invoice

To memorize the rent invoice:

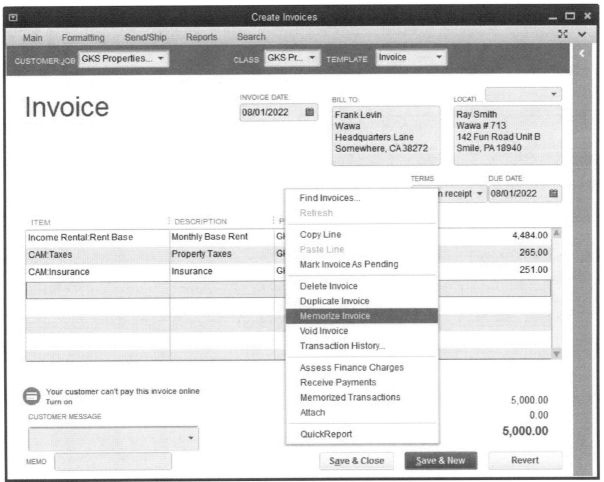

Screen Shot 178 Memorize Invoice

- Right-click on the invoice
- Select Memorize Invoice

INVOICES

Screen Shot 179 Memorize Transaction in Group

- Complete the fields as follows:

Field	Data
Name	R for rent, Property, and Tenant This will let you sort by rent invoices and the property name
How Often	Monthly
Next Date	Enter date of next month's invoice
Number Remaining	Term of lease (in months) minus one month
Days In Advance To Enter	As needed - 10 days is recommended
Click **OK**	

Table 45 Memorize Transaction in Group

This will bring you back to the invoice on the screen.

- Click **Save & Close** to record the invoice

> **NOTE**
> You can always open a saved invoice and memorize it.

REPORT: OPEN INVOICE REPORT

To view the open invoice report:

- Click **MemRpts** on the Icon Bar
- Double-click Open Invoices under Invoices

www.RealEstateAccounting.com
Open Invoices
All Transactions

Type	Date	Num	Terms	Due Date	Open Balance
GKS Properties					
Fun Road 142					
Levin, Frank					
Invoice	08/01/2022	50	Due on receipt	08/01/2022	5,000.00
Total Levin, Frank					5,000.00
Total Fun Road 142					5,000.00
Total GKS Properties					5,000.00
Rentals in PA					
Plumly Way					
Delicious Pizza					
Invoice	08/01/2022	51	Due on receipt	08/01/2022	5,425.00
Total Delicious Pizza					5,425.00
Total Plumly Way					5,425.00
Total Rentals in PA					5,425.00
TOTAL					**10,425.00**

Report 16 Open Invoices

VIEW MEMORIZED TRANSACTION LIST

After you have memorized the invoices, view the memorized transaction list.

Let's say Wawa's lease started on 2/1/2022 and rent escalates each year on February 1st. Enter the date and Number Remaining for six rent invoices. After all the invoices have been entered the number remaining will be zero. This will serve as an indication that the rent is due to be increased.

- Click **MemTx** on the Icon Bar

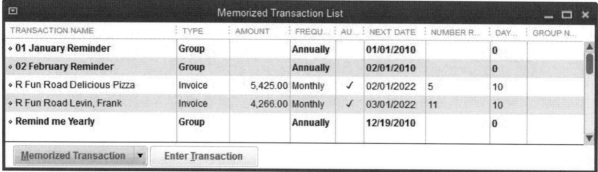

Screen Shot 180 Memorized Transaction List

CHAPTER 40 PAYMENTS AND DEPOSITS

Tenants make payments when they receive invoices or when they know a regular payment, such as a rent payment, is due. These payments need to be entered under the tenant's name and deposited into the bank account.

Sometimes the tenant's payment will include payment for current, next, or prior month invoices. The payment received should be applied to the invoices dated before the Owner's Proceed Statement date.

For example, if the payment was received on January 15th and applied to an invoice dated in February, the payment will not be reflected in the January report. It will show up in the February report.

When payment for an invoice is received in full, QuickBooks will automatically stamp the invoice PAID with the date.

Objectives

Upon completion of this chapter, you will be able to:

- Record Payments
- Make Deposits
- View Reports

CURRENT MONTH INVOICES

Apply, the tenant's payment, received against the invoice that was created.

To receive payments:

- Click **Payment** on the Icon Bar

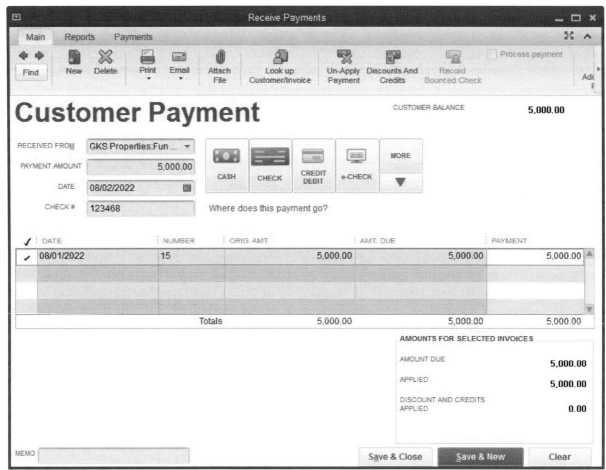

Screen Shot 181 Tenant Payment for Current Month

PAYMENTS AND DEPOSITS

- Complete the fields as follows:

Field	Data
Received From	Type in tenant's last name and field should prefill OR Type in the unit name and select the tenant's name
Amount	Amount of tenant's check
Date	Date the payment was received
Pmt. Method	Select from the drop down menu
Reference #	Number on the check or money order
Memo	As needed. Anything entered in this field can be viewed in Tenant Center or Customer Center and reports.
Card No.	As needed
Exp. Date	As needed
Payment	You can change the payment amount to be applied to each invoice
When the amount of the payment equals the amount of the invoice, QuickBooks will automatically enter a check mark in that line item. You can manually unclick and click on the check mark to apply the payment to the appropriate invoices.	
Click **Save & Close**	

Table 46 Tenant Payment for Current Month

MAKE DEPOSITS

When you receive payments, QuickBooks will record the amounts you receive in a holding account known as Undeposited Funds until you make a deposit.

To Make Deposits:

- Click **Deposit** on the Icon Bar
- View Payments to Deposit screen to see the list of payments you received
- Click on each payment that will be included on the deposit slip. The Payments Subtotal should equal the amount of the deposit slip.
- Click **OK**

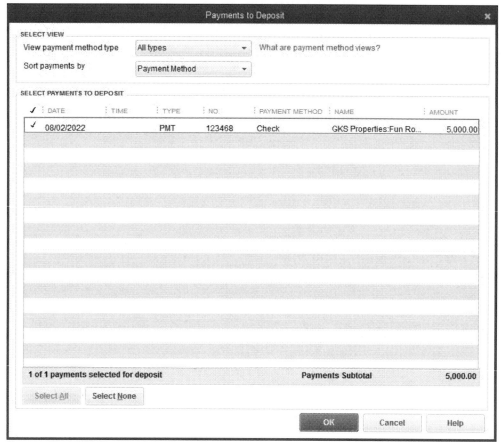

Screen Shot 182 Payments to Deposit

The Make Deposits screen will open. The Make Deposits window is a re-creation of the deposit slip.

PAYMENTS AND DEPOSITS

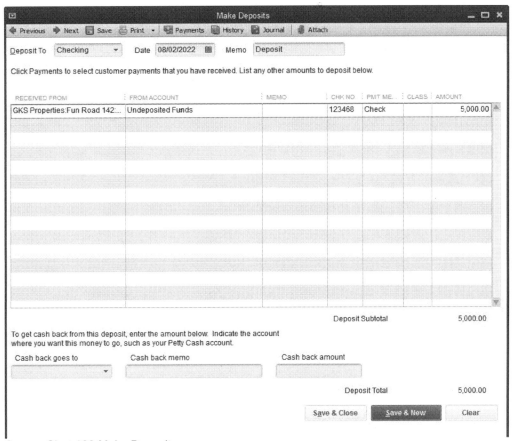

Screen Shot 183 Make Deposits

- Complete the fields as follows:

Field	Data
Deposit To	Bank Account
Date	Date on the deposit slip
Memo	As needed
Received From From Account Memo Chk No. Pmt Meth. Class Amount	Should prefill – if not, click **Payments** and select the payments deposited
Deposit Total	Deposit Total should equal the total on the Deposit Slip
Click **Save & Close**	

Table 47 Make Deposits

REPORT: PROFIT & LOSS

To view the payment received for current and prior month invoices:

- Click **MemRpts** on the Icon Bar
- Double-click Profit & Loss under Company

www.RealEstateAccounting.com
Profit & Loss
August 2, 2022

	Aug 2, 22
Ordinary Income/Expense	
Income	
Application Fees	50.00
Total Rent	
Rental	5,000.00
Total Total Rent	5,000.00
Total Income	5,050.00
Gross Profit	5,050.00
Net Ordinary Income	5,050.00
Net Income	**5,050.00**

Report 17 Profit & Loss

REPORT: DEPOSIT DETAIL

To view the Deposit Detail report:

- Click **MemRpts** on the Icon Bar
- Double-click Deposit Detail under Banking

www.RealEstateAccounting.com
Deposit Detail
August 1 - 3, 2022

Type	Num	Date	Name	Account	Amount
Deposit		08/01/2022		Checking	12,425.00
Payment	785	08/01/2022	GKS Properties:Fu...	Undeposited Funds	-10,000.00
Sales Receipt	4	08/01/2022	GKS Properties:Fu...	Undeposited Funds	-2,425.00
TOTAL					-12,425.00
Deposit		08/02/2022		Checking	50.00
Sales Receipt	2	08/02/2022	GKS Properties:Fu...	Undeposited Funds	-50.00
TOTAL					-50.00
Deposit		08/03/2022		Checking	5,000.00
Payment	1234...	08/02/2022	GKS Properties:Fu...	Undeposited Funds	-5,000.00
TOTAL					-5,000.00

Report 18 Deposit Detail

REPORT: DEPOSIT - BANK ACCOUNTS

To view the Bank Accounts report:

- Click **MemRpts** on the Icon Bar
- Double-click Bank Accounts under Company

www.RealEstateAccounting.com
Bank Accounts
As of August 30, 2022

Type	Date	Num	Source Name	Memo	Amount	Balance
Checking						16,343.88
Deposit	08/01/2022			Deposit	12,425.00	28,768.88
Deposit	08/02/2022			Deposit	50.00	28,818.88
Deposit	08/03/2022			Deposit	5,000.00	33,818.88
Total Checking					17,475.00	33,818.88
TOTAL					17,475.00	33,818.88

Report 19 Deposit - Bank Accounts

CHAPTER 41 LATE FEES

Late fees are charged to a tenant when rent payments are not paid promptly according to the lease terms.

Depending who retains the late fee use the appropriate class, Property or Your Company.

> **IMPORTANT**
> Late Fees Preferences: QuickBooks does not calculate the interest rate as per our industry standard practice. The percentage is charged by the day, not by the month.
>
> I **strongly do not** recommend using the Assess Finance Charge feature as it does not give you the option to use Class.

Objectives

Upon completion of this chapter, you will be able to:

- Determine which Tenants are Assessed Late Fees
- Automate Invoices
- Charge Late Fees
- View Reports

LATE FEES

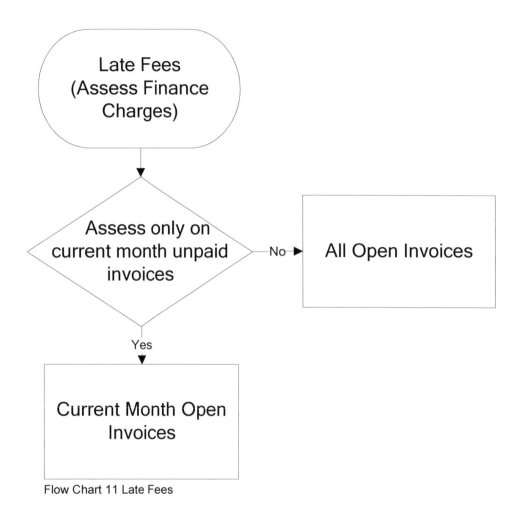

Flow Chart 11 Late Fees

REPORT: THIS MONTH'S OPEN INVOICES

We will be assessing late fees ONLY for current month's unpaid invoices.

To view this month's open invoices:

- Click **MemRpts** on the Icon Bar
- Double-click This Month's Open Invoices or Open Invoices under Rent Due

www.RealEstateAccounting.com
This Month's Open Invoices
As of August 31, 2022

Type	Date	Num	Terms	Due Date	Aging	Open Balance
GKS Properties						
Swamp Road						
Flippet, Groue						
Invoice	08/01/2022	18	5 Days	08/06/2022	25	2,500.00
Total Flippet, Groue						2,500.00
Total Swamp Road						2,500.00
Total GKS Properties						2,500.00
TOTAL						**2,500.00**

Report 20 This Month's Open Invoices

Determine whether you are charging late fees for the current month only or all unpaid (open) invoices.

A default late fee will show when assessing finance charges in QuickBooks. You may change the amount for each tenant as needed.

Late Fees payable to the Property Management Co.

If the Property Management Company retains the late fees, use batch invoicing to create invoices for multiple tenants. When creating an invoice, use Overhead (Your Company) as the Class. Refer to chapter Batch Invoicing.

Late Fees Payable to the Owner

If the property owner retains the late fees, create invoices for each tenant. Indicate Late Fees as the item and designate the specific property as the Class.

A good practice would be to create invoices for late fees and memorize either for each property or multiple tenants. If you create it for only one property, then all you have to do is change the name.

Print Statements

For further instruction to print statements, refer to chapter Statement.

Chapter 42 Pass Thru Charges

You may incur expenses for services, repairs, or materials, which are reimbursable to you by the tenant. These expenses are called reimbursable expenses or pass-thru charges.

Objectives

Upon completion of this chapter, you will be able to:

- Invoice for Pass Thru Charges
- Steps for Pro, Premier and Enterprise
- View Reports

PASS THRU CHARGES

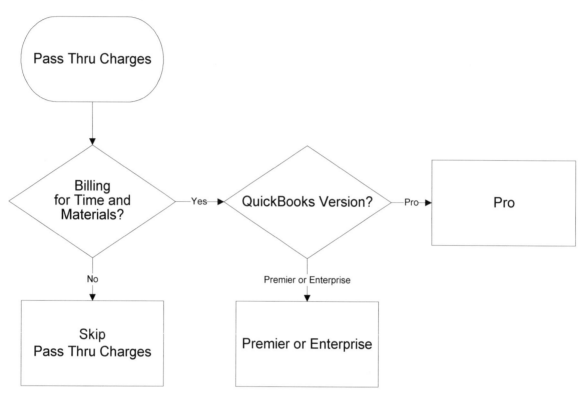

Flow Chart 12 Pass Thru Charges

You may wish to create invoices for reimbursable expenses if you charge more than you pay for services and maintenance (refer to the chapter on Markups), To record data for correct reflection on your reports, refer to the chapter on Categorizing Records.

> **NOTE**
> When you spend money on behalf of the tenant, you must create invoices for pass-thru charges. The method you use depends on the version of QuickBooks you have. Refer to the section which corresponds to your version.

REPORT: UNBILLED COSTS BY JOB (BEFORE)

Before you invoice for pass-thru charges, regardless of which version of QuickBooks you are using, view the Unbilled Cost by Job report and update the terms and send method for each property, unit, or tenant, as needed. Refer to the chapters in the Manage Names section.

To view unbilled costs by property, unit, and tenant:

- Click **MemRpts** on the Icon Bar
- Double-click Unbilled Costs by Job under Invoices

www.RealEstateAccounting.com
Unbilled Costs by Job
All Transactions

Type	Date	Source Name	Memo	Account	Billing Status	Amount
GKS Properties						
Fun Road 142						
Levin, Frank						
Bill	03/31/2022	Ala Zachery	(03/01/2022...	Property Repairs	Unbilled	25.00
Bill	03/31/2022	Ala Zachery	(03/01/2022...	Property Repairs	Unbilled	25.00
Bill	05/04/2022	Home Depot		Property Repairs	Unbilled	99.00
Total Levin, Frank						149.00
Total Fun Road 142						149.00
Total GKS Properties						149.00
TOTAL						**149.00**

Report 21 Unbilled Costs by Job

INVOICE FOR PASS THRU CHARGES

To access the Income Tracker:

- Click on **Tenants**

Screen Shot 184 Customer Center Menu Bar

- Click on **Income Tracker**
- Under Action select Create Invoice or Choose Billables to verify the time and costs.

Screen Shot 185 Income Tracker

Alternatively, To invoice for reimbursable expenses:

- Click **Tenant** on the Icon Bar
- Enter the owner or tenant name and tab to go to the next field

The Billable Time/Costs window appears.

PASS THRU CHARGES

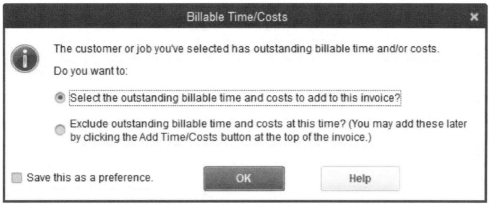
Screen Shot 186 Billable Time/Costs

- Select the outstanding billable time and costs to add to this invoice?
- Click **OK**

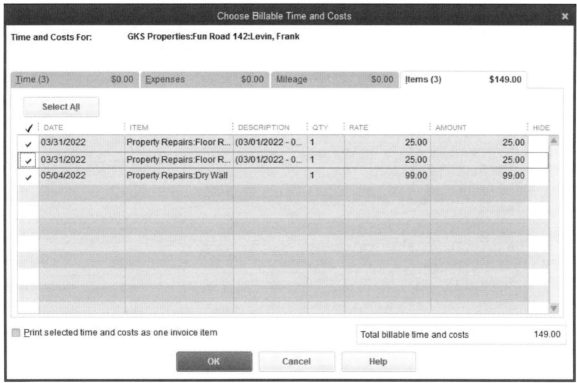
Screen Shot 187 Choose Billable Time and Costs

- Click **Time**, **Expenses**, **Mileage**, and **Items** tabs and select the billable items by clicking on the line
- Click **OK**
- Modify the invoice as needed
- Click **Save & Close** or **Save & New** to enter another invoice.

PASS THRU CHARGES

INVOICE FOR PASS THRU CHARGES (NOT AVAILABLE IN PRO VERSION)

IMPORTANT
The following function is only available for QuickBooks Premier Accountant and Enterprise users.

You should have already marked expenses as billable. Invoice the tenant for those charges.

To invoice for reimbursable expenses:

- Click **Customers** on the Menu Bar
- Select Invoice for Time & Expenses
- Choose the date range
- Select the template

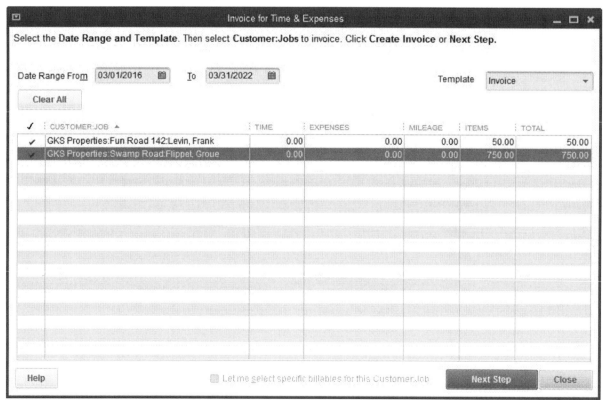
Screen Shot 188 Invoice for Time & Expenses

Commercial Property Management for Managers: QuickBooks Desktop

PASS THRU CHARGES

- Click the left column to select the Customer:Job
- Click **Next Step**

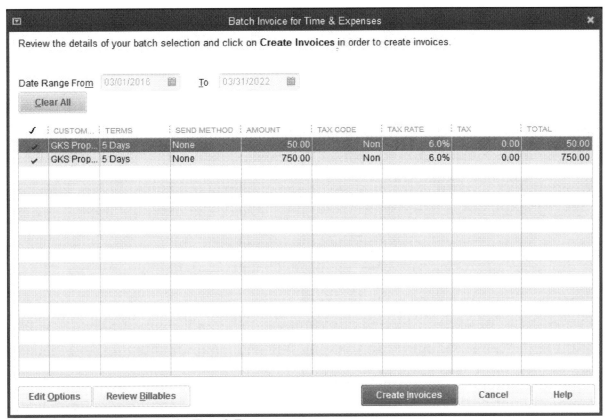
Screen Shot 189 Batch Invoice for Time & Expenses

- Click **Edit Options** to select options for transferring time, mileage, and markups.
- Click **Review Billables** to review and select the appropriate items.
- Click **Create Invoices**

A confirmation window appears.

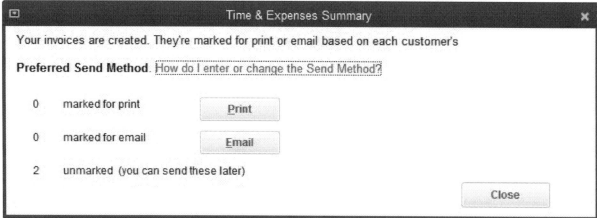

Screen Shot 190 Time & Expenses Summary

- Choose to either print or email the invoices
- Click **Close** twice to return to the original screen

> **NOTE**
> If you select only one Customer:Job to be invoiced, the invoice screen appears. Review the details on the invoice and click **Save**.

REPORT: UNBILLED COSTS BY JOB (AFTER)

To view the expenses incurred yet to be invoiced:

- Click **MemRpts** on the Icon Bar
- Double-click Unbilled Costs by Job under Markup

Since we created invoices for all the costs, the report shows no transactions.

CHAPTER 43 BOUNCED CHECK

A check is returned when there is not enough money in the bank account to cover the check amount. Should you have the unfortunate experience of having a tenant's check returned for insufficient funds, you will find out that the bank will charge an NSF (Non-Sufficient Funds) fee.

Objectives

Upon completion of this chapter, you will be able to:

- Record the Bank Service Fee (Non-Sufficient Funds)
- Record the Bounced Check
- Re-invoice for the bounced check and Bank Fees
- View Reports

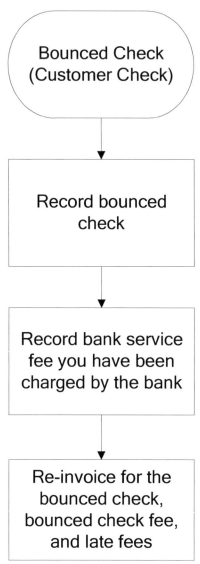

Flow Chart 13 Bounced Check

RECORD THE BANK SERVICE FEE

When a tenant's check bounces, record the Bank Service Fee by writing a separate check to the bank. Refer to the chapter on Writing Checks for additional information. Use Bank Service Fees as the Item, and the Name as the Customer:Job.

Depending on who is retaining the bank fee received, you will use the class accordingly, Property or Your Company

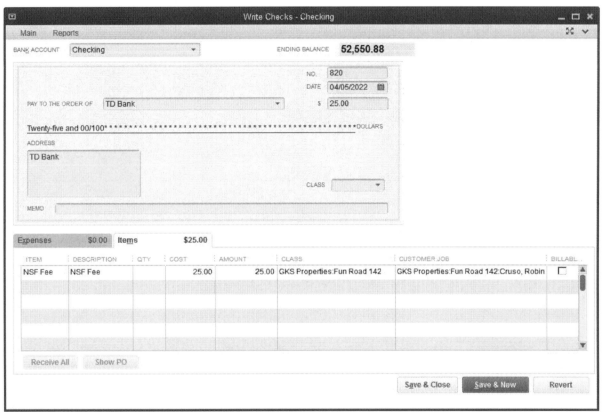

Screen Shot 191 Write Check for Bank Service Fee

RECORD BOUNCED CHECK

In addition to the check for the Bank Service Fee, record another for the bounced check amount. Creating this check it will record it as a deposit in your bank account.

To record a tenant's bounced check:

- Click **Customer** on the Menu Bar
- Select Customer Center
- Select the Property, Unit, or Tenant Name on the left column
- On the right bottom section, double-click on the Invoice (that you previously applied the payment to)
- Click **Refund/Credit**

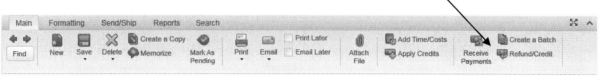
Screen Shot 192 Refund/Credit

Creating a credit will reflect the right line items and amount, reduce the tax payable amount, and decrease the money received on the reports.

- Add the word Bounced in the Credit No. field for reference
- Click **Use credit to give a refund**

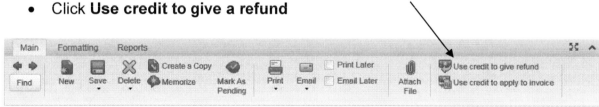
Screen Shot 193 Use credit to give refund

This step ensures that the bounced check is reflected on the bank register.

BOUNCED CHECK

The Issue a Refund screen appears.

![Issue a Refund screen]

Screen Shot 194 Issue a Refund

- Verify the data
- Type Bounced in the Memo field
- Uncheck the To be printed box
- Remove the text from the Ref/Check No. field
- Click **OK**

After you enter the credit memo, writing a check and re-invoice for the bounced payment view the Tenant center for the transactions.

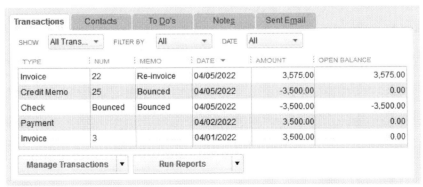

Screen Shot 195 Transactions List

Commercial Property Management for Managers: QuickBooks Desktop

BOUNCED CHECK

RE-INVOICE

Once you have accounted for the bank service fee and lack of payment, create another invoice for the tenant for the original amount, NSF charge, and appropriate late fees. If you know that you are never going to receive the payment, do not re-invoice the tenant.

To re-invoice the tenant:

- Click **Customer** on the Menu Bar
- Select Customer Center
- Select the Property, Unit, or Tenant Name on the left column
- On the right bottom section, double-click on the Invoice (that you previously applied the payment to)
- Right-click the Invoice and select Duplicate Invoice

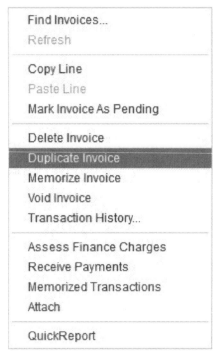

Screen Shot 196 Duplicate Invoice

- Verify the details for accuracy
- Add a line for Bank Charges and Late Fees (optional)
- Click **Save & Close**

Commercial Property Management for Managers: QuickBooks Desktop

CHAPTER 44 CREDIT OR WRITE OFF

Uncollected rent and reimbursable expenses are delinquent amounts due from tenants which are not collected at a future date. Usually, this amount is written off as a bad debt toward tenants' invoices. You may also need to credit a tenant's account for another reason. Keeping your tenants happy is your number one priority.

Another reason to use the credit feature is in the case of uncollected rent or unpaid reimbursable expenses. These unpaid amounts, which you do not expect to collect in the future, are typically written off as a bad debt toward the tenant's invoice.

Sometimes you may know in advance that a tenant account should be credited, but other times you may not know until after the tenant has been invoiced.

Objectives

Upon completion of this chapter, you will be able to:

- Credit a Tenant
- Write Off Unpaid Tenant Debt
- Handle Cancellations
- View Reports

CREDIT MEMO

Creating a credit memo is the same concept as creating an invoice.

To create a credit memo:

- Click on **Customers** on the Menu Bar
- Select Credit Memos/Refunds

CREDIT A TENANT

A credit reflects the correct line items and amount, reduces the tax payable amount, and decreases the money received on reports. If you give a credit on rent, it will reduce the tax payable amount. You may choose to write off the amount as uncollected. In that case, use the same items that you did not receive the money for.

To record credit for a tenant:

- Click **Customer** on the Menu Bar
- Select Customer Center
- Select the Property, Unit, or Tenant Name on the left column
- On the bottom right section, double-click on the Invoice (that you applied the payment to)

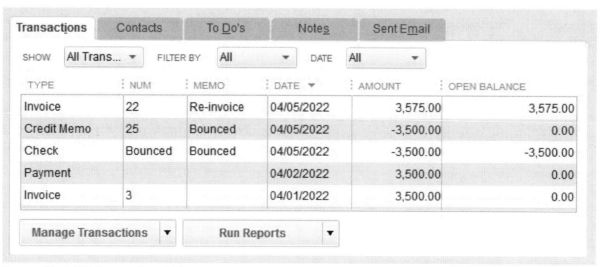

Screen Shot 197 Transactions List

CREDIT OR WRITE OFF

- Click **Refund/Credit**

Screen Shot 198 Refund/Credit

- Click **Use credit to apply to invoice** (to an open balance)

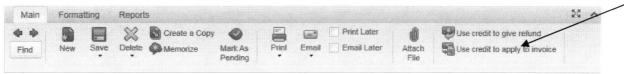

Screen Shot 199 Use credit to apply to invoice

The Available Credit screen appears.

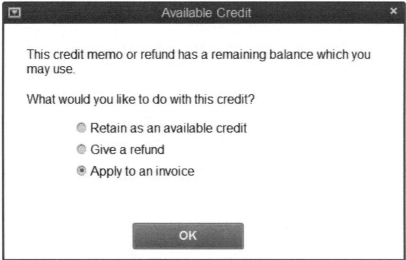

Screen Shot 200 Available Credit

- Select Apply to an invoice
- Click **OK**

Commercial Property Management for Managers: QuickBooks Desktop

CREDIT OR WRITE OFF

Apply Credit to Invoice screen will appear.

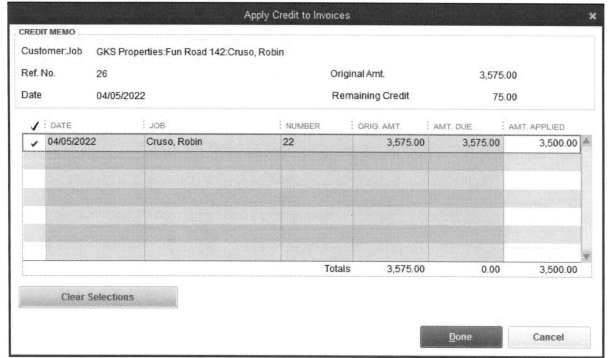

Screen Shot 201 Apply Credit to Invoices

- Add a check mark next to the Invoice you want to apply the credit to
- Change the amount to be applied to the invoice. It could be different from the amount due
- Click **Done**

It takes you back to the Credit Memo screen, which is already open. On the bottom right there may be a Remaining Credit balance depending on whether you applied the full amount of invoice due.

- Click **Use credit to give refund**

Screen Shot 202 Use credit to give a refund

The Issue a Refund screen appears.

Screen Shot 203 Issue a Refund

- Verify the data
- Mark To be printed
- Click **OK** to save

WRITE OFF

When you want to track the amount you write off on your reports, you should - Create a credit memo by using the Item Write-off or Bad Debt and then apply it to the open invoice.

CREDIT OR WRITE OFF

To print the check:

- Click **Reports** on top ribbon of the Credit Memo screen
- Click **Transaction History** on the top of the screen

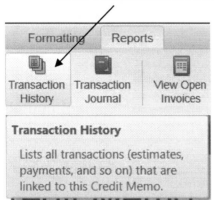
Screen Shot 204 Transaction History

The Transaction History – Credit Memo screen appears.

- Double-click Check
- Click **Print**
- Click **Save & Close** on the Credit Memo screen

You may also print checks at any time by clicking **File – Print Forms** and selecting Checks.

If you hold deposit funds in an escrow account, transfer the amount to an operating account.

REPORTS FOR TENANT CREDITS

To view related reports:

- Click **MemRpts** on the Icon Bar
- Select by double-clicking the following under Tenant Credits:
    - Checks Issued for Credits
    - Credit Memo Details
    - Credit Memo – Refunded
    - Credit Memo – Not Refunded

CHAPTER 45 COLLECTIONS, EVICTIONS, AND STATEMENTS

Your rental property business revolves around collecting payments for rent, taxes, fees, etc., from tenants. It is important to manage tenant payments, as well as view overdue and almost due invoices regularly.

If you are recording tenant names, you can use statements to track balances. Statements list outstanding rent and other charges owed by tenants. Customize statements and send notices to tenants by mail or email.

If you are not entering tenant names, you will not be able to pull up a balance, invoice, or payment details.

Objectives

Upon completion of this chapter, you will be able to:

- Open the Collections Center
- Notify Tenants Regarding Overdue Invoices
- Add Notes or Warnings to Invoices
- View Overdue and Almost Overdue Invoices
- Create and Print Statements

COLLECTIONS, EVICTIONS AND STATEMENTS

OPEN COLLECTIONS CENTER

To open the Collections Center:

- Click **Tenants** on the Icon Bar
- Click **Collections Center** on the top bar in the Customer Center
- Select either the Overdue or the Almost Due tab

Screen Shot 205 Collections Center

View all of the overdue invoices for properties, units, and tenants. Double-click to open an overdue invoice and add notes.

Under the Notes/Warnings column, the envelope icon indicates that the email address is missing. Click on the icon and enter an email address for future use. You can also add or view pending notes and tasks.

SEND EMAILS FOR OVERDUE INVOICES

Click **Select and Send Email** in the upper right corner to send an email to overdue or almost overdue accounts. Choose tenants to include in the email by selecting the desired invoices. If none of the listed customers have a valid email address, this button will not show.

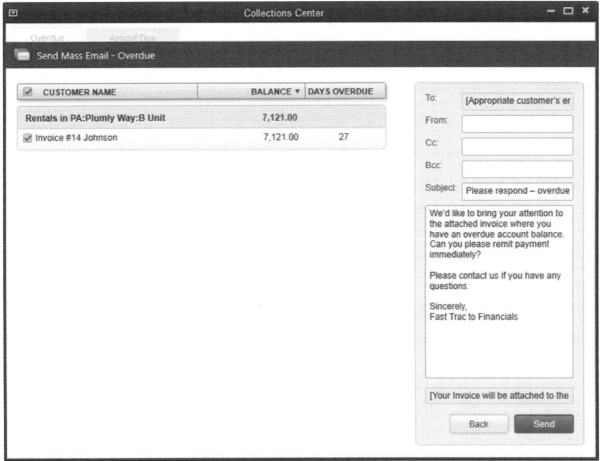

Screen Shot 206 Send Email for Overdue Invoices from Collections Center

If you send emails through the Collections Center, QuickBooks will automatically timestamp when the notices are sent.

To create:

- Letters: Refer to chapter Letter and Envelopes
- Templates: Refer to chapter Templates
- Statements: Refer to chapter Statements

View or Edit Notes and Warnings

To view or edit notes and warnings:

- Click on the notepad icon to open Notes
- Add notes after the automated date and time stamp
- Click **Save**

View Overdue Invoices

To view overdue invoices in the Customer Center:

- Click **Tenants** on the Icon Bar
- Select Customers with Overdue Invoices from the drop down menu

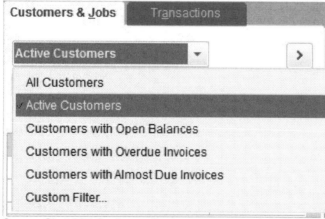
Screen Shot 207 Customer Center

From the same drop down menu, select Customers with Almost Due Invoices to view those invoices. You can also view all customers with open balances.

Evictions

Two options, customize a statement template or write a letter. Refer to chapter Letters and Envelopes and Statement.

CHAPTER 46 VACANCY LOSS

Would you like to be the best property manager in town? If you answered **YES**, it is a good practice to track the vacancy rent loss and hand the report to your client.

Vacancy rent loss is the amount of income lost due to the vacancy. To track the amount of rent lost due to vacancy, create an estimate. The amount will not be reflected on the Profit & Loss or Balance Sheet reports.

When the tenant moves out or is evicted, change the Job Status to vacant by editing the Unit or the Property. Doing so will enable you to track the vacancies, size of the unit, the amount of rent anticipated (rent roll), vacancy expenses, and losses.

Failure to anticipate the loss of rental income from vacant units and non-payment of rent will reduce the profitability of your clients' income-producing real estate investments.

Vacancy Loss chapter is optional

Objectives

Upon completion of this chapter, you will be able to:

- Record Vacancy Loss
- View Reports

ENTER RENT LOSS

Create an estimate using the vacant unit as a Customer:Job and Vacancy Loss as the Item.

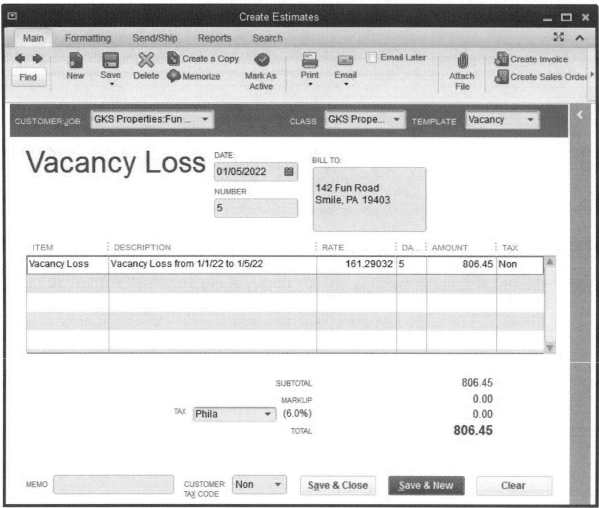

Screen Shot 208 Enter Rent Loss

VACANCY LOSS

- Complete the fields as follows:

Field	Data
Customer:Job	Property or Unit
Estimate Active	Click on it to Mark As Inactive
Class	Property
Template	Vacancy
Date	Last date of the vacancy
No.	Prefills
Bill To	Prefills
Property Location (Ship To)	Prefills
Item	Vacancy Loss
Description	From and to dates
Rate	Take the monthly rent and divide it by days in the month
Days	Number of days it is vacant
Amount	Auto-populates
Memo	As needed
Click **Save & Close**	

Table 48 Enter Rent Loss

Report: Vacancy Rent Loss

To view the Vacancy Rent Loss report:

- Click **MemRpts** on the Icon Bar
- Double-click Vacancy Loss Report under Vacancy

www.RealEstateAccounting.com
Vacancy Rent Loss
All Transactions

Date	Memo	Amount
GKS Properties		
Fun Road 142		
01/05/2022	Vacancy Loss from 1/1/22 to 1/5/22	806.45
Total Fun Road 142		806.45
Swamp Road		
03/24/2022	Vacancy Loss from 3/15/22 to 3/24/22	322.58
Total Swamp Road		322.58
Total GKS Properties		1,129.03
TOTAL		**1,129.03**

Report 22 Vacancy Rent Loss

SECTION 7

MANAGE ORDERS AND TIME

You may hire employees or subcontractors to do work or provide services. Track their job, and either pay them by time or by task completed.

Orders can be used for the purchase of supplies, to keep track of maintenance, or for noting repairs expected to occur. Enter an order to track supplies and/or avoid overpaying a supplier. When you decide to rehab or repair, complete an order to track the need and finally completion of the work.

Track orders by the property. If you have a similar problem later, you will know when the problem was reported, the date of the original repair, and who did the work. Also, track whether you provided proper notice and received permission to enter the unit.

VENDORS PURCHASE

Vendors Menu

To enter transactions:

- Click **Vendors** on the Menu Bar
- Select one to enter

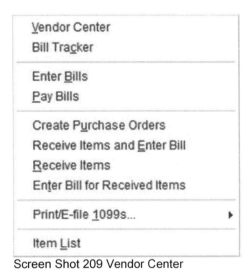

Screen Shot 209 Vendor Center

Purchase Reports

To view reports:

- Click **Reports** on the Menu Bar
- Select Report Center
- Click on **Purchases** under Standard tab
- Select one of the reports

```
Purchases by Vendor Summary
Purchases by Vendor Detail
Purchases by Item Summary
Purchases by Item Detail
Open Purchase Orders
Open Purchase Orders Detail
Open Purchase Orders by Job
```

Screen Shot 210 Report List

Additional reports can be found in the file provided by me, and a list can be found in chapter Customized Reports For You.

CHAPTER 47 PURCHASE ORDERS

Purchase orders are helpful when hiring contractors or buying supplies for repairs. Not only is it useful to track whom you are hiring with purchase orders, but the date of the repair, the amount spent, etc.

Objectives

Upon completion of this chapter, you will be able to:

- Understand the Process Working with Contractors
- Track Supplies Ordered

CONTRACTORS

You may use outside contractors to perform some or all of your maintenance tasks. Once you and the contractor have agreed to the terms of a job, you should have a contract or an estimate of anticipated costs. Sometimes you may agree to purchase and supply the materials; other times the contractor may include materials in the estimate. Be sure to include supplies regarding your agreement.

SUPPLIES

When ordering supplies, create a work order after agreeing to the terms. Such terms will be entered on the purchase order to serve as an additional record. Complete an order when ordering supplies from a vendor and record them when you receive the materials. As supplies are received, receive the Items in QuickBooks.

Enter a bill or write a check toward the purchase order entered. When the entire quantity ordered is applied to the bill or check, the purchase order closes automatically. If the total quantity ordered is not going to be received, close the purchase order manually when the work is completed.

You may question the necessity of completing purchase orders. QuickBooks is as good a place as any to enter the data. If a purchase order is entered in QuickBooks at the time the bill is created, the information will prefill, saving you from entering it twice.

> **NOTE**
> In QuickBooks, purchase orders are handled the same way as work orders. Refer to the chapter on Work Orders for step-by-step instructions on how to create a purchase order, enter a bill against a purchase order, and close a purchase order manually or automatically.

Chapter 48 Work Orders

Work orders are used for tracking materials ordered and repairs made by in-house employees or contractors. Entering a work order will help you avoid overpaying a contractor, as well as allow you to track contracts and estimates.

Objectives

Upon completion of this chapter, you will be able to:

- Create Work Orders
- Receive Items
- Complete a Work Order
- View Reports

WORK ORDERS

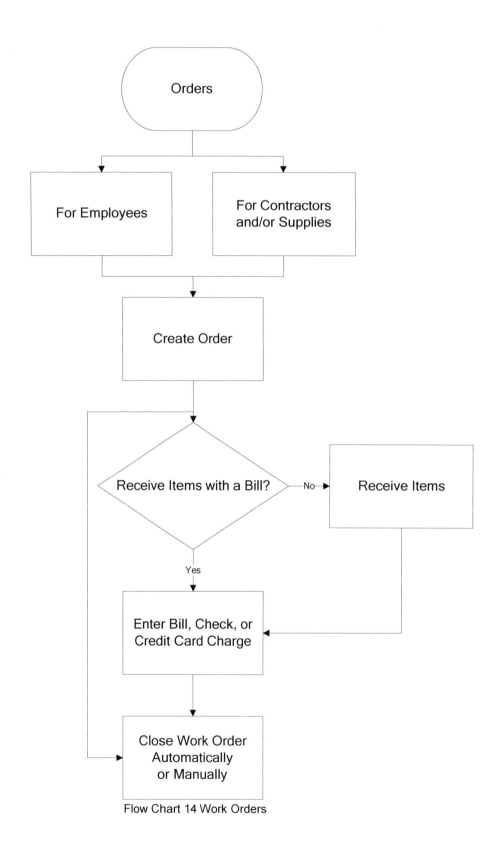

Flow Chart 14 Work Orders

EMPLOYEES VS. VENDORS

> **IMPORTANT**
> If an in-house employee is assigned a work order, enter the employee's name as a Vendor. Especially, if you are running payroll in QuickBooks. Be sure to differentiate vendor names from employee names. Refer to the chapter on Vendors.

Using work orders enables you to track which jobs need to be completed, who is assigned the job, and when the job is completed. Create a work order when a repair is needed or requested.

If you have in-house employees, they earn wages regardless of what work is assigned to them or when they complete a job. You do not have to complete the rate and amount fields unless you track employee productivity in that manner. Simply assign the task of completing the work order to your in-house employee.

Close the work order when the work is completed. If an in-house employee is handling the request, there will not be an estimate, contract, or bill.

CREATE WORK ORDERS

Create work orders for all repairs, contractors' estimates, and supplies ordered.

To create a work order:

- Click **Work Order** on the Icon Bar

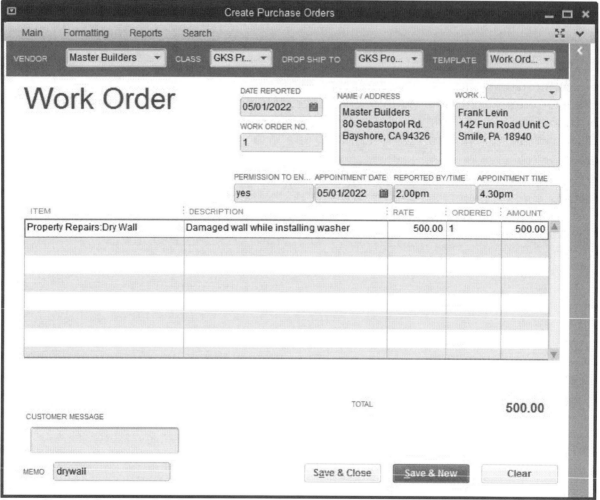

Screen Shot 211 Create Work Order

WORK ORDERS

- Complete the fields as follows:

Field	Data
Vendor	Company Name/Name of the repair person
Class	Property Name
Drop Ship To	Location of the repair or where the product is to be delivered
Template	Work Orders
Date Reported	Date
Work Order No.	Prefills
Name/Address	
Work	Select from the drop down menu
Permission to Enter	Yes or No
Terms	Select from the drop down menu
Due Date	As needed
Appointment Date	
Reported by/Time	
Appointment Time	
Item	Kind of repair to be done (For example, plumbing or painting)
Description	Details of the problem
Rate	Total amount or per unit price
Ordered	Number of units ordered
Amount	Prefills
Customer Message	As needed
Memo	Write a brief description to be used later when entering a bill, check, or credit card charge
Click **Save & Close** or **Save & New** to enter another order	

Table 49 Create Work Order

*If you decide to only track work orders and not receipt or completion of orders, save the order, reopen and then close the work order by adding a check mark to each line item under CLSD column.

RECEIVE ITEMS WITHOUT BILL

In most cases, work will be completed, or you will receive items before the bill comes from a vendor. Although you have yet to receive the bill, record receipt of the items as soon as the work has been completed.

To receive items:

- Click **Vendors** on the Menu Bar
- Select Receive Items
- Enter the Vendor Name

QuickBooks alerts you to the existence of open orders.

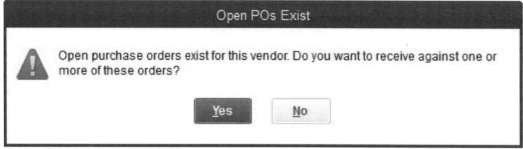

Screen Shot 212 Open POs Exist

- Click **Yes**

WORK ORDERS

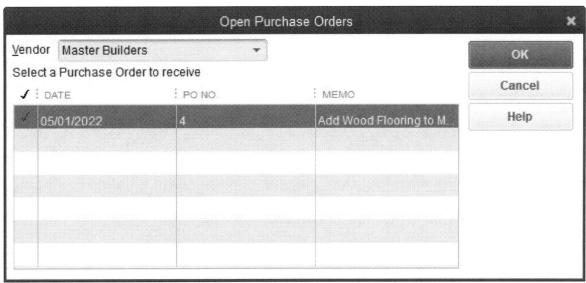

Screen Shot 213 Open Purchase Orders

- Select the work order which contains the items you have received
- Click **OK**

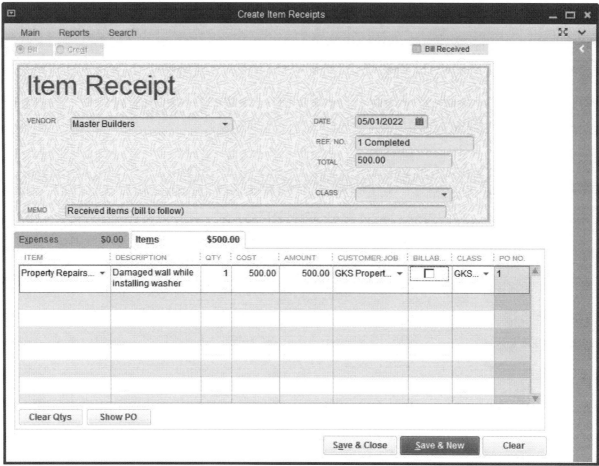

Screen Shot 214 Create Item Receipts

> **NOTE**
> For all purchase/work orders, details prefill under the Items tab, whether or not the Class you selected is a property or your Company.

- Complete the fields as follows:

Field	Data
Bill Received	Uncheck
Vendor	Prefills
Date	Date that the items are received
Ref. No.	As needed
Total	Total value of items received
Class	Change as needed
Memo	
Items tab	
Item	Prefills – do not change (if you do select clear and then change Show PO to make the changes
Description	Change as needed
Qty	
Cost	
Amount	
Customer:Job	
Billable?	
Class	
PO No.	Prefills
Click **Save & Close** or **Save & New** to receive additional items	

Table 50 Create Item Receipts

Once you receive the bill, select Bill Received in the top right of the window to convert it to a bill automatically. Add the bill number as the Ref. No. Refer to the chapter on Entering Bills.

RECEIVE ITEMS WITH BILL

When you receive the bill at the same time as the work is completed, follow the same steps as to receive items without a bill, click on Bill Received, but enter the bill and reference number right away. Refer to the chapter on Entering Bills.

CLOSE WORK ORDER - AUTOMATICALLY

The work order automatically is stamped RECEIVED IN FULL and is considered closed after one or more of the following has occurred:

- The work has been completed
- The total quantity ordered has been received
- A bill, check, or credit card charge is entered against the entire work order

Refer to the chapter on Entering Bills.

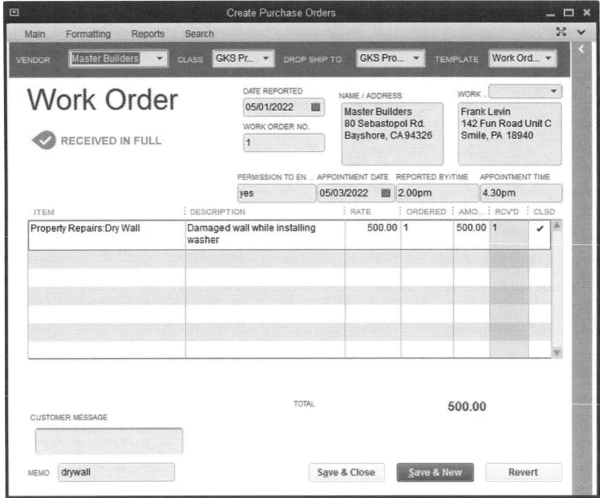

Screen Shot 215 Work Order Closed Automatically

CLOSE WORK ORDER - MANUALLY

There are several scenarios for which you may need to close a work order manually.

If an in-house employee completes the work and there is no bill, close the work order, so it does not appear in the Open Work Orders report. If you want to consider a supply order as received in full, even though it may not have been, you can close the work order.

When you do not receive a bill, or you cancel an order, enter the reason in the Memo field, and close the work order.

To close a work order manually:

- Click on **Mark As Closed** on the top of the screen
- Confirm the work order is stamped CLOSED
- Click **Save & Close** or **Save & New** to review another work order

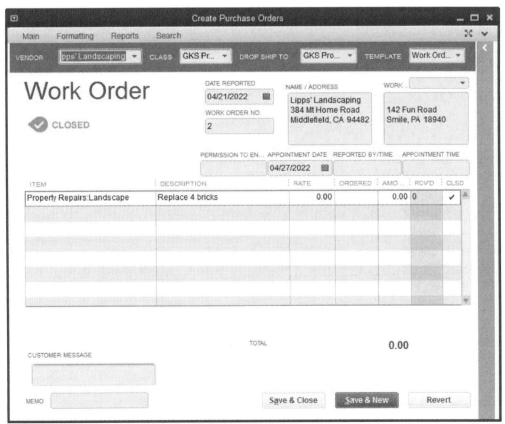

Screen Shot 216 Work Order Closed Manually

WORK ORDERS

REPORT: OPEN WORK ORDERS BY CONTRACTORS

To view the Open Work Orders by Contractors report:

- Click **MemRpts** on the Icon Bar
- Double-click All Work

www.RealEstateAccounting.com
All Work Orders
All Transactions

Date	Name	Memo	Deliv Date	Class	Amount
04/21/20...	Lipps' Landscap...		04/27/2022	GKS Properties:Fun Road 142	0.00
05/01/20...	Master Builders	drywall	05/03/2022	GKS Properties:Fun Road 142	500.00
Total					500.00

Report 23 All Work Orders

To view related reports:

- Click **MemRpts** on the Icon Bar
- Select by double-clicking the following under Work Orders:
    - Open Work Orders
    - Open Work Orders by Property
    - Open Work Orders by Contractor
    - Closed Work Orders
    - Closed Work Orders by Property
    - Closed Work Orders by Contractor
    - All Work Orders
    - All Work Orders by Property
    - All Work Orders by Contractor

CHAPTER 49 TRACK TIME AND TASKS

When employees or vendors perform tasks for which you pay them, you may track their work by time or by task completed.

For example, you may pay for cleaning, repairs, and other work on an hourly basis or by the job. If you pay for the work on an hourly basis, or you wish to track work performed by one person at multiple properties, use timesheets.

The goal is to make the billing process as simple as possible for your office, so consider this when entering timesheet data.

Objectives

Upon completion of this chapter, you will be able to:

- Enter Weekly Timesheets
- Copy the Last Timesheet
- View Reports

ENTER WEEKLY TIMESHEETS

Timesheets are entered only on a weekly basis.

> **NOTE**
> You must use items when creating timesheets.

To enter a new weekly timesheet:

- Click **Employees** on the Menu Bar
- Select Enter Time
- Select Use Weekly Timesheet

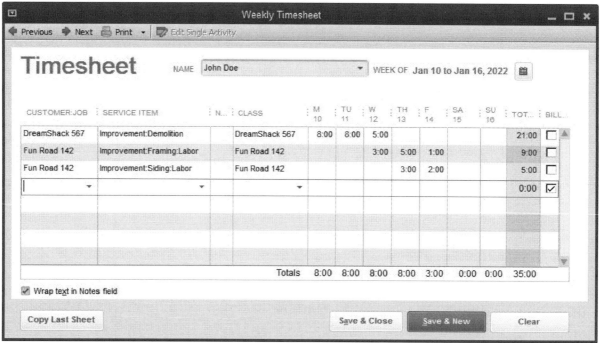
Screen Shot 217 Weekly Timesheet

Track Time and Tasks

- Complete the fields as follows:

Field	Data
Name	Your Company as a Vendor Name, Vendor, or Employee's Name
Week of	Select last day of the week
Customer:Job	Property Name
Service Item	Work performed
Notes	As needed
Class	Property Name
M, TU, W, TH, F, SA, SU	Enter the time or quantity you are paying for on the appropriate day of the week
Total	Prefills
Billable?	Mark if you are going to create an invoice for the Customer
Click **Save & Close** or **Save & New** to enter another timesheet	

Table 51 Weekly Timesheet

When the same service is performed, is non-billable, for the same Customer:Job, enter the numbers on the same line.

When you are creating an invoice for the same numbers you entered, repeat the name on the second line and mark it billable. To check for accuracy, view the Unbilled Costs by Property report.

COPY THE LAST TIMESHEET

When an employee or vendor performs work on the same property week after week, save time by duplicating the timesheet and making changes reflecting the weekly details.

To copy a vendor or employee timesheet from the previous week:

- Click **Employees** on the Menu Bar
- Select Enter Time
- Select Use Weekly Timesheet
- Select the name of the employee
- On the bottom left, click **Copy Last Sheet**
- All details from the previous week will prefill
- Change the time or quantity on the timesheet, as needed
- Click **Save & Close** or **Save & New** to enter another timesheet

Report: Quantity & Time by Property

To view the time by property report:

- Click **Reports** on the Menu Bar
- Select Jobs, Time & Mileage
- Click **Time by Job Summary**

www.RealEstateAccounting.com
Time by Job Summary
January 1 - 15, 2022

	Jan 1 - 15, 22
DreamShack 567	
Improvement:Demolition	21:00
Total DreamShack 567	21:00
Fun Road 142	
Improvement:Framing:Labor	9:00
Improvement:Siding:Labor	5:00
Total Fun Road 142	14:00
TOTAL	**35:00**

Report 24 Time by Job Summary

Reports for Timesheets

To view related reports for Timesheets:

- Click **MemRpts** on the Icon Bar
- Select by double-clicking the following under Timesheets:
    - Quantity & Time by Property
    - Time by Name
    - Time by Property Detail
    - Time by Property Summary for Your Company
    - Time by Work Performed

Tasks

Refer to chapter Notes, To Do List and Reminders.

SECTION 8

MANAGE VENDORS

As money comes in, it also goes out!

Your business is likely to split between managing tenants and vendors. As you purchase goods, supplies, and services from insurance companies, contractors, utility companies, and other suppliers, track these products and services, bills, and payments.

The following chapters will show you how to track every interaction with vendors from deposits at the beginning of a job to credits after paying for completed work. We will cover how to enter and pay bills, either online or by using a credit card, petty cash, or your checking account. Including tracking reimbursable expenses, and markups.

VENDORS

Vendors Menu

To enter transactions:

- Click **Vendors** on the Menu Bar
- Select one to enter

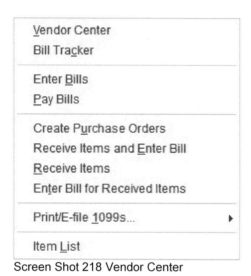

Screen Shot 218 Vendor Center

Vendors & Payables Reports

To view reports:

- Click **Reports** on the Menu Bar
- Select Report Center
- Click on **Vendors & Payables** under Standard tab
- Select one of the reports

```
A/P Aging Summary
A/P Aging Detail
Vendor Balance Summary
Vendor Balance Detail
Unpaid Bills Detail
Accounts Payable Graph
Transaction List by Vendor

1099 Summary
1099 Detail

Vendor Phone List
Vendor Contact List
```

Screen Shot 219 Report List

Additional reports can be found in the file provided by me, and a list can be found in chapter Customized Reports For You.

Chapter 50 Writing Checks

Occasionally, you may have the opportunity to write a check or make a payment online without having already entered a bill. Be sure to use the Pay Bill feature if you have already entered a bill, referring to the chapter on Paying Bills.

Objectives

Upon completion of this chapter, you will be able to:

- Write a Check
- View Reports

WRITING CHECKS

WRITE A CHECK

When writing a check for a specific property expense, refer to Entering Bills for details on Items tab.

To write a check:

- Click **Banking** on the Menu Bar
- Select Write Checks

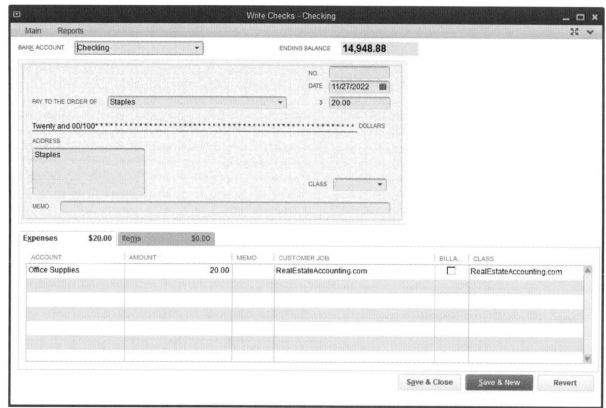

Screen Shot 220 Write Checks

Commercial Property Management for Managers: QuickBooks Desktop   376

Writing Checks

- Complete the fields as follows:

Field	Data
Bank Account	Select bank account
No.	Check number or Online
Date	Date
Pay to the Order of	Vendor Name
$	Amount paid
Address	Prefills
Class	Property, Unit, Tenant, CAM or Non-CAM or Your Company
Memo	As needed
Expenses tab*	Use for Your Company
Account	Select from the drop down menu
Amount	Amount
Memo	As needed
Customer:Job	Your Company
Billable?	Leave blank
Class	Your Company
Items tab*	Use for particular property
Item	Select from the drop down menu
Description	As needed
Qty	1 or as needed
Cost	Amount due per Item
Amount	Prefills
Customer:Job	Property, Unit, Tenant, CAM or Non-CAM
Billable?	As needed
Class	Property Name
Click **Save & Close** or **Save & New** to enter another check	

Table 52 Write Checks

*To split the amount across two or more accounts, create multiple line entries and divide the amounts.

Report: Check Detail

To view the Check Detail report:

- Click **MemRpts** on the Icon Bar
- Double-click Check Detail under Banking

www.RealEstateAccounting.com

Check Detail
November 3 - 27, 2022

Type	Num	Date	Name	Account	Class	Paid Amount
Check		11/27/2022	Staples	Checking		
			RealEstateAccoun...	Office Supplies	RealEstateAc...	-20.00
TOTAL						-20.00
Check	818	11/27/2022	John Greenlane	Checking		
				Petty Cash	RealEstateAc...	-20.00
TOTAL						-20.00
Check	819	11/03/2022	Ala Zachery	Checking		
				Property Repairs	GKS Properti...	-750.00
				Property Repairs	GKS Properti...	-2,000.00
				Property Repairs	GKS Properti...	-1,598.00
TOTAL						-4,348.00

Report 25 Check Detail

CHAPTER 51 PETTY CASH

Petty cash is money held in the office for small cash expenses, such as buying lunch, gas, stamps, or postage. To maintain petty cash, withdraw money from a bank account and keep it on site. As you spend it, you will maintain a record of the expenses and withdraw additional cash from the bank to replenish your supply.

Objectives

Upon completion of this chapter, you will be able to:

- Withdraw Money from Petty Cash
- Record Expenses
- View Register

WITHDRAW MONEY FOR PETTY CASH

Withdraw money from the bank account in QuickBooks to accurately reflect the bank balance and the petty cash amount. This could be for a formal withdrawal or an ATM withdrawal.

For example, if you decide to withdraw $100 from the checking account to use as Petty Cash, write a check to withdraw money from the bank and use Petty Cash as the account name on the Expenses tab.

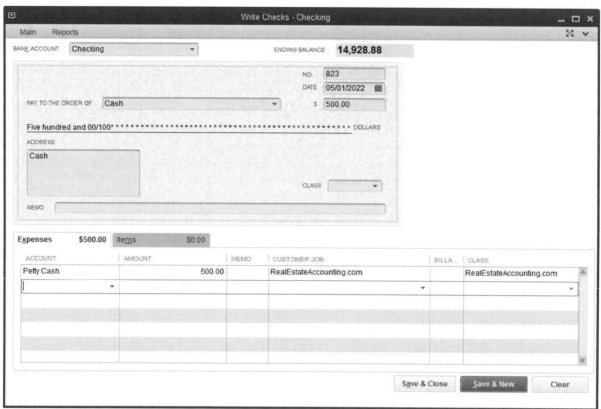

Screen Shot 221 Write a Check to Withdraw Money for Petty Cash

> **NOTE**
> Using Petty Cash as the expense account increases the Petty Cash account balance.

RECORD EXPENSES

To accurately reflect your expenses by Vendor and Class, record expenses paid in cash just as you would record expenses paid by check.

Write a check selecting Petty Cash as the bank account to register each expense from the Petty Cash bank account, reducing the amount, so the account balance always matches your cash on hand.

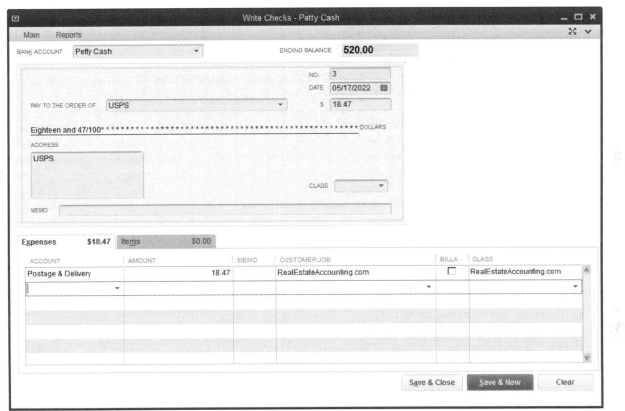

Screen Shot 222 Write a Check to Record Petty Cash Expenses

VIEW PETTY CASH REGISTER

The Petty Cash register lists all cash withdrawals to the petty cash account, as well as all expenses paid in cash.

To view the Petty Cash register:

- Click **Accnt** on the Icon Bar
- Double-click on the Petty Cash account

Screen Shot 223 Use Register

- Select Petty Cash from the drop down menu
- Click **OK**

Screen Shot 224 Petty Cash Register

CHAPTER 52 ENTERING BILLS

A bill shows how much you owe a vendor and what the expense is for. Entering vendor bills allows you to track expenses and pay bills on time, whether or not you enter work orders. Bills should be associated with a particular property when appropriate.

If you use credit cards to make purchases, track expenses and cash flow for those expenditures, too.

> **IMPORTANT**
> To fully understand the concept of entering bills, refer to the chapter on Categorizing Records before you begin.

Objectives

Upon completion of this chapter, you will be able to:

- Manage Reimbursable Expenses
- Enter Bills
- Enter Credit Card Charges
- Enter and Apply Vendor Credit
- Enter Bills using Time
- Handle Recurring Bills
- View Reports

ENTERING BILLS

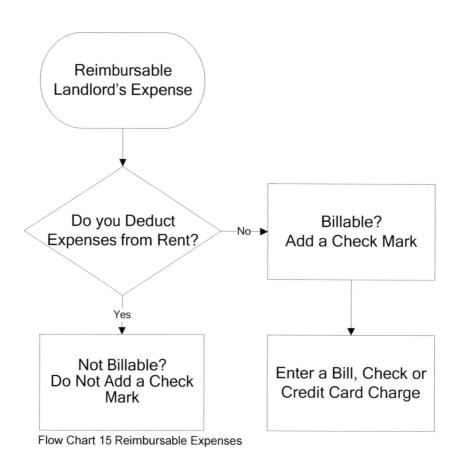

Flow Chart 15 Reimbursable Expenses

ENTERING BILLS

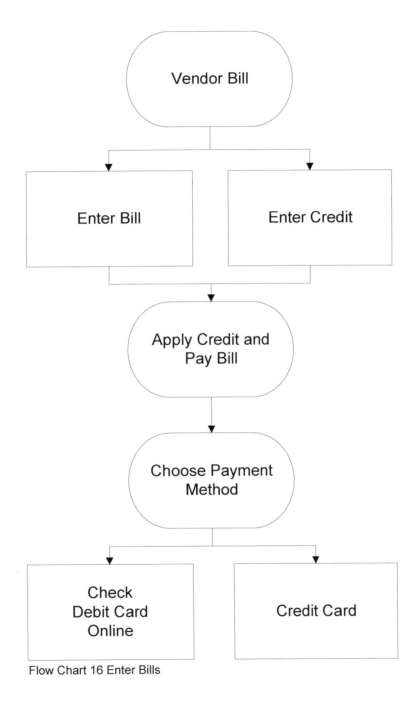

Flow Chart 16 Enter Bills

ENTERING BILLS

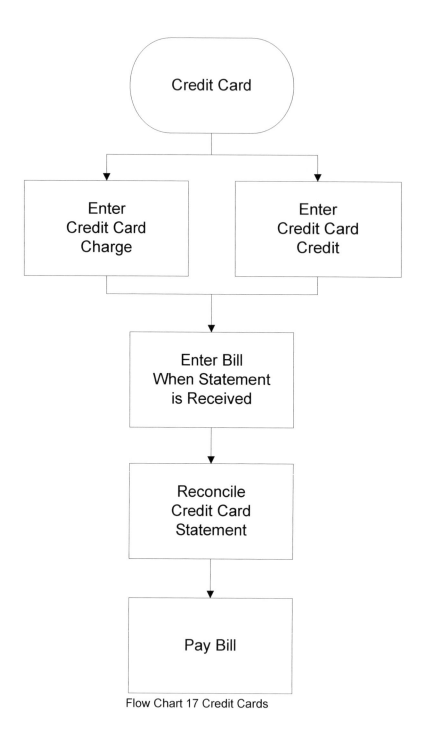

Flow Chart 17 Credit Cards

ENTER REIMBURSABLE EXPENSES

When managing rentals properties, you will probably incur expenses for services, repairs, or materials, which are reimbursable. These costs can also be referred to as pass-thru charges.

When do you add a check mark in the Billable? Column?

- Only if you are going to invoice the owner or the tenant, for the amount you in entered in the line item. Refer to chapter Markup and Pass Thru Charges
- DO NOT add a check mark if you are going to deduct the expenses from owner proceed check. As you are receiving and paying on behalf of the owner's fund.

If **you already have charged the tenant**, you do not need to mark the Billable? Column or create invoices, as the money has already been charged or paid by the tenant at some point.

If **you did not yet collect payment** but did spend money, be sure to mark the expense as billable by placing a check mark in the Billable? column. Then create invoices for reimbursement. If you charge a markup, include the amount. Refer to the chapter on Pass Thru Charges.

Screen Shot 225 Mark Billable Expenses

FOR MANAGERS: Any expenses incurred on behalf of the owner and is going to be deducted from the rental income, uncheck the Billable box.

ENTER A BILL AGAINST A WORK ORDER

When you receive a bill from a vendor, enter the bill, check, or credit card charge as quickly and accurately as possible, as the information from the work order flows directly to the form.

Let's suppose you receive a bill from Master Builders for pool supplies and work performed for a property (Fun Road) that is previously entered as a purchase order.

To enter the bill:

- Click **Bill** on the Icon Bar
- If the Open PO's Exist message appears, click **Yes**

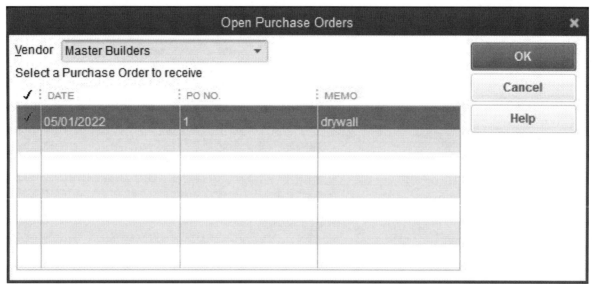

Screen Shot 226 Open Purchase Orders

- Select appropriate purchase order
- Click **OK**

Entering Bills

All the details from the work order will be copied into a bill.

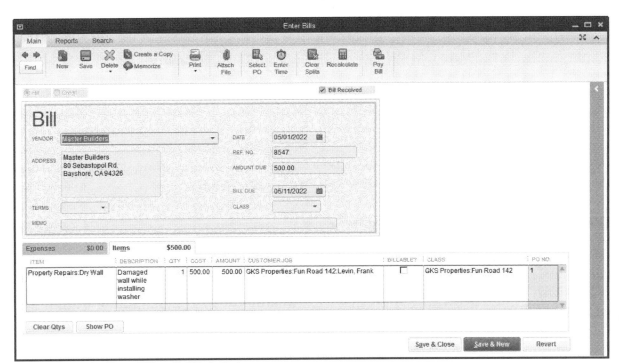

Screen Shot 227 Enter Bills with Work Order

- Complete the fields as follows:

Field	Data
Date	Date bill is received
Ref No.	Bill number
Amount Due	Equals to Expenses plus Items tab
Bill Due	As needed
Terms	Select from the drop down menu
Qty	Actual quantity received
Cost	Change as needed
Billable?	
Class	
The other fields prefill from the work order.	
Click **Save & Close** or **Save & New** to enter another bill	

Table 53 Enter Bills with Work Order

Work orders remain open until all Items are received or until the work orders are closed manually.

ENTER A BILL WITHOUT A WORK ORDER

You may enter a material expense like a bill where no work order is needed.

For example, you order materials for the Fun Road property and receive the bill from Home Depot instantly.

> **NOTE**
> Use the Expenses tab for Your Company expenses and the Items tab for specific property expenses.

To enter a bill without a work order:

- Click **Bill** on the Icon Bar

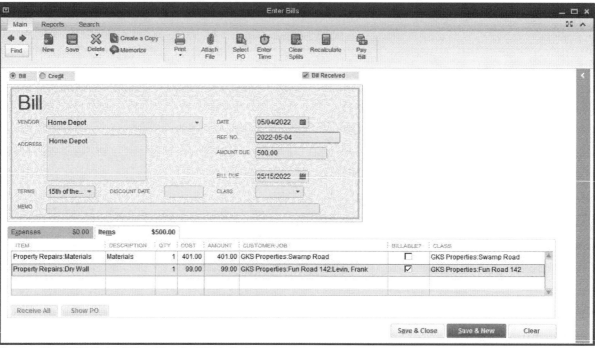

Screen Shot 228 Enter Bills without a Work Order

ENTERING BILLS

- Complete the fields as follows:

Field	Data
Vendor	Vendor Name
Address	Prefills
Date	Date of the bill
Ref. No.	Bill number or date of the bill
Amount Due	Total amount due
Bill Due	Date
Terms	Select from the drop down menu
Discount Date	
Class	As needed
Memo	
Expenses tab*	Use for Your Company expenses
Account	Select from the drop down menu
Amount	Amount of check
Memo	As needed
Customer:Job	Your Company
Billable?	Leave blank
Class	Your Company
Items tab*	Use for specific property
Item	Select from the drop down menu
Description	As needed
Qty	1 or as needed
Cost	Amount due per item
Amount	Prefills
Customer:Job	Property, Unit, Tenant, CAM or Non-CAM
Billable?	As needed
Class	Property Name
Click **Save & Close** or **Save & New** to enter another bill	

Table 54 Enter Bills without a Work Order

*The amounts in the Expenses tab and Items tab must equal Amount Due.

ENTERING BILLS

REPORT: UNPAID BILLS DETAIL

To view the Unpaid Bills Detail report:

- Click **MemRpts** on the Icon Bar
- Double-click Unpaid Bills Detail under Vendors

www.RealEstateAccounting.com
Unpaid Bills Detail
As of May 22, 2022

Type	Date	Num	Due Date	Aging	Open Balance
Home Depot					
Bill	05/04/2022	2022-05-04	05/15/2022	7	500.00
Total Home Depot					500.00
Master Builders					
Bill	05/01/2022	8547	05/11/2022	11	500.00
Total Master Builders					500.00
TOTAL					**1,000.00**

Report 26 Unpaid Bills Detail

CREDIT CARD CHARGES

To set up your credit card accounts, refer to the chapter on Company File.

At times, it may be appropriate to pay vendors with a credit card on the spot. Enter credit card charges at the date of purchase or when you receive the statement.

If you enter the charges upon receipt of the statement, add any finance charges or late fees and reconcile the statement against your transactions. Refer to the chapter on Reconciling Accounts.

> **IMPORTANT**
> Only enter a credit card charge if you did not enter a bill for the transaction. If you have already entered a bill and wish to pay by credit card, refer to the chapter on Paying Bills.

Let's say, an employee, Andy C., pays a Staples bill for supplies with his American Express card. He enters the charge directly without entering a bill.

ENTERING BILLS

To enter a credit card charge:

- Click **CCard** on the Icon Bar

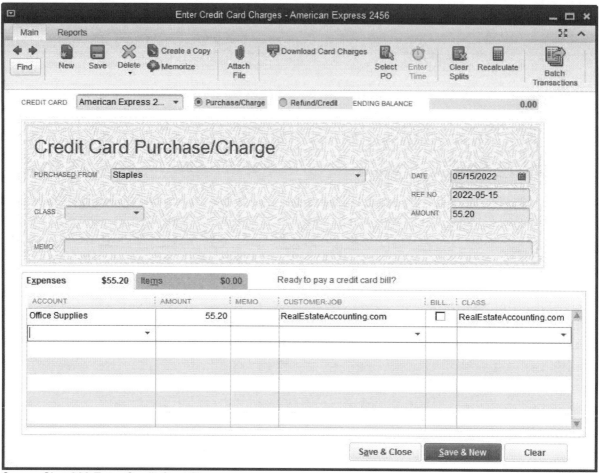

Screen Shot 229 Enter Credit Card Charges

Commercial Property Management for Managers: QuickBooks Desktop

ENTERING BILLS

- Complete the fields as follows:

Field	Data
Credit Card	Select credit card and cardholder account
Purchase/Charge	Select
Refund/Credit	Unselect
Purchased From	Vendor Name
Date	Date of charge
Ref No.	Leave blank or enter the bill number
Amount	Total amount of the charge
Class	As needed
Memo	
Expenses tab*	Use for Your Company expenses
Account	Select from the drop down menu
Amount	Amount paid
Memo	As needed
Customer:Job	Your Company
Billable?	Leave blank
Class	Your Company
Items tab*	Use for specific property
Item	Select from the drop down menu
Description	As needed
Qty	1 or as needed
Cost	Amount due per item
Amount	Prefills
Customer:Job	Property, Unit, Tenant, CAM or Non-CAM
Billable?	As needed
Class	Property Name
Click **Save & Close** or **Save & New** to enter another credit card charge	

Table 55 Enter Credit Card Charges

*To split the amount across two or more accounts, create multiple line entries and divide the amounts.

Commercial Property Management for Managers: QuickBooks Desktop

ENTERING BILLS

REPORT: CREDIT CARD ACCOUNTS

To view Credit Card Accounts:

- Click **MemRpts** on the Icon Bar
- Double-click Credit Card Accounts under Company

NOTE
In the report, "Type" refers to Credit Card account

www.RealEstateAccounting.com
Credit Card Accounts
As of May 31, 2022

Type	Date	Num	Source Name	Memo	Amount
American Express 2456					
Payments Only					
Bill	05/30/2022	2022...	American Express		-6,104.01
Total Payments Only					-6,104.01
American Express 2456 - Other					
Credit Card Charge	05/15/2022	2022...	Staples		55.20
Total American Express 2456 - Other					55.20
Total American Express 2456					-6,048.81
TOTAL					**-6,048.81**

Report 27 Credit Card Accounts

ENTER BILLS TO PAY CREDIT CARD BALANCE

Regardless of the outstanding balance, enter a bill to reconcile the credit card statement with the transactions entered in QuickBooks and track the card balance. This simplifies the process of reconciling QuickBooks entries with the credit card statement.

The total balance owed on the statement is the compilation of the prior month's balances, current charges, payments made, and credits for the statement period.

The total balance owed for the statement period is equal to purchases, interest, and finance or other charges minus any credits for the specified date range. Credits do not include any payments made before the statement date.

To calculate your current statement amount:

- Add charges (purchases)
- Subtract all credits (not payments)
- Add late fees and finance charges

ENTERING BILLS

To enter a bill to pay a credit card balance:

- Click **Bill** on the Icon Bar

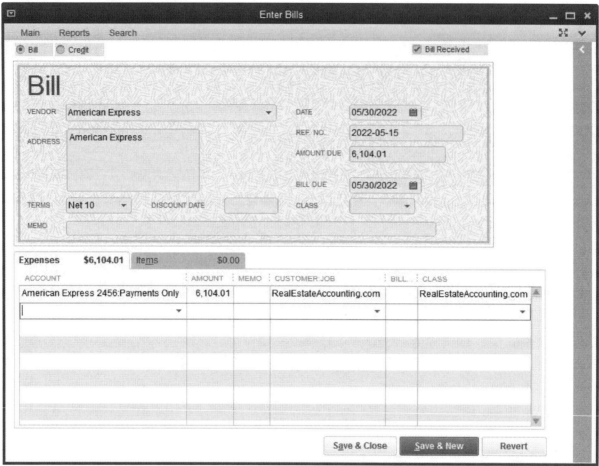

Screen Shot 230 Enter Bills to Pay Credit Card Balance

Entering Bills

- Complete the fields as follows:

Field	Data
Vendor	Credit Card
Date	Closing date of statement
Address	Prefills
Ref. No.	Closing date of statement
Amount Due	Total amount of new transactions (purchases + finance charge + additional charges - credits)
Bill Due	Payment due date
Terms	Leave blank
Class	Your Company
Memo	As needed
Expenses tab	
Account	Credit card payments only account
Amount	Prefills
Memo	As needed
Customer:Job	Your Company
Billable?	Leave blank
Class	Your Company

Click **Save & Close** or **Save & New** to enter another bill

Table 56 Enter Bills to Pay Credit Card Balance

ENTERING BILLS

USE TIME TO ENTER BILLS

> **NOTE**
> To enter weekly timesheets, refer to the chapter on Tracking Time and Tasks. Be sure to check your reports before you enter bills.

To enter a bill using timesheet data:

- Click **Vendor** or **Banking** on the Menu Bar
- Select Bill, Check, or Credit Card Charge
- Enter the Vendor Name

The Pay for Time Worked window appears.

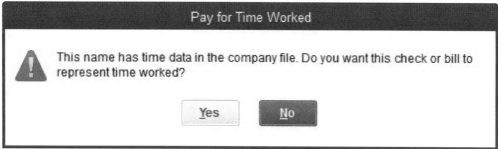

Screen Shot 231 Pay for Time Worked

- Click **Yes**

The Select Time Period window appears.

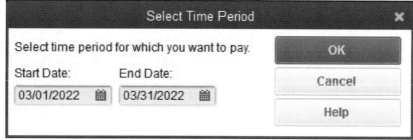

Screen Shot 232 Select Time Period

- Select the time period for which you want to enter the transaction

Commercial Property Management for Managers: QuickBooks Desktop

Entering Bills

Timesheet data will prefill.

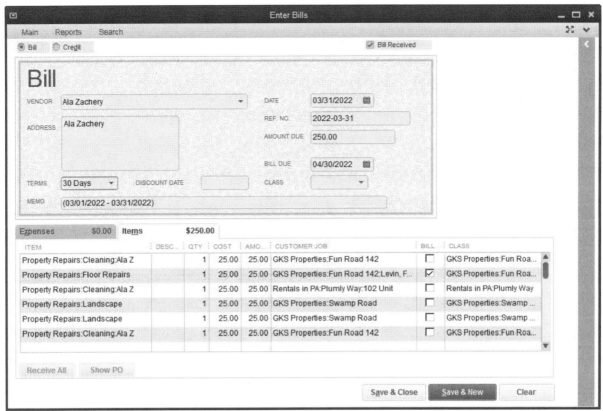

Screen Shot 233 Enter Transaction using Timesheet Data

- Check the date, time, amount, and names for accuracy
- Click **Save & Close** or **Save & New** to enter another transaction

Recurring Bills

Some bills may be recurring. For example, a utility company may charge you money on a monthly basis.

Memorize a check or bill for the utility company with a line item for each property, unit, or tenant. Make the charge billable if you will charge the exact amount to the tenant.

Refer to the chapter on Recurring Transactions.

Reports for Vendors

To view related reports:

- Click **MemRpts** on the Icon Bar
- Select by double-clicking the following under Vendors:
    - A/P Aging Summary
    - Expenses by Vendor Detail
    - Expenses by Vendor Summary
    - Transaction List by Vendor
    - Unpaid Bills by Property and Unit
    - Unpaid Bills Detail
    - Vendor Balance Detail
    - Vendor Balance Summary
    - Vendor Contact List
    - Vendor Phone List

CHAPTER 53 VENDOR DEPOSITS

When working with vendors, you may be asked to give an advance deposit as partial payment for such things as utility set up or a contractor's work to be performed. The deposit may either be for a particular property, or for Your Business as a whole (Overhead).

Objectives

Upon completion of this chapter, you will be able to:

- Record a Deposit
- Apply Expenses against Deposits
- Transfer Deposits
- View Reports

VENDOR DEPOSITS

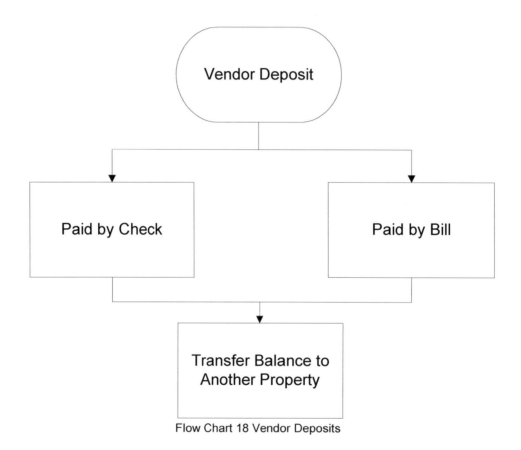

Flow Chart 18 Vendor Deposits

VENDOR DEPOSITS

Enter a bill or write a check for the deposit amount using the Items tab. Refer to the chapters on Entering Bills and Writing Checks.

FOR PROPERTIES

When giving a deposit for services or work to be performed by a contractor for a particular property, it is an expense that the manager will attribute to that particular property (Class). This deposit will be reflected on the Owner's Proceed report as an Expense account.

For example, if you make a deposit to the contractor to fix the roof on one of the owner's properties, then it is a property expense.

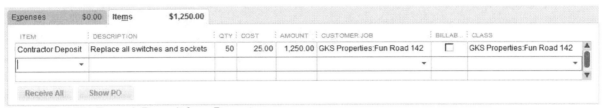
Screen Shot 234 Record, Deposit for a Property

Commercial Property Management for Managers: QuickBooks Desktop

VENDOR DEPOSITS

FOR YOUR COMPANY

When giving a deposit for services or work to be performed by a contractor for your office, it is an asset attributed to Your Company (Class). This deposit will be reflected on the Balance Sheet as an Asset account.

For example, if you make a deposit to the electric company for your office, then it is considered as Your Company expense.

Apply Expense to a Vendor Deposit

If there is **no balance due**, enter a check from the Petty Cash bank account after the work has been completed. The deposit and the cost of the electrical work, in this case, will be the same, bringing the balance of Items to zero. The check amount will be zero, as well.

By writing a check from the Petty Cash bank account, you are only reflecting that the work has been completed and paid in full.

Screen Shot 235 Apply Deposit to Property when No Balance is Due

Pay By Check

When there is a **balance to be paid**, write a check using the appropriate item name under the Items tab. Add a line item to deduct the deposit.

For example, an electrician does a job for your Company, and he applies a $150 deposit to the total cost of $350.

Screen Shot 236 Apply Deposit to Property when Balance is to be Paid

Enter a Bill

IMPORTANT
This section is only applicable if you have created a bill to pay for a vendor deposit.

When applying the deposit to expense, deduct the deposit from the bill by following the steps below:

- Enter Bill: Credit for the amount of the deposit you want to apply to the bill (Refer to the chapter on Entering Bills)
- Pay Bill: Select the bill you want to apply the deposit to and change the amount (Refer to the chapter on Paying Bills)
- Set Credit: Apply the credit towards the bill
- Address Balance:
    - If there is a balance, make a payment and select the method of said payment
    - If there is a zero balance, make a payment by selecting the Petty Cash account as the Payment Method

REPORTS FOR VENDOR DEPOSITS

To view related reports:

- Click **MemRpts** on the Icon Bar
- Select by double-clicking the following:
    - Balance Sheet under Company
    - Profit & Loss under Company
    - Bills Entered under Vendors
    - Unpaid Bills Detail under Vendors
    - Vendor Deposits under Vendors

VENDOR DEPOSITS

TRANSFER DEPOSIT TO ANOTHER PROPERTY

There may come a time when you must transfer a deposit from one property or project to another.

To do this, write a check from the Petty Cash bank account. The deposit and the total cost will be the same, bringing the balance of Items to zero. The check amount will be zero, as well.

This changes the property under Customer:Job and Class. You can also transfer a deposit from property to Your Company, or vice versa.

For example, your Company completes a project with the electrician at the Fun Road property. They did such an excellent job that you hire them for work at the Swamp Road property, as well. You will need to transfer the vendor deposit from the Fun Road property (negative amount) to the Swamp Road property (positive amount).

Screen Shot 237 Transfer Deposit

IMPORTANT
Before you transfer the deposit, be sure you have recorded the actual expense incurred (excluding the deposit amount) by entering a bill or check. To confirm you have entered it properly, check the Balance Sheet.

CHAPTER 54 PREPAID EXPENSES

At times, you may have to pay insurance, taxes, or other charges to vendors in advance. Keep track of these expenses, so you do not overpay or lose track of vendor balances.

> **IMPORTANT**
> This chapter applies only to Your Company expenses.
>
> All prepaid expenses made on behalf of the owner is considered to be an expense.

Objectives

Upon completion of this chapter, you will be able to:

- Enter Prepaid Expenses
- Record Incurred Expenses
- View Reports

FOR PROPERTIES

When prepaying for services or work to be performed by a contractor for a particular property, it is an expense that the manager will attribute to that particular property (Class). This payment in advance will be reflected on the Owner's Proceed report as an Expense account.

For example, if you make a deposit to the contractor to fix the roof on one of the owner's properties, then it is a property expense.

FOR YOUR COMPANY

When prepaying for services or work to be performed by a contractor for your office, it is an asset attributed to Your Company (Class). This deposit will be reflected on the Balance Sheet as an Asset account.

For example, if you make a deposit to the electric company for your office, then it is considered as Your Company expense.

ENTER PREPAID EXPENSES

For money owed to a Vendor (Accounts Payable), create a bill to document the unpaid balance or credit to the account.

To enter a bill, check, or credit card charge for prepaid expenses:

- Click **Bill** or **Check** on the Icon Bar

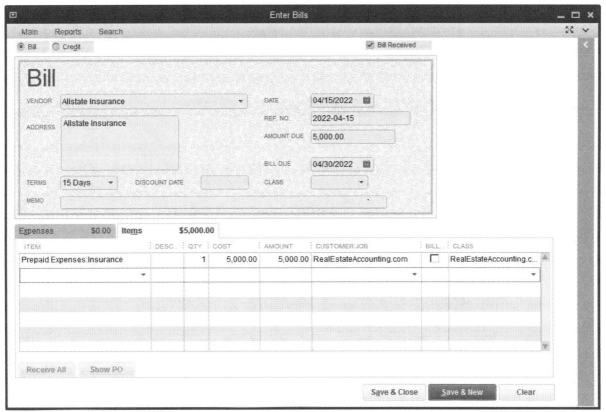

Screen Shot 238 Enter Bills or Check for Prepaid Expenses

- Enter all the details needed to enter an expense
- Enter Prepaid Expenses
    - For Your Business: under the Expenses tab
    - For Property: under the Items tab
- Click **Save & Close**

Review your Profit & Loss and Balance Sheet reports for accuracy.

PREPAID EXPENSES

RECORD INCURRED EXPENSES

Memorize a check to transfer the amount from the Balance Sheet to the Profit & Loss expense account. Memorize the check for the number of transactions to be entered automatically. Refer to the chapter on Recurring Transactions.

> **IMPORTANT**
> Do NOT save the check after you memorize it.

To transfer the amount from the prepaid expense account to the current expense account:

- Click **Check** on the Icon Bar

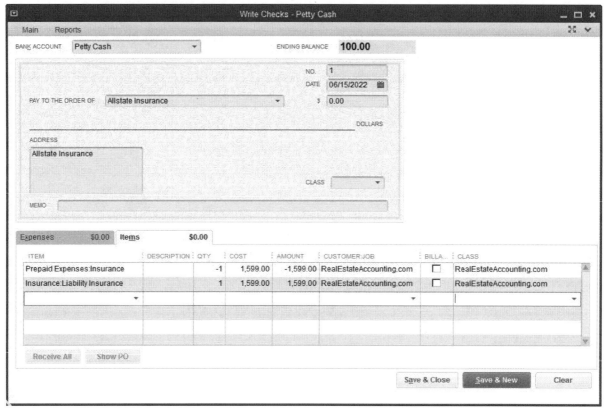

Screen Shot 239 Write Check to Transfer Amount

Commercial Property Management for Managers: QuickBooks Desktop   412

PREPAID EXPENSES

- Complete the fields as follows:

Field	Data	
Bank Account	Petty Cash	
Date	Date of transfer	
Pay to the Order of	Vendor Name	
$	ZERO	
Address	Prefills	
Class	Your Company	
Memo	As needed	
Expenses tab		
Split Lines	Account	Amount
Line 1	Prepaid Expenses:Insurance	Negative
Line 2	Insurance:Liability Insurance	Positive
Memo	As needed	
Customer:Job	Your Company	
Billable?	Leave blank	
Class	Your Company	
Right-click and memorize the check (refer to the chapter on Recurring Transactions)		
Click **Clear** – Do NOT save the check		

Table 57 Write Check to Transfer Amount

After you record the memorized transaction, check both the Profit & Loss report and Balance Sheet for the account balances.

Report: Profit & Loss

To view the Profit & Loss report:

- Click **MemRpts** on the Icon Bar
- Double-click Profit & Loss under Accountant (partial report)

Report 28 Profit & Loss

Report: Balance Sheet (After)

To view the Balance Sheet:

- Click **MemRpts** on the Icon Bar
- Double-click Balance Sheet under Accountant (partial report)

Report 29 Balance Sheet

CHAPTER 55 MARKUPS

Markups are defined as the difference between the actual cost of a service and the amount you charge the tenant. The markup is income earned by your company, for each property.

Objectives

Upon completion of this chapter, you will be able to:

- Enter Expenses and Markups
- Apply Flat Fee or Percentage Markups
- Create Invoices
- Track Unbilled Expenses
- View Reports

ENTER EXPENSES AND MARKUPS

There are two ways to charge a tenant for markups. You may choose always to charge a flat fee for certain services. Alternatively, you may charge a percentage of a particular expense.

Enter the transaction as a bill, check, or credit card charge.

Flat Fee on Expenses

You may have the policy to charge a certain amount and may bill for each expense as it is incurred. In this case, add the markup cost as a flat fee.

For example, you may receive a bill for $380, but charge the tenant $475 for that expense. The total amount of $475 appears as the electric expenses; $95 is the markup earned.

Customer:Job: Enter property name to track markup income for each property

Class: Do you want to show the markup income on Your Business or Property report? Enter class accordingly.

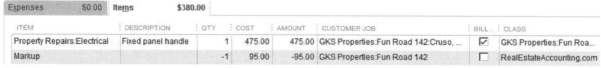

Screen Shot 240 Markup as a Flat Fee

Percentage of Expenses

You may charge markup by calculating a percentage. For example, you may mark up a repair by ten percent, as shown below.

For example, you may receive a bill for $380, but charge the tenant $475 for that expense. The total amount of $475 appears as the electric expenses; 20% is the markup earned.

Customer:Job: Enter property name to track markup income for each property

Class: Do you want to show the markup income on Your Business or Property report? Enter class accordingly.

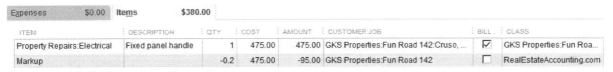

Screen Shot 241 Markup as a Percentage

TIP
Mark the Billable? Column on the first line if you are going to create an invoice. Either way, be sure you uncheck it on the Markup line.

MARKUPS

REPORT: PROFIT & LOSS

To view the Profit & Loss report:

- Click **Reports** on the Menu Bar
- Select Profit & Loss under Company & Financial

In this example, you will see that there is an expense for $475 for the property. The markup of $95 shows as income for your property.

www.RealEstateAccounting.com
Profit & Loss by Class
April 15, 2022

	RealEstateAccounting.com	Fun Road 142 (GKS Properties)	Total...	TOTAL
▼ Ordinary Income/Expense				
▼ Income				
Markup	95.00	0.00	0.00	95.00
Total Income	95.00	0.00	0.00	95.00
▼ Cost of Goods Sold				
Property Repairs	0.00	475.00	475.00	475.00
Total COGS	0.00	475.00	475.00	475.00
Gross Profit	95.00	-475.00	-475.00	-380.00
Net Ordinary Income	95.00	-475.00	-475.00	-380.00
Net Income	95.00	-475.00	-475.00	-380.00

Report 30 Profit & Loss by Class

TRACK UNBILLED EXPENSES

Knowing that you have decided to mark up expense, the next step is to create an invoice to track how much money a tenant owes you.

To track unbilled expenses:

- Click **Tenants** (Customer Center)
- Open the Income Tracker by clicking the link on the right
- Note the time and expenditures that were marked billable and select the appropriate tenant name from the drop down menu, Customer:Job

Screen Shot 242 Track Unbilled Expenses with Income Tracker

- Select the item by checkmark in the first column on the left
- Then select Create Invoice from the drop down menu under the Action column on the far right

Once you select Create Invoice, all the data will be copied to an invoice, and you will be able to view that Invoice. Verify the data and save it.

To receive the payment, once the tenant makes it, refer to the chapter on Tenant Charges and Payments.

UTILITY BILLING

Utility bills, such as an electric bill or water bill, may have different amounts due each month depending on usage.

Memorize a check or bill to the utility company with a line item for each tenant. Make the charge Billable if you will charge the exact amount to the tenant.

If you do not charge the same amount to the tenant, create one line item for the total sum due. Memorize an invoice for each tenant to bill utility expenses to update charges each month easily.

CHAPTER 56 VENDOR CREDITS AND REFUNDS

If you overpay a vendor for a bill, you may receive a check for the difference or a credit to apply to an unpaid bill. For example, insurance companies may refund excess payments when insurance premiums are re-evaluated.

> **IMPORTANT**
> Use the Expenses tab for Your Company expenses and the Items tab for specific property expenses.

Objectives

Upon completion of this chapter, you will be able to:

- Enter a Bill or Credit Card Credit
- Enter a Refund
- View Reports

VENDOR CREDITS AND REFUNDS

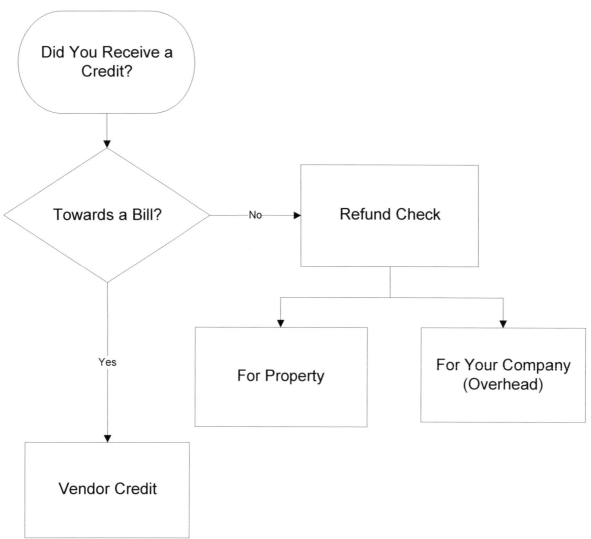

Flow Chart 19 Vendor Credits and Refunds

VENDOR CREDIT

A vendor credit can be applied to an outstanding or future bill. To apply the credit to a bill that has been entered, refer to the chapter on Paying Bills.

For example, if Home Depot credits you $45.24 for returned materials, the credit is applied to future purchases.

To enter a vendor credit:

- Click **Bill** on the Icon Bar OR click **Credit Card Charges** under Banking on the Menu Bar
- Select Credit on the top left
- Enter the credit number as the Ref. No.
- Enter the credit using the same account as the original bill
- Click **Save & Close** or **Save & New** to enter another credit

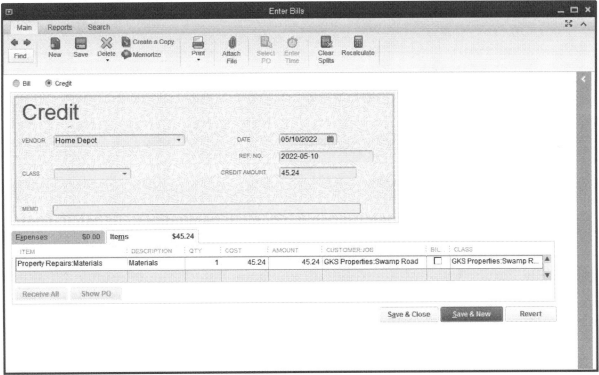

Screen Shot 243 Enter Bill to Record Vendor Credit

IMPORTANT
At the time of paying a vendor bill, deduct the credit amount from the bill. Refer to chapter Paying Bills to apply the credit against the bill.

VENDOR REFUND

If your Company was overbilled or dissatisfied with a service related to a specific property, a vendor might offer a refund for that expense. Enter that vendor's refund, so the amount reflects on the Profit & Loss Summary report and is deposited in the bank account.

Let's say; you were dissatisfied with the work East West Imported Carpets did at the Fun Road property. East West Imported Carpets agrees to refund the total amount of the job.

To enter a vendor refund for property or Your Company expense:

- Click **Check** on the Icon Bar

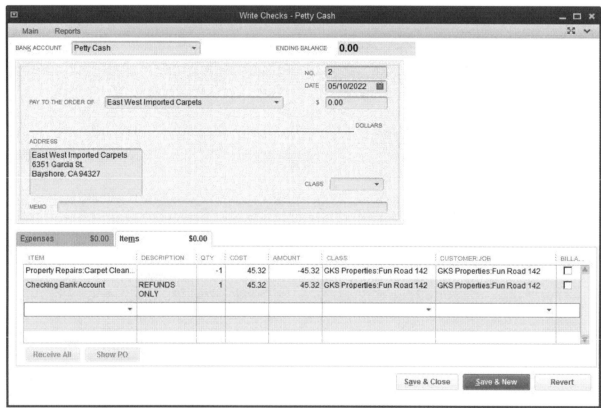

Screen Shot 244 Write Check to Record Vendor Refund Property Expense

VENDOR CREDITS AND REFUNDS

- Complete the fields as follows:

Field	Data			
Bank Account	Petty Cash			
Pay to the order of	Vendor Name			
No.	As needed			
Date	Date of refund			
$	ZERO			
Address	Prefills			
Class	Only available in Enterprise version (use if the class is the same for all line items)			
Memo	Prefills			
Items tab				
Split Lines	Item	Qty	Cost	Amount
Line 1	Type or select from drop down menu	-1	Amount	Prefills
Line 2	Bank Account	1		
Description	As needed			
Customer:Job	Property, Unit, Tenant, CAM or Non-CAM			
Billable?	Leave blank			
Class	Property Name or Your Company			
Click **Save & Close** or **Save & New** to enter another check				

Table 58 Write Check to Record Vendor Refund Property Expense

REPORT: EXPENSES BY VENDOR DETAIL

To view the vendor credits, deposit, and refunds:

- Click **MemRpts** on the Icon Bar
- Double-click Expenses by Vendor Detail under Vendors

www.RealEstateAccounting.com
Expenses by Vendor Detail
May 2022

Type	Date	Num	Memo	Item	Account	Class	Amount
East West Imported Carpets							
Check	05/10/2022	2		Property Repairs:Carpet ...	Property Repairs	GKS Properties:Fun Road 142	-45.32
Total East West Imported Carpets							-45.32
Home Depot							
Bill	05/04/2022	2022...	Materials	Property Repairs:Materials	Property Repairs	GKS Properties:Swamp Road	401.00
Bill	05/04/2022	2022...		Property Repairs:Dry Wall	Property Repairs	GKS Properties:Fun Road 142	99.00
Credit	05/10/2022	2022...	Materials	Property Repairs:Materials	Property Repairs	GKS Properties:Swamp Road	-45.24
Total Home Depot							454.76
Master Builders							
Bill	05/01/2022	8547	Damaged w...	Property Repairs:Dry Wall	Property Repairs	GKS Properties:Fun Road 142	500.00
Total Master Builders							500.00
Staples							
Credit Card Char...	05/15/2022	2022...			Office Supplies	RealEstateAccounting.com	55.20
Total Staples							55.20
TOTAL							964.64

Report 31 Expenses by Vendor Detail

CHAPTER 57 PAYING BILLS

After entering bills, pay your expenses online or with cash, checks, debit cards, or credit cards. You may pay multiple bills at one time using one of these payment methods. Track all bill payments and associate with the property, as needed, to maintain current vendor balances.

Objectives

Upon completion of this chapter, you will be able to:

- Understand Payment Methods
- Pay Bills
- Print Checks
- View Reports

PAYING BILLS

PAYMENT METHODS

Whichever method you use to receive money and make payments to others determines how you should enter the data into QuickBooks. Use the table below as a guide:

You make a payment by	Enter in QuickBooks as
Check	Write a check or Pay a bill (if you entered a bill)
Online payment	
Debit card	
Handwritten check	
Cash	
Credit on account	Enter a bill (click on credit – top right corner) and apply to existing bill
Check received for refund	Make a deposit (only for Your Company) Enter a sales receipt (for property)
Credit card credit	Enter credit card charge (click on credit – top right corner)

Table 59 Payment Methods in QuickBooks

If you handwrite the check, you will have to enter that payment into QuickBooks at a later time. How you enter the payment depends on whether you have already entered the bill or not.

PAY BILLS NOT ENTERED IN QUICKBOOKS

If you have not entered the bill in QuickBooks, you have the option to write a check to make a payment. If you charge an expense on a debit card, you will need to enter that expense. Refer to the chapter on Writing Checks.

PAY BILLS ENTERED IN QUICKBOOKS

You may <u>handwrite the entire check</u> for the bill already entered in QuickBooks, especially if you are not on your computer. In that case, pay bills easily using the Pay Bills QuickBooks feature only if you have entered the bills.

Despite doing the work twice (once on the handwritten check and a second time entering the information in QuickBooks), keeping track of bills and payments this way is an invaluable tracking tool.

Remember to view and apply vendor discounts and available credits as you go through the bill paying process. If you are paying bills by check, manually assign check numbers, so that your check numbers remain sequential in QuickBooks.

To check if all your expenses have been entered, reconcile your bank account and credit card. Refer to the chapter on Reconciling Accounts.

PAYING BILLS

To pay bills that have been entered in QuickBooks:

- Click **Pay Bills** on the Icon Bar

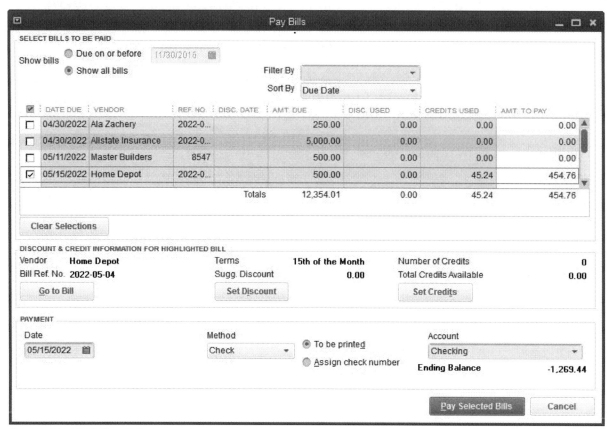

Screen Shot 245 Pay Bills

PAYING BILLS

- Complete the fields as follows:

Field	Data
Show Bills	Select Due on or before or Show all bills
Filter By	Select from the drop down menu
Sort By	
Click left column to select the bill(s) to be paid	
Enter the amount to pay	
Discount & Credit Information for Highlighted Bill	
Go to Bill	Click **Go to Bill** to view
Set Discount	Click to deduct discount
Set Credits	
If there is a credit balance, select credits to be applied and click **Done**	
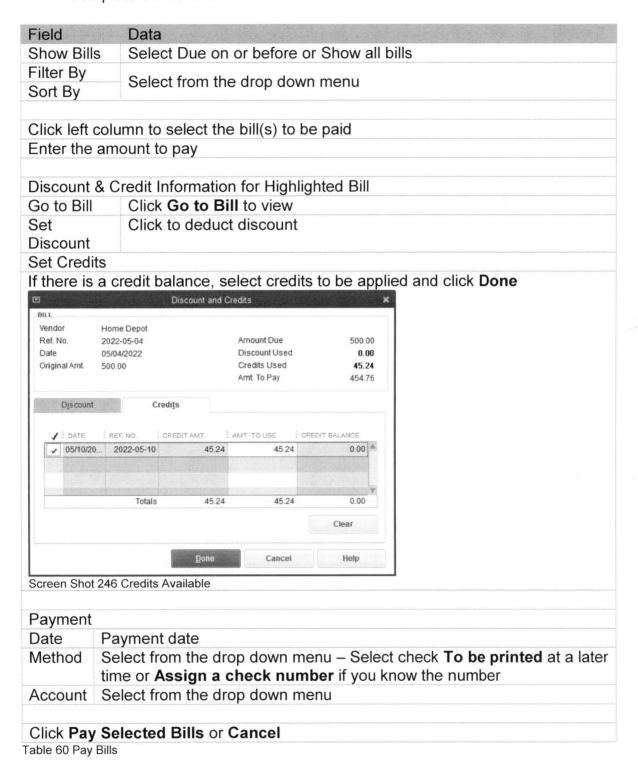	
Screen Shot 246 Credits Available	
Payment	
Date	Payment date
Method	Select from the drop down menu – Select check **To be printed** at a later time or **Assign a check number** if you know the number
Account	Select from the drop down menu
Click **Pay Selected Bills** or **Cancel**	

Table 60 Pay Bills

Commercial Property Management for Managers: QuickBooks Desktop

The Payment Summary screen appears.

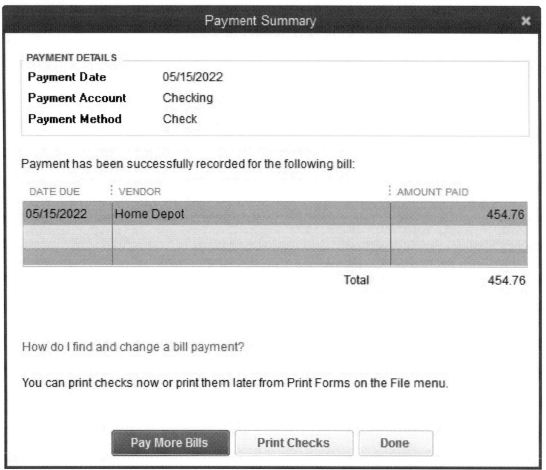

Screen Shot 247 Payment Summary

- Click **Pay More Bills**, **Print Checks**, or **Done**

PAYING BILLS

PRINT CHECKS

If you select Print Checks, the following screen appears:

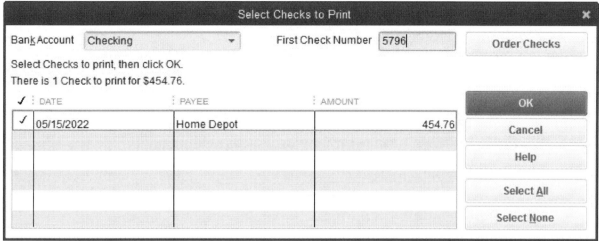

Screen Shot 248 Select Checks to Print

- Complete the fields as follows:

Field	Data
Bank Account	Account from which the checks were issued
First Check Number	First check number to be printed
Click left column of each check you wish to print	
Click **OK**	

Table 61 Select Checks to Print

- Follow the steps on the screen to select the printer
- Click **Print**

TIP
If ever you miss printing a check, go to Print Forms on the File menu and select one or multiple items to print.

PAYING BILLS

PAYMENT METHODS

Pay by Check by Selecting To be printed

In the Payment section of the Pay Bills screen, select check as the payment method, To be printed, and the bank account you are paying from. After selecting Pay Selected Bills, the Payment Summary screen appears.

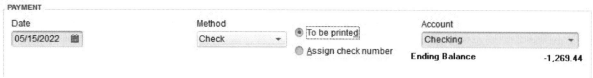

Screen Shot 249 Pay Bill by Check To be printed

- Click **Pay More Bills**, **Print Checks**, or **Done**

Pay by Check Select Assign check number

In the Payment section of the Pay Bills screen, select check as the payment method, assign the check number, and the bank account you are paying from. After selecting Pay Selected Bills, the Assign Check Numbers screen appears.

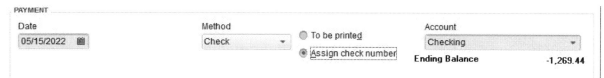

Screen Shot 250 Pay Bill by Check and Assign check number

- Select the appropriate option to assign check numbers
- If you select Let QuickBooks assign check numbers. QuickBooks will automatically select the next sequential check number and enter it.
- If you choose Let me assign the check numbers, below, fill in the check number(s), debit, or online
- Click **Pay More Bills** or **Done**

Commercial Property Management for Managers: QuickBooks Desktop

PAYING BILLS

Pay by Credit Card

In the Payment section of the Pay Bills screen, select credit card as the payment method and the credit card account you are paying from.

After selecting Pay Selected Bills, the Payment Summary screen appears.

Screen Shot 251 Pay Bill by Credit Card

- Click **Pay More Bills**, **Print Payment Stub**, or **Done**

REPORTS FOR PAID BILLS

To view related reports:

- Click **MemRpts** on the Icon Bar
- Select by double-clicking the following:
    - Credit Card Accounts under Company
    - Balance Sheet under Company
    - Profit & Loss under Company
    - Bills Entered under Vendors
    - Unpaid Bills Detail under Vendors
    - Expenses by Vendor Detail under Vendors
    - Expenses by Vendor Summary under Vendors

REPORT: BANK ACCOUNTS

To view the Bank Accounts report:

- Click **MemRpts** on the Icon Bar
- Double-click Bank Accounts under Company

www.RealEstateAccounting.com
Bank Accounts
As of May 30, 2022

Type	Date	Num	Source Name	Memo	Amount	Balance
Checking						**-480.00**
Check	05/10/2022	2	East West Imported C...	REFUNDS ONLY	45.32	-434.68
Bill Pmt -Che...	05/15/2022	3	Home Depot		-454.76	-889.44
Bill Pmt -Che...	05/15/2022	123	Ala Zachery	(03/01/2022 - 03...	-250.00	-1,139.44
Total Checking					-659.44	-1,139.44
Petty Cash						**100.00**
Check	05/10/2022	2	East West Imported C...		0.00	100.00
Total Petty Cash					0.00	100.00
TOTAL					**-659.44**	**-1,039.44**

Report 32 Bank Accounts

CHAPTER 58 TAX PAYMENTS

It is your responsibility to collect taxes and pay them for each rental property. In many cases, the tax may be collected, but not passed on to the tenant as a separate item. If taxes are included in the rent, it is still your important that you track, verify, and pay taxes, as appropriate.

We have covered the most common tax situations for most of the United States. If you are located in Hawaii or another country, please contact the author directly for instructions.

Objectives

Upon completion of this chapter, you will be able to:

- View Tax Reports
- Adjust Sales Tax (discounts)
- Record Tax Payments
- View Reports

Before you pay sales tax, review the Sales Tax Liability report and the Sales Tax Revenue Summary report to check that tax has been collected accurately.

> **IMPORTANT**
>
> Pay attention to dates. Sales amounts are dependent on when you reflect income received as income.
>
> If you use the Tax and Customer Tax Code fields and select Non when entering invoices or sales receipts, the amount will be reflected in the Always ZERO – Tax line.
>
> Check with the appropriate tax authority to determine the amounts that should be included in Total Sales and Non-Taxable Sales.
>
> You can always double-check from the report by double-clicking on the amount to view details.

REPORT: SALES TAX LIABILITY

To view the Sales Tax Liability report:

- Click **Vendors** on the Menu Bar
- Select Sales Tax Liability under Sales Tax

www.RealEstateAccounting.com
Sales Tax Liability
April 2022

	Total Sales	Non-Taxable Sales	Taxable Sales	Tax Rate	Tax Collected	Sales Tax Payable As of Apr 30, 22
PA Dept of Revenue						
Phila	5,100.00	100.00	5,000.00	6.0%	300.00	300.00
Total PA Dept of Reve...	5,100.00	100.00	5,000.00		300.00	300.00
TOTAL	5,100.00	100.00	5,000.00		300.00	300.00

Report 33 Sales Tax Liability

ADJUST SALES TAX

To record a sales tax adjustment or discount before making a payment:

- Click **Vendors** on the Menu Bar
- Select Sales Tax
- Click **Adjust Sales Tax Due…**

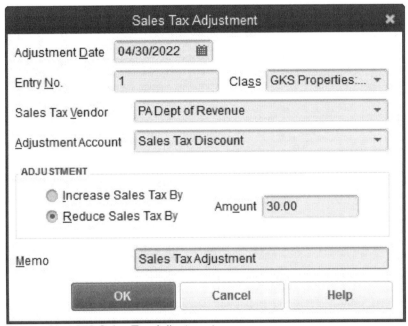

Screen Shot 252 Sales Tax Adjustment

- Complete the fields as follows:

Field	Data
Adjustment Date	Show Sales tax due through
Entry No.	Year-month
Class	Your Company, Property or Unit
Sales Tax Vendor	Name of the authority
Adjustment Account	Sales Tax Discount
Increase Sales Tax By	
Reduce Sales Tax By	As needed
Amount	
Memo	As needed
Click **OK** and select the adjustment and the total amount due	

Table 62 Sales Tax Adjustment

RECORD TAX PAYMENTS

When you make a tax payment online, record it in QuickBooks. If you print and mail a check, refer to the chapter on Paying Bills. For either, use the Pay Sales Tax feature to record the tax payment in QuickBooks.

Many times, tax authorities may give you a discount for timely payments. For example, your payment may be reduced by 1%. If this occurs, make the adjustment from the Pay Sales Tax window.

To record a sales tax payment:

- Click **Vendors** on the Menu Bar
- Select Sales Tax
- Click **Pay Sales Tax…**

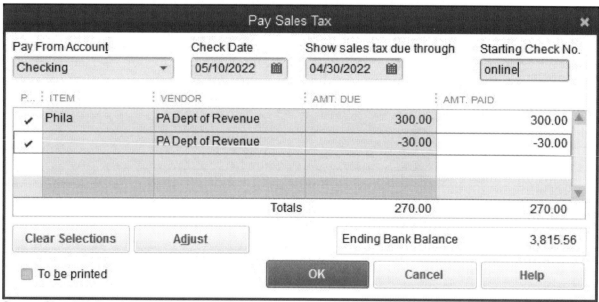

Screen Shot 253 Pay Sales Tax

TAX PAYMENTS

- Complete the fields as follows:

Field	Data
Pay From Account	Bank Account
Check Date	Date of payment
Show sales tax due through	The last date of the month for which you are paying sales tax
Starting Check No.	Check number
Pay	Mark to make a payment
Item	Tax Item
Vendor	Vendor Name
Amt. Due	Total Amount Due in QuickBooks
Amt. Paid	Amount you will pay
Adjust	Check the next page to apply discount
To be printed	As needed
Click **OK**	

Table 63 Pay Sales Tax

Report: Sales Tax Revenue Summary

To view the Sales Tax Revenue Summary report:

- Click **Vendors** on the Menu Bar
- Select Sales Tax Revenue Summary under Sales Tax

www.RealEstateAccounting.com
Sales Tax Revenue Summary
April 2022

	Taxable Sales	Non-Taxable Sales	TOTAL
PA Dept of Revenue			
Phila	5,000.00	100.00	5,100.00
Total PA Dept of Reve...	5,000.00	100.00	5,100.00
TOTAL	5,000.00	100.00	5,100.00

Report 34 Sales Tax Revenue Summary

CHAPTER 59 VOIDING A CHECK

In the case of a mistake or a misplaced check, you may need to void it. A voided check may affect your reports, so it is important that you handle it correctly. Two methods are depending on whether you have already reconciled your bank account, shared the reports with your CPA, or filed tax returns. Before deciding on which method is best for you, you should also determine for which month you are voiding the check.

Objectives

Upon completion of this chapter, you will be able to:

- Decide Your Method
- Void a Check
- Reconcile the Account

Voiding a Check

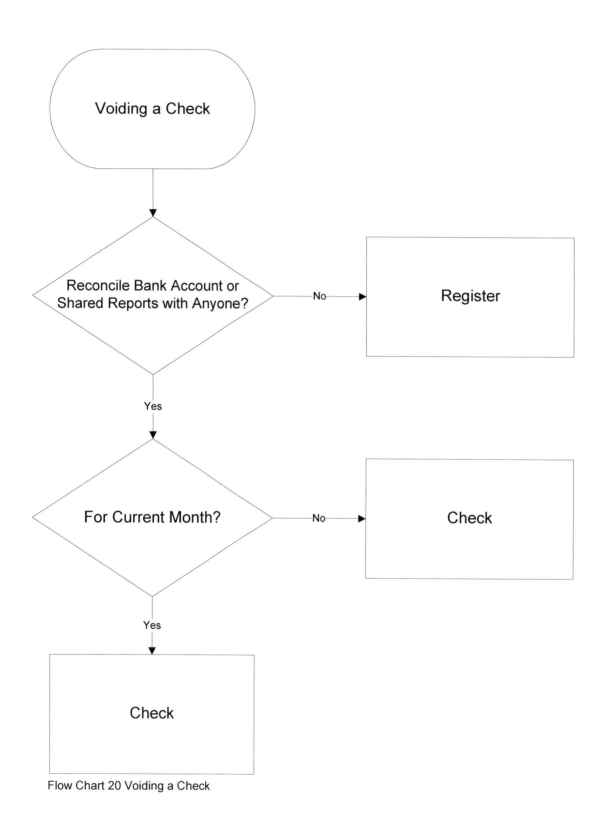

Flow Chart 20 Voiding a Check

VOIDING A CHECK

REGISTER

Void a check using the bank register, if it is for the current month and you have not shared your reports.

To void a check using the bank register:

- Click **Accnt** on the Icon Bar
- Double-click on the bank account to open the register
- Right-click on the check to be voided
- Click **Void Check**

The amount will change to zero and QuickBooks automatically adds VOID to the memo field.

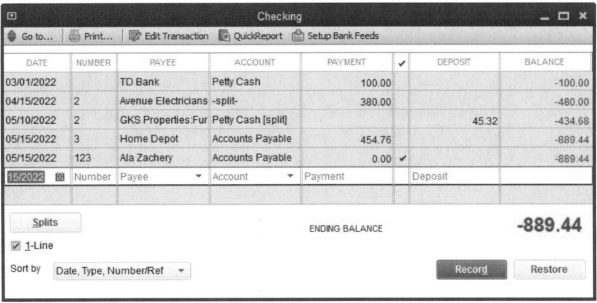

Screen Shot 254 View Voided Check

Commercial Property Management for Managers: QuickBooks Desktop

CHECK

If the check to be voided is not for the current month, you have already reconciled your account, or you have shared reports, create a check to deduct the expense.

Create a check from the Petty Cash bank account, using the Vendor name, Item, and Account of the original check. For accurate reporting, use the same account, Customer:Job, and Class as you did when you first entered the expense.

Enter a negative amount in the expense account (reducing the expense account) and a positive amount in the bank account (creating a deposit in your bank account). The balance is brought to zero.

Screen Shot 255 Void check by using Petty Cash Bank Account

RECONCILE BANK ACCOUNT

If you void a check using the Register method, the check will reflect on the Deposits and Other Credits column on the Reconciling screen.

If you have used the Check method to void a check, both the check you originally wrote and the Petty Cash deposit will reflect on Checks and Payments and Deposits and Other Credits column on the Reconciling screen.

Add a check mark next to the check and deposit. Refer to the chapter on Reconciling Accounts.

CHAPTER 60 VENDOR BOUNCED CHECK

If your payment to a vendor bounces due to insufficient funds, the bank will reverse the charge it had already recorded. Since your bank deducts the amount of that check, the bank will then add that amount back to your account. Be aware that your bank will likely charge you a fee.

Objectives

Upon completion of this chapter, you will be able to:

- Record a Bounced Check
- Record a Bank Service Fee
- View Reports

BOUNCED CHECK

When a check for either a property or your company expense bounces, create two checks, one for the bank charge and another to reflect the property expense.

To enter a bounced check for a property or your company expense:

- Click **Check** on the Icon Bar

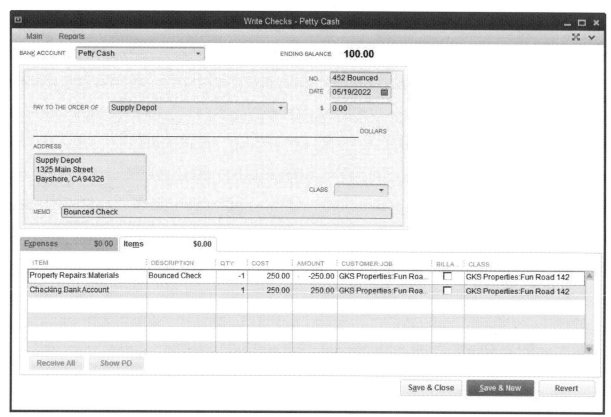

Screen Shot 256 Write Check to Enter Bounced Check for Property

Vendor Bounced Check

- Complete the fields as follows:

Field	Data			
Bank Account	Petty Cash			
No.	Check number that bounced			
Date	Date of bounced check			
Pay to the Order of	Vendor			
$	ZERO			
Address	Prefills			
Memo	As needed			
Items tab				
Split Lines	Item	Qty	Cost	Amount
Line 1	Same Item used on original	-1	Amount	Prefills
Line 2	Checking bank account	1		
Description	As needed			
Customer:Job	Property, Unit, Tenant, CAM or Non-CAM or Your Company			
Billable?	Leave blank			
Class	Property, Unit, Tenant, CAM or Non-CAM or Your Company			
Click **Save & Close** or **Save & New** to write another check				

Table 64 Write Check to Enter Bounced Check for Property

This step reduces the balance of the Item for that specific property and adds a deposit to the bank account in one step.

IMPORTANT
You may choose to issue another vendor check or enter another bill for payment at a later date.

VENDOR BOUNCED CHECK

BANK CHARGE

If your bank charges you a fee for a bounced check, determine the correct Customer:Job and Class for the bank charge. Enter it by entering a check using the Bank Fees as the account name, as shown below. Using a specific property or your company may be appropriate. Add a memo, as needed.

ACCOUNT	AMOUNT	MEMO	CUSTOMER:JOB	BILLABLE?	CLASS
Bank Service Charges	25.00		RealEstateAccounting.com	☐	RealEstateAccounting.com

Expenses $25.00 Items $0.00

Screen Shot 257 Write Check to Enter Bank Charge

REPORT: BANK ACCOUNTS

To view the Bank Accounts report:

- Click **MemRpts** on the Icon Bar
- Double-click Bank Accounts under Company

www.RealEstateAccounting.com
Bank Accounts
As of May 19, 2022

Type	Date	Num	Source Name	Memo	Amount	Balance
Checking						**4,110.56**
Check	05/16/2022	125	Supply Depot		-250.00	3,860.56
Check	05/19/2022	45...	Supply Depot	Bounced Check	250.00	4,110.56
Check	05/19/2022	124	TD Bank		-25.00	4,085.56
Total Checking					-25.00	4,085.56
Petty Cash						**100.00**
Check	05/19/2022	45...	Supply Depot	Bounced Check	0.00	100.00
Total Petty Cash					0.00	100.00
TOTAL					-25.00	4,185.56

Report 35 Bank Accounts

Commercial Property Management for Managers: QuickBooks Desktop

SECTION 9

MANAGE EQUITY AND LOANS

As a business owner, you will most likely find your Company in the position of borrowing or invest money at some point. The source of these funds may be an equity holder or a lending institution. Account for all loans to make sure your Company does not miss any payments.

Easy Way Out

If you are looking for an easy way out, then create the following for each loan:

- Vendor name
- Account name

To enter:

- Money received or withdrawn: Make a deposit
- Money paid back: Write a check

Caution

OK, so you are reading this. My question to you is: Do you want to track money approved, withdrawn and paid back. Did you say YES, then you are truly looking to increase your wealth. Wait did you say NO, then take the Easy Way Out.

My way will show you and track money approved, withdrawn and paid back by property and financiers.

However, again; it is your call.

Yes, I want to Track Details

Okay, let us do it. It is very easy after you learn it. The steps are very similar whether it is a hard money or a soft money loan.

Reports

Customized reports can be found under the Report Center:

- Click **Reports**
- Select Report Center
- Select Memorized on the tab and double click on the report you want to veiw.

Chapter 61 Investment, Draw, Personal Loans, & Reimbursements

Equity holders are individuals or entities that have a personal interest in your Company's success. They may make purchases for your Company or lend additional funds. At some point, an equity holder may request that your Company make a purchase on his or her behalf or give money for personal reasons. The money that an equity holder contributes to the business is considered either an investment or a loan. The money that an equity holder withdraws from the business is either a draw, loan repayment or profit share.

Record loans and reimbursements to and from equity holders, and track cash flow in and out of business. By now you should be a pro in entering a bill, check, credit card charge and deposits.

Objectives

Upon completion of this chapter, you will be able to:

- Record Investments and Draws
- Record Loans To and From
- Reimburse Owner's Expense

INVESTMENT OR LOAN FROM

When investment or loan is received from an equity holder or investors into your Company, enter a sales receipt for the amount received (borrowed) and make a deposit.

When you want to track all money received by property, below the steps below.

INVESTMENT OR LOAN FROM CHECKLIST

	Task	Refer to Chapter
☐	Create Sales Receipts of Investment or Loan	Invoices
☐	Write a Check to Reimburse Loan Amount	Writing Checks
☐	View Reports	Understanding Reporting

Checklist 15 Investment or Loan From

For example, John Greenlane, a partner, lends your Company $10,000 to buy a new computer. You deposit the money into the Company checking account. At a later time, you will reimburse John Greenlane for the money he contributed for the computer.

PERSONAL MONEY DEPOSITED

When you want to track money you are depositing for a specific property or to run your business:

My Way: Create a Sales Receipt and Make Deposit refer to chapter Payments and Deposits

Easy Way Out: Make Deposit

Reimbursement, Draw, or Personal Loan

When reimbursing an investor or when an equity holder borrows money from the Company for personal reasons, record a draw by writing a check using the draw or loan account under the Items tab.

Use your Company or a particular property as the Customer:Job and Class.

For example, John Greenlane borrows $2,500 from the business. You would write a check to John Greenlane for the borrowed amount, and when he repays the business, deposit the funds.

Reimbursing Expenses

There are two ways to handle reimbursing expenses. You may choose to write a check at the time the expense was incurred or record the transaction to be paid back at a later date (considered a loan).

Reimburse When an Expense Occurs

If you wish to repay the expense when it occurs, write a check directly to the equity holder reimbursing for the purchase using the appropriate account name, Customer:Job and Class. Refer to the Draw section above. Be aware that when you do this, you will not be able to track expenses by vendor name when running reports.

I call this the EASY WAY OUT and do not recommend it.

Reimburse When an Expense Occurs (Vendor)

Tracking the vendor name is crucial to track the expenses incurred for that specific name. It is a two step process:

- Create a check using the Petty Cash bank account to record the expense occurred using the vendor name. Just as you would enter any other expense.
- Moreover, to reimburse the funds, create a check from the Checking bank account, payable to the equity holder or a lending company using the expense account as Petty Cash bank account.
- Review your petty cash bank account

| 11/27/2022 | | Staples | Office Supplies | 20.00 | | -20.00 |
| 11/27/2022 | 818 | John Greenlane | Checking | | 20.00 | 0.00 |

Screen Shot 258 Petty Cash Bank Account

Enter Expenses and as Investment or Loan

If you are going to reimburse the equity holder, at a later time for the purchases, record the expense and credit the equity or loan account. This method allows you to keep track of where and when the reimbursed money was spent, in case you need to contact the vendor.

Write a check using the Petty Cash bank account and vendor name, with the total amount being zero. Enter a positive amount on the first line for the expense. On the second line, enter the equity or loan account in a negative amount. Select your Company for an overhead cost or a particular property, if applicable.

Screen Shot 259 Reimburse Expenses as a Loan

CHAPTER 62 LINE OF CREDIT

A line of credit is an account from which amounts can be borrowed at your Company's discretion. You only pay interest on amounts withdrawn and then pay the principal and interest amount to the lender at a specified time. Just as with any loan, withdraw as needed and make a deposit into your bank account. Then make payments, applying for money against loan and interest.

Objectives

Upon completion of this chapter, you will be able to:

- Make a Withdraw
- Make Payments
- View Reports

Money Received

Money withdrawn from the line of credit account is usually deposited in your Company's bank account or paid out directly to a vendor.

In QuickBooks, the line of credit works the same way as the detailed in this section. All you have to remember is to use the right names.

For all money received, enter Sales Receipt and Make Deposit.

Enter Payments

Enter and make a payment towards the borrowed account and the amount by writing a check and using the Items tab. Remember to use Customer:Job as the LOC name and not the property name.

This will let you view reports for the LOC approved, withdrawn and paid back.

SECTION 10

MANAGE BANK ACCOUNTS

Regular banking tasks, like writing checks, cross-checking your bank and credit card accounts with online statements, moving money from one account to another, and reconciling accounts, are valuable to your business if done properly. A simple mistake can quickly wreak havoc on your books. Learn how to perform these simple procedures the right way and do so regularly to easily manage your bank accounts and business.

MANAGE BANK ACCOUNTS

BANKING

Banking Menu

To enter transactions:

- Click **Banking** on the Menu Bar
- Select one to enter

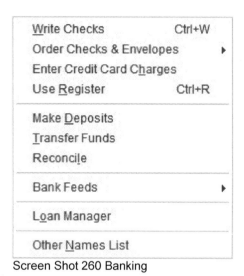
Screen Shot 260 Banking

Banking Reports

To view reports:

- Click **Reports** on the Menu Bar
- Select Report Center
- Click on **Banking** under Standard tab
- Select one of the reports

Screen Shot 261 Report List

Additional reports can be found in the file provided by me, and a list can be found in chapter Customized Reports For You.

CHAPTER 63 TRANSFERRING FUNDS

If you need to pay a bill or you are saving for the next big project, you can transfer funds between bank accounts online or by manually depositing funds at the bank. You can also transfer funds between properties.

Objectives

Upon completion of this chapter, you will be able to:

- Transfer Funds Between Properties
- Record Bank Transfers

Transfer Funds Between Properties

You may reallocate funds in your bank account for specific properties. To move funds from one property to another using the same account, write a check from the Petty Cash bank account for a zero amount.

The account from where the money is transferred has a positive amount and the account where the money is transferred to has a negative amount. The check must equal zero.

Transfer	Split Lines	Account	Customer:Job/Class
Funds Remain in the Same Account	Line 1	Same Account Name	Funds From Property
	Line 2		Funds To Property

Table 65 Transfer Funds Between Properties

To transfer funds between accounts and properties, write a check from the Petty Cash bank account for a zero amount.

Transfer	Split Lines	Account	Customer:Job/Class
Funds from One Account to Another	Line 1	Funds From Account	Funds From Property
	Line 2	Funds To Account	Funds To Property

Table 66 Transfer Funds Between Accounts and Properties

Check the Balance Sheet by Class report to view the transferred amounts.

For example, your Company transfers $5,000 initially allocated to the Fun Road property from the checking account to the savings account for the Swamp Road property.

Screen Shot 262 Transfer Funds Between Properties

ONLINE TRANSFER

When making an online transfer from one bank account to another, write a check to record the transaction.

For example, your Company makes an online transfer of $5,000 from the checking account to the savings account.

Screen Shot 263 Online Transfer

Select the account where the money is transferred from as the bank account. Use the account where the money is moved to as the account on the Expenses tab. Enter your Company as the Customer:Job and Class.

This transaction will decrease the balance in one account and increase the balance in the other. Refer to the chapter on Writing Checks.

Manual (Paper) Transfer

To record a manual (paper) transfer, write and print a check and make a deposit into the appropriate bank account.

> **IMPORTANT**
> In QuickBooks, writing a check is the only required transaction to record a manual transfer. In real life, you would go to the bank and deposit the check into the appropriate account.

If the bank accounts are in the same QuickBooks file, follow the same steps as for an online transfer (previous page).

If the bank accounts are in different QuickBooks files, write a check using the appropriate account name. Refer to the chapter on Writing Checks.

CHAPTER 64 ONLINE SERVICES

As technology advances, managing your bank accounts and credit cards is getting easier. When charges are incurred, you can check your records against bank and credit card online statements right away and potentially discover fraudulent use early on. Checking online records is also a valuable tool for reconciling your accounts.

Objectives

Upon completion of this chapter, you will be able to:

- Consider Pros and Cons
- Set up Bank and Credit Card Accounts
- Download Cleared Transactions and Charges

Consider Pros and Cons

QuickBooks's Online Services connects your financial institutions' data to your QuickBooks file. There are pros and cons to consider before deciding to use this feature.

If you do use Online Services:

- QuickBooks automatically matches the downloaded transactions to the transactions entered in QuickBooks
- QuickBooks automatically displays which transactions have cleared at your financial institutions

However, there are a few challenges:

- QuickBooks records transactions from the downloaded entries, but it does not automatically use Items and Classes
- You must manually enter the Items for property-related transactions and the Class for all transactions

Online Services

Set up Bank and Credit Card Accounts

Compare the bank's cleared amounts and credit card charges against QuickBooks transactions to discover any uncleared transactions, errors, omissions, new fees, or fraudulent activity on your accounts.

The following errors can cause a discrepancy when setting up a new account:

- Failing to create a check
- Failing to enter a deposit
- Creating a duplicate transaction
- Entering a wrong check number
- Failing to enter a bank fee and finance charge
- Entering a wrong amount

Check with your bank and credit card companies before signing up for Online Services.

ONLINE SERVICES

To connect to your financial institution and set up accounts:

- Click **Banking** on the Menu Bar
- Select Bank Feeds
- Click **Set Up Bank Feed for an Account**

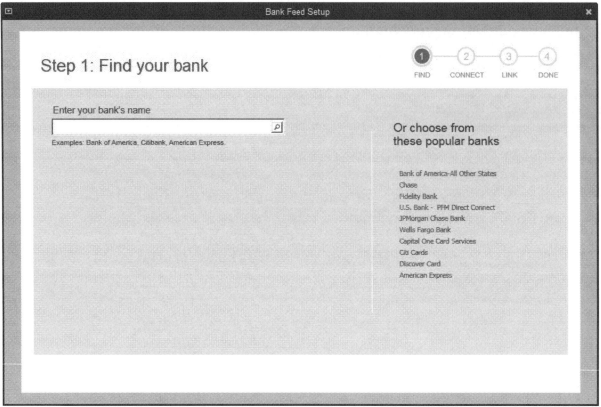

Screen Shot 264 Set Up Account for Online Services

- Search for and select your bank's name
- Click **Continue** and follow the prompts

DOWNLOAD TRANSACTIONS

To download bank and credit card transactions:

- Click **Banking** on the Menu Bar
- Select Bank Feeds
- Click **Bank Feeds Center**

The Online Banking Center window appears.

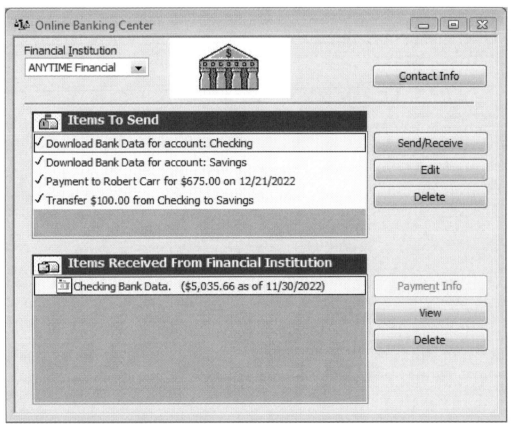

Screen Shot 265 Online Banking Center

- Click **Send/Receive**
- Enter your password to download transactions

ONLINE SERVICES

The transactions download and the bank balance is updated.

- Click **View** to see detailed transactions
- Click **Add One to Register**, **Add Multiple…**, or **Match**

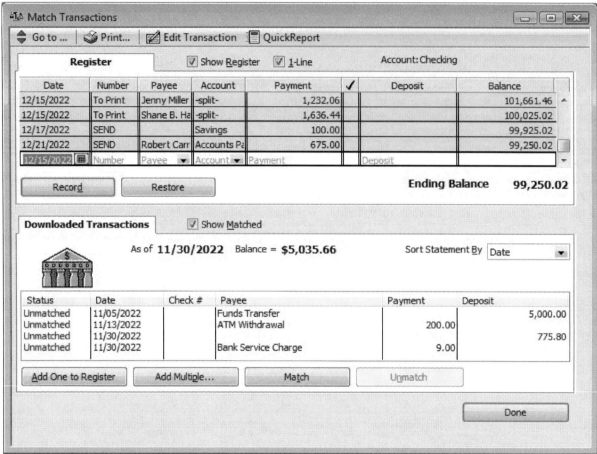

Screen Shot 266 Match Transactions

To learn more about the available options, click **Help** on the Menu Bar.

CHAPTER 65 RECONCILE ACCOUNTS

Reconciling accounts ensures that your financial records match your bank and credit card statements. Things such as an unentered deposit or check, duplicated transactions, an unentered bank charge, or an unentered bounced check can impact the accuracy of your balances. To accurately manage your accounts, reconcile your records against received bank, credit card, and loan statements on a monthly basis.

Objectives

Upon completion of this chapter, you will be able to:

- Reconcile Asset Accounts
- Reconcile Liability Accounts

RECONCILE A BANK ACCOUNT

Before you reconcile a bank account, check your statement for bank service charges and interest earned. If necessary, write a check to the bank to enter the bank service charge, or make a deposit to register interest received.

> **IMPORTANT**
> The Account, Statement Date, Beginning Balance, and Ending Balance fields should match the bank statement.

To reconcile a bank statement:

- Click **Banking** on the Menu Bar
- Select Reconcile

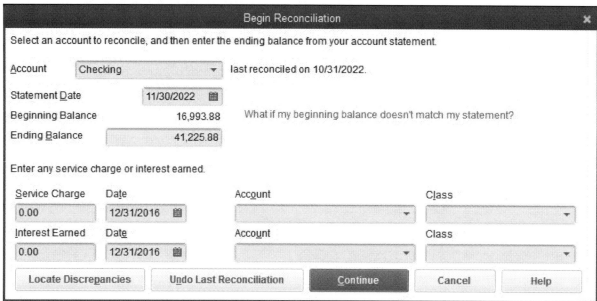

Screen Shot 267 Reconcile Bank Account

Reconcile Accounts

- Complete the fields as follows:

Field	Data
Account	Select the bank account
Statement Date	Ending date from the statement
Beginning Balance	Should equal the statement beginning balance
Ending Balance	Enter the ending balance as per the statement
Service Charge and Interest Earned	
Amount	As needed
Date	Ending date from the statement
Account	Select from the drop down menu
Class	Property Name or Your Company (Overhead)
Click **Continue**	

Table 67 Reconcile Bank Account

RECONCILE ACCOUNTS

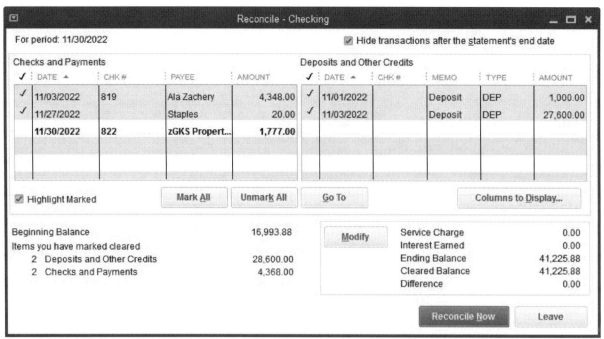

Screen Shot 268 Select Transactions

- Add a check mark to select Hide transactions after the statement's end date
- Select the Checks and Payment transactions that match the bank statement, making sure that the total Checks and Payments marked in the lower left match the statement
- Select the Deposits and Other Credits transactions that match the bank statement, making sure that the total Deposits and Other Credits marked in the lower left match the statement

IMPORTANT
The Difference should always be zero. If Difference is NOT zero, enter the missing transactions. If you wish to reconcile the accounts at a later time, click **Leave**.

- When the Difference is zero, click **Reconcile Now**

RECONCILE ACCOUNTS

The Select Reconciliation Report window appears.

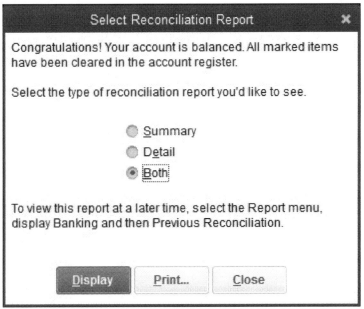

Screen Shot 269 Select Reconciliation Report

To review the reports for cleared, uncleared, and new transactions:

- Select Both
- Click **Display** to view the reconciliation reports
- Click **Print** and attach the reports to your bank statements

RECONCILE A CREDIT CARD ACCOUNT

Reconcile credit card statements monthly to be sure your credit card account balance matches the issuer's records. Not only does this help catch discrepancies, but it also verifies all credit card purchases and protects against fraud.

To reconcile a credit card statement:

- Click **Banking** on the Menu Bar
- Select Reconcile

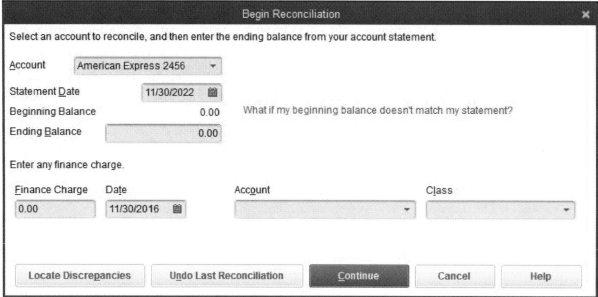

Screen Shot 270 Reconcile Credit Card Account

RECONCILE ACCOUNTS

- Complete the fields as follows:

Field	Data
Account	Select the credit card
Statement Date	Closing date of the statement
Beginning Balance	ZERO
Ending Balance	
Finance Charge	Leave blank
Date	
Account	
Class	
Click **Continue**	

Table 68 Reconcile Credit Card Account

- Select the Charges and Cash Advance transactions that match the credit card statement, making sure that the total Charges and Cash Advances marked in the bottom left match the statement
- Select the Payments and Credit transactions that match the credit card statement, making sure that the Total Payments and Credits marked on the bottom left to match the statement

IMPORTANT
The Difference should always be zero. If Difference is NOT zero, enter the missing transactions. If you wish to reconcile the accounts at a later time, click **Leave.**

- When the Difference is zero, click **Reconcile Now**

The Select Reconciliation Report window appears.

To review the reports for cleared, uncleared, and new transactions:

- Select Both
- Click **Display** to view reconciliation reports
- Click **Print** and attach the reports to your bank statements

RECONCILE LOAN AND DEPOSIT ACCOUNT

Reconciling loan and deposit account to ensure the balances match the statements. Be sure only to select the amounts that were received against the payee's name.

To reconcile a deposit account:

- Click **Banking** on the Menu Bar
- Select Reconcile
- Select the account and Statement Date
- Enter zero as the Ending Balance
- Click **Continue**
- Select the money received, paid, reimbursed or offset for each property.

The Difference should always be zero. If Difference is NOT zero, enter the missing transactions or reclassify the transactions already entered.

- Click **Reconcile Now**

To review the reports for cleared, uncleared, and new transactions:

- Select Both
- You may choose to select to either Display or Print the statements

SECTION 11

MANAGE OWNERS AND PROPERTIES

As a property manager, you will collect money from a tenant, pay vendors, charge management fee, and the balance will be payable to the owner or transferred to reserve fund, or the owner may be liable to pay the balance to you to cover money spent over and above the money received from the tenant.

In this section, you will learn how to process the management fees correctly, track reserve funds if applicable, record and view the relevant reports to forward the owners proceed a payment and reports in detail, summary and year-to-date.

CHAPTER 66 MANAGEMENT FEES

Management fees represent the cost for services performed by a management company to operate the property as a whole. Your management fees may be a flat charge, a percentage of the rental property income, or you may charge fees for each service or repair provided.

NOTE
If you are tracking balances, entering invoices, and receiving payments in QuickBooks, we recommend you purchase either QuickBooks Premier, Accountant or Enterprise Accountant version.

Objectives

Upon completion of this chapter, you will be able to:

- Record Management Fees
- Transfer Funds
- View Reports

MANAGEMENT FEES

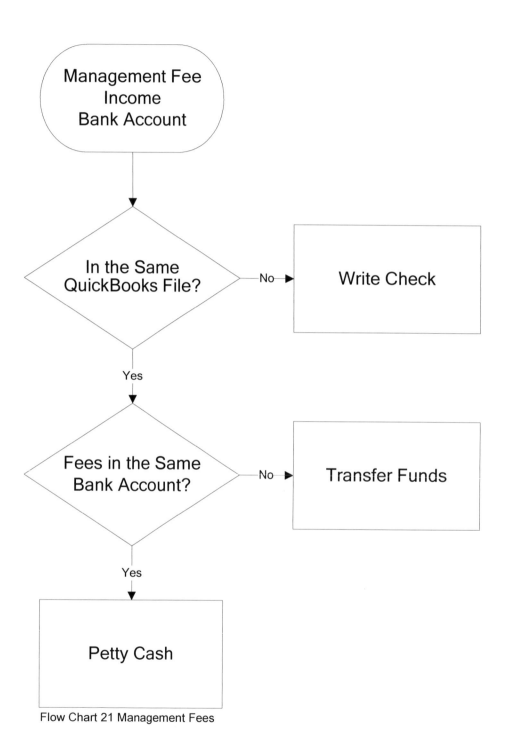

Flow Chart 21 Management Fees

MANAGEMENT FEES - FIRST TIME CHECKLIST

Management Fees
☐ Apply the Payments to Invoices (if applicable)
☐ View Owner's Proceed Summary Report
☐ View Rental Income by Property Report
☐ Write Check for Management Fees
☐ Memorize Check (Replace if you made changes)

Checklist 16 Management Fees – First Time

FLAT OR CALCULATED MANAGEMENT FEES

If you **charge a flat rate** for management services, create and memorize one check with the owner's fees to be automatically entered on a specified date.

If and when there are changes, you will be able to update the memorized check as needed. Refer to the chapter on Recurring Transactions.

If you **do not charge a flat fee**, calculate the fees on a regular basis following the steps outlined in this chapter. Think back to when you defined your business policies, and be sure you have determined how much and how often you will charge for your services. Be consistent with your procedure for all property owners.

IMPORTANT
You MUST review the Open Invoices report and apply the negative amounts to the appropriate invoices BEFORE recording management fees and issuing owner's proceed to check if you want the amount to be accurate. Refer to the next page.

REPORT: OPEN INVOICES

When you see a negative amount in the Open Invoices report, that amount will not be recorded in the Owner's Proceed Summary report unless you apply the payment to the invoice.

To view Open Invoices report:

- Click **MemRpts** on the Icon Bar
- Double-click Open Invoices under Management Fees

www.RealEstateAccounting.com
Open Invoices
As of December 1, 2022

Type	Date	Num	Terms	Due Date	Aging	Open Balance
Rentals in PA						
Plumly Way						
101 Unit						
Lewis, Frank						
Payment	12/01/2022					-100.00
Payment	11/02/2022					-800.00
Payment	10/19/2022					-100.00
Invoice	11/01/2022	4	Due on receipt	11/01/2022	30	1,000.00
Total Lewis, Frank						0.00
Total 101 Unit						0.00
Total Plumly Way						0.00
Total Rentals in PA						0.00
TOTAL						**0.00**

Report 36 Open Invoices

APPLY PAYMENTS TO INVOICES

When did you decide to pay the owner? In the month you receive the payment, or the invoice is dated?

Let us look at this example and determine which step applies to you. The invoice is dated November for $1000.00, and payment received:

- $200 in October (this amount will reflect in the month of November)
- $350 in November (this amount will reflect in the month of November)
- $500 in December (this amount will reflect in the month of December)

If you have agreed to **pay an owner on receipt of payment**, then you need to create an invoice for $200 for rent paid in advance and apply the payment to that specific invoice. Doing so $200 will be reflected in your owner's report in October. Remember to change the rent invoice by adding a line item Rent Paid in Advance with a negative amount 200, reducing the total amount of the invoice to $800.

If you agreed to **pay an owner on the invoice date**, then you need to apply the payment received in October and November to the invoice. Doing so $550 will be reflected on your owner's report in November. Now review you Open Invoice report there will be a balance of $450.00

To **apply negative amounts** to an invoice, double-click on the amounts to open the Receive Payments screen, select the appropriate open invoices and apply the negative amounts. The money received will then be reflected on the Owner's Proceed Summary report.

$500 payment received in December, when applied to the invoice will reflect on the December report.

This can be time-consuming when using QuickBooks Pro, which is why we recommend QuickBooks Premier Accountant or the Enterprise Accountant version.

MANAGEMENT FEES

REPORTS : MANAGEMENT FEE REVIEW

Are you going to charge management fees on rent received in advance? If you do, calculate the management fee accordingly and charge the owner.

Review the reports and verify the rent income before you charge the management fee. To view the reports:

- Click **MemRpts** on the Icon Bar
- Double-click on the ... under Management Fees
    - Open Invoices (apply negative amount to invoices)
    - Rent for Management Fees report reflects rent collected.
    - Management Fees: This report will take into account the management fee charged

The total amount of rent received from Profit & Loss by Class should match to the Rent for Management Fees report

- Click **MemRpts** on the Icon Bar
- Double-click the Rent for Management Fees Report under Management Fees

www.RealEstateAccounting.com
Rent for Management Fees
November 2022

	TOTAL
▼ GKS Properties	
▼ Fun Road 142	
Levin, Frank	5,000.00
Total Fun Road 142	5,000.00
▼ Swamp Road	
Flippet, Groue	2,500.00
Total Swamp Road	2,500.00
Total GKS Properties	7,500.00
TOTAL	**7,500.00**

Report 37 Rent for Management Fees

RECORD MANAGEMENT FEES FOR DEPOSIT

Once you have verified the correct amount, calculate the fee, and write a check. Record the management fees for all properties on one check to avoid entering separate checks for each property.

> **IMPORTANT**
> After you have created the check, memorize the check. You will be able to access it each time to record the management fees WITHOUT having to re-enter all the accounts and Properties (Class).
>
> For each subsequent check, you will only need to change the date, and the rent received an amount(s) under Cost for each property.

MANAGEMENT FEES

WRITE CHECK

Write a check to transfer management fees from one account to another.

To write a check for management fees:

- Click **Check** on the Icon Bar

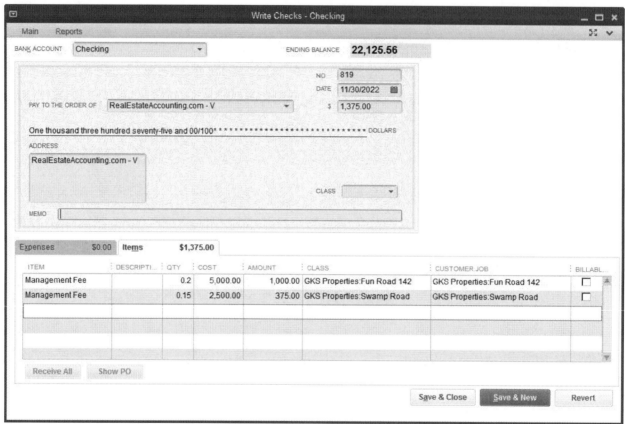

Screen Shot 271 Record Management Fees Expense

Add multiple lines for each property management fee. For example, if you have 10 property, you will have 10 Management Fee lines.

MANAGEMENT FEES

- Complete the fields as follows:

Field	Data
Bank Account	Checking
No.	To Print
Date	Date of check
Pay to the Order of	Your Company
$	Auto calculates
Address	Prefills
Class	Property Name
Memo	As needed
Items tab	
Item	Management Fees – if you want to split the amount into two or more Items, create a second line entry and divide the amount
Description	Prefills
Qty	Convert management rate into decimals e.g. 10% fee = 0.1
Cost	Rent received for the month (view Profit & Loss by Class report and enter the total rent received)
Amount	Prefills
Customer:Job	Property Name
Billable?	Leave blank
Class	Property Name
Do NOT click **Save & Close** until after you have memorized the check	

Table 69 Write Check for Management Fees

MANAGEMENT FEES

To memorize the Owner's Proceed check:

- Right-click on the check
- Select Memorize Check

Screen Shot 272 Memorize Management Fee Check

- Type your Company in the Name field
- Select Add to Group
- Select Management Fees from the Group Name drop-down menu
- Click **OK**

The Memorize Transaction window closes. On the Check screen, click **Save & Close** to save the check or **Print** to print and deposit the check.

When you deposit the check; make a deposit in the QuickBooks file for that bank account reflecting the amount of management fee income. Refer to the chapter on Deposits.

TRANSFER FUNDS

Instead of making a deposit or keeping the funds in one account, you may decide to transfer the money online from one bank account to another. For example, you may transfer the funds from checking to a savings account.

To record a transfer from one bank account to another:

- Write a check from the checking account for the amount of the management fee that is being transferred
- Use your Company as the Customer:Job and Class
- Add a line at the end for Management Fee Income with (-1) negative Qty and the Cost being the total amount of the management fee
- Add an another line for the savings bank account with (1) positive Qty and the Cost being the total amount of the management fee
- Use your Company as the Customer:Job and Class
- Memorize the check for future use.

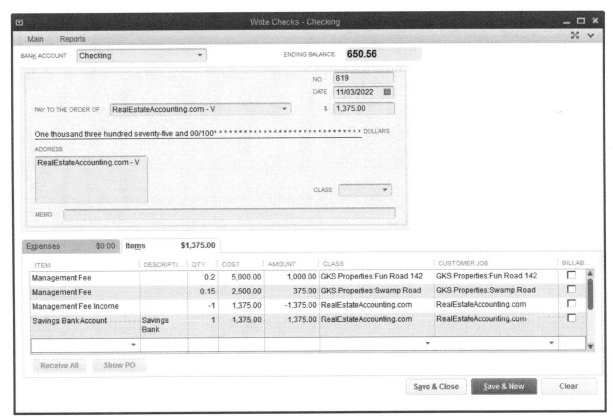

Screen Shot 273 Record Management Fee and Transfer

PETTY CASH

When recording management fees, you may choose to leave the income in the same bank account, rather than make a deposit to another bank account.

To record management fees, leaving income in the same account:

- Write a check from the Petty Cash bank account amounting to zero
- Add a line at the end for Management Fee Income
- Make the Qty negative (-1) and the Cost the total amount of the management fee
- Use your Company as Customer:Job and Class.

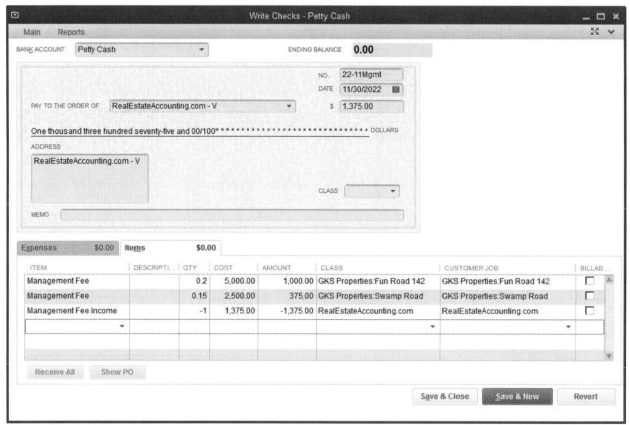

Screen Shot 274 Record Management Fees Expense and Income

- Click **Save & Close** or **Save & New** to write another check
- Remember to memorize the check for future use

MANAGEMENT FEE – EACH SUBSEQUENT TIME CHECKLIST

	Task
☑	Double-check Open Invoices Report
☑	View Profit & Loss by Class Report
☑	Edit Memorized Check
☑	Make Deposit
☑	Verify Profit & Loss by Class Report

Checklist 17 Management Fee - Each Subsequent Time

SUBSEQUENT MANAGEMENT FEES CHECKS

To recall a memorized transaction for next month:

- Click **MemTx** on the Icon Bar
- Double-click Management Fees – Check

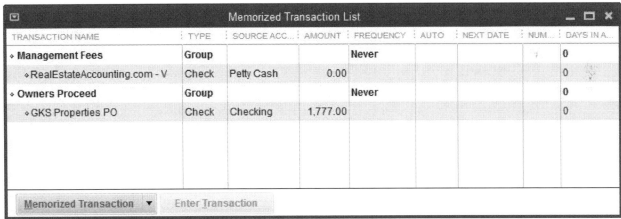

Screen Shot 275 Memorized Transaction List

For each subsequent check, you only need to:

- Change the date
- Change the rent received amount under Cost for each property
- Click **Save & Close**

REPORT: MANAGEMENT FEES

To view the Management Fees report:

- Click **MemRpts** on the Icon Bar
- Double-click the Profit & Loss Class Report under Company

www.RealEstateAccounting.com
Profit & Loss by Class
November 2022

	Swamp Road (GKS Properties)	Fun Road 142 (GKS Properties)	Total GKS Properties
Ordinary Income/Expense			
Income			
Total Rent			
Rental	2,500.00	5,000.00	7,500.00
Total Total Rent	2,500.00	5,000.00	7,500.00
Total Income	2,500.00	5,000.00	7,500.00
Gross Profit	2,500.00	5,000.00	7,500.00
Expense			
Management Fee	375.00	1,000.00	1,375.00
Total Expense	375.00	1,000.00	1,375.00
Net Ordinary Income	2,125.00	4,000.00	6,125.00
Net Income	**2,125.00**	**4,000.00**	**6,125.00**

Report 38 Profit & Loss by Class

CHAPTER 67 RESERVE FUNDS

A Reserve Fund is money received from the Owner to cover expenses over and above the rent received.

Objectives

Upon completion of this chapter, you will be able to:

- Enter a Reserve Fund
- Apply Funds to Owner's Proceed
- Transfer Funds
- View Reports

Working with Reserve Funds

Most property management companies collect reserve funds from owners for each property. In QuickBooks, the owner's Reserve Fund is similar to a security deposit.

The first step is to check the Open Invoice Report for negative balances. If there are negative balances, apply them to the appropriate invoices. Refer to the chapter on Management Fees.

At times, the total balance (Net Income) for a property may be **negative** in the Owner's Proceed Summary report. When this happens, transfer money from the Reserve Fund account to offset the negative income thus reducing the Reserve Fund account balance. Then, either invoice the owner or deduct the money from the next month's proceeds.

The objective is to have a Total Net Income of zero for all columns except Your Company on the Profit & Loss by Class report.

If you choose to **request the funds** from the Property Owner right away, enter an invoice for the amount, using Reserve Fund as the Item and record payment when received.

If you wish to **apply the balance to the next months,** proceed, create a Transfer To check this month and a Transfer From check dated the first day of the next month following the steps below.

Other times, the total balance (Net Income) for a property may be **positive** in the Owner's Proceed Summary report. When this happens, you may either:

- Write the owner a proceed check
- Transfer the money to the Reserve Fund for the current month and transfer it back, as needed, to cover the expenses
- For owner's with multiple properties, offset the negative amount for one property with the positive amount of another property, if agreed upon with the owner.

To reconcile the Reserve Fund, refer to the chapter on Reconciling Accounts.

RESERVE FUNDS

CHECKLIST

Reserve Fund
☐ Check Open Invoices Report
☐ View Owner's Proceed Summary Report
☐ Transfer Funds
☐ Create Invoice
☐ Verify Reports

Checklist 18 Reserve Fund

REPORT: OWNER'S PROCEED SUMMARY

After you have transferred the amount, the Owner Proceed Summary report reflects the owners proceed amount transferred to and from the Reserve Fund.

To view the Owner's Proceed Summary report:

- Click **MemRpts** on the Icon Bar
- Double-click the owner's name under Owner's Proceed

www.RealEstateAccounting.com
Profit & Loss
August through November 2022

	Aug 22	Sep 22	Oct 22	Nov 22	TOTAL
Ordinary Income/Expense	1,000.00	1,000.00	-450.00	1,000.00	2,550.00
Other Income/Expense					
▼ Other Expense					
Transfer to/from Reserve F...	450.00	-450.00	-450.00	450.00	0.00
Total Other Expense	450.00	-450.00	-450.00	450.00	0.00
Net Other Income	-450.00	450.00	450.00	-450.00	0.00
Net Income	550.00	1,450.00	0.00	550.00	2,550.00

Report 39 Profit & Loss (Reserve Fund)

TRANSFER TO

Transfer to Reserve Fund:

- When income has a negative balance, transfer the negative balance to reserve fund. Example view the report for the month of October. (it is good practice to reverse the entry and bring the amount back to the Owner's Proceed Summary report for the next period. an example is on the next page).
- Transfer money from the reserve fund to increase the balance of owners proceed. Example view the report for the month of September

To transfer to reserve fund:

- Click **Check** on the Icon Bar

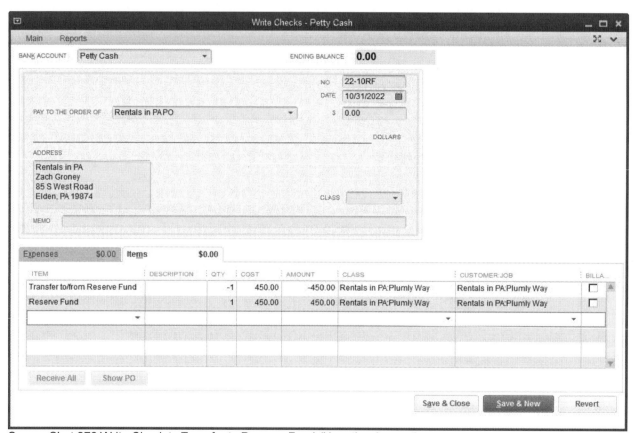

Screen Shot 276 Write Check to Transfer to Reserve Fund (Negative Amount)

Reserve Funds

- Complete the fields as follows:

Field	Data
Bank Account	Account
No.	As needed
Date	Last day of the Owner's Proceed Summary report
Pay to the Order of	Property Owner - Vendor
$	ZERO
Address	Prefills
Class	Property Name
Memo	As needed
Items Tab	

Split Lines	Item	Description	Qty	Cost	Amount
Line 1	Transfer TO Reserve Funds	Transfer TO Reserve Funds	-1	Amount	Negative balance
Line 2	Deposits:Reserve Funds	Reserve Funds	1	Amount	Positive balance

Field	Data
Customer:Job	Property Name
Billable?	Leave blank
Class	Property Name

Click **Save & Close** or **Save & New** to write another check

Table 70 Write Check to Transfer to Reserve Fund (Negative Amount)

TRANSFER FROM TO DECREASE BALANCE

To transfer from Reserve Fund:

- Transfer money from the reserve fund to decrease the balance of owners proceeds. Example view the report for the month of August and November
- Click **Check** on the Icon Bar

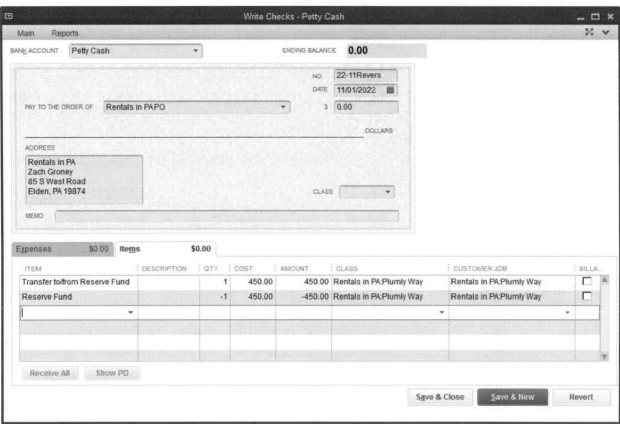

Screen Shot 277 Write Check to Transfer to Reserve Fund (Positive Amount)

Reserve Funds

- Complete the fields as follows:

Field	Data
Bank Account	Account
No.	As needed
Date	Last day of the Owner's Proceed Summary report
Pay to the Order of	Property Owner - Vendor
$	ZERO
Address	Prefills
Class	Property Name
Memo	As needed
Items Tab	

Split Lines	Item	Description	Qty	Cost	Amount
Line 1	Transfer TO Reserve Funds	Transfer TO Reserve Funds	1	Amount	Positive balance
Line 2	Deposits: Reserve Funds	Reserve Funds	-1	Amount	Negative balance

Field	Data
Customer:Job	Property Name
Billable?	Leave blank
Class	Property Name

Click **Save & Close** or **Save & New** to write another check

Table 71 Write Check to Transfer to Reserve Fund (Positive Amount)

REPORT: RESERVE FUND

The Reserve Fund report reflects the invoice created, and after the invoice is received in full the Invoice in the Paid column will show as "Paid."

To view the Reserve Fund report:

- Click **MemRpts** on the Icon Bar
- Double-click Reserve Fund under Reserve Funds

www.RealEstateAccounting.com
Reserve Funds
All Transactions

Type	Date	Num	Paid Amount	Balance
Rentals in PA				
Plumly Way				
Check	08/31/2022	22-08	450.00	450.00
Check	09/30/2022	22-09	-450.00	0.00
Check	10/31/2022	22-10RF	-450.00	-450.00
Check	11/01/2022	22-11Revers	450.00	0.00
Total Plumly Way			0.00	0.00
Total Rentals in PA			0.00	0.00
TOTAL			**0.00**	**0.00**

Report 40 Reserve Funds

Chapter 68 Owner's Proceed

Owners proceed equal to the net amount of rent and other income, after deducting all incurred costs for a property. Managers typically provide periodic reports and payments to the owner showing the proceeds of each property. The Owner's Proceed Summary report is on a cash basis.

TIP
We recommend running reports for the January to the last day of owners report and verify the Net Income/Loss is ZERO.

Objectives

Upon completion of this chapter, you will be able to:

- Determine Amount of Owner's Proceed
- Write a Check
- View Reports

OWNER'S CHECK – FIRST TIME CHECKLIST

Owner's Proceed
☐ Check Open Invoices Report
☐ Apply the Payments to Invoices
☐ View Owner's Proceed Summary Report
☐ Write Check to the Property Owner
☐ Memorize Check
☐ Verify Profit & Loss by Class Report
☐ Enter Closing Date

Checklist 19 Owner's Check – First Time

Report: Owner's Proceed Summary (Before)

Before you begin to calculate an owner's proceeds, check the Open Invoices report for negative balances. The credit amounts to invoices and then check the Owner's Proceed Summary report.

The Owner's Proceed Summary report shows a net income or a net loss (negative balance) for each property. The total is paid to the property owner. When the owner owns multiple properties, each column is each property's total. The owner's column will represent the totals of all properties combined.

> **IMPORTANT**
> The objective is to have a Total Net Income of zero for all columns except Overhead.

OWNER'S PROCEED

To view the Owner's Proceed Summary report:

- Click **MemRpts** on the Icon Bar
- Double-click owner's name under Owner's Proceed

www.RealEstateAccounting.com
Profit & Loss by Class
November 2022

	Swamp Road (GKS Properties)	Fun Road 142 (GKS Properties)	Total GKS Properties
Ordinary Income/Expense			
▼ Income			
▼ Total Rent			
Rental	2,500.00	5,000.00	7,500.00
Total Total Rent	2,500.00	5,000.00	7,500.00
Total Income	2,500.00	5,000.00	7,500.00
▼ Cost of Goods Sold			
Property Repairs	2,750.00	1,598.00	4,348.00
Total COGS	2,750.00	1,598.00	4,348.00
Gross Profit	-250.00	3,402.00	3,152.00
▼ Expense			
Management Fee	375.00	1,000.00	1,375.00
Total Expense	375.00	1,000.00	1,375.00
Net Ordinary Income	-625.00	2,402.00	1,777.00
Net Income	**-625.00**	**2,402.00**	**1,777.00**

Report 41 Profit & Loss by Class

On this report, Swamp Road shows a Net Income (negative balance) of $625.00 and Fun Road shows a Net Income (positive balance) of $2,402 totaling $1,777 as the proceed. After you have saved the check, the report will reflect proceed (Net Income) balances as zero for each property and the owner (Total).

WRITE A CHECK TO OWNER

To track proceed for each property and pay the owner, write a check for the total amount with a separate line for each property under the Items tab.

> **IMPORTANT**
> Once you have initially memorized the check, you will be able to access it each time you want to make a payment to that owner WITHOUT having to re-enter all the accounts and properties (Class). Refer to the chapter on Recurring Transactions.
>
> For each subsequent check, change the date and the payment amount(s) for each property.

Owner's Proceed

Create one check for each owner and memorize it (not to be automatically entered) under Group.

To write a check for owner's proceed:

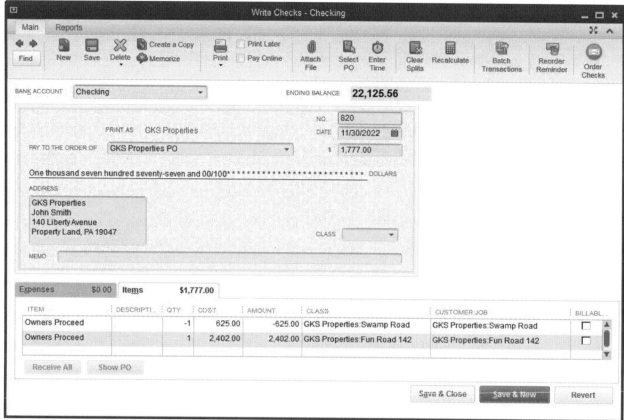

Screen Shot 278 Owner's Proceed Check

Owner's Proceed

- Complete the fields as follows:

Field	Data
Bank Account	Account name you are transferring the money from
No.	Leave blank
Date	Date
Pay to the Order of	Name of Property Owner - Vendor
$	Amount to be paid
Address	Prefills
Class	Property Name
Memo	As needed
Items Tab		
Split Lines	Account	Amount
Line 1	Owner's Proceed	Net Income (negative balance in this case)
Line 2	Owner's Proceed	Net Income (positive balance in this case)
Memo		As needed
Customer:Job		Property Name
Billable?		Leave blank
Class		Property Name
Do NOT click **Save & Close** until after you have memorized the check		

Table 72 Owner's Proceed Check

OWNER'S PROCEED

MEMORIZE OWNER'S CHECK

After writing the check, memorize it to save all the accounts and property names. You will be able to access it each time you want to send the Owner a payment without re-entering all the Property information.

To memorize the Owner's Proceed check:

- Right-click on the check
- Select Memorize Check

Screen Shot 279 Memorize Owner's Proceed Check

- Select Add to Group
- Select Owner's Proceed from the drop down box in the Group Name field
- Click **OK**

The Memorize Transaction window closes. On the Check screen, click **Save & Close** to save the check or **Print** to print it.

Commercial Property Management for Managers: QuickBooks Desktop

OWNER'S PROCEED

OWNER'S CHECK – EACH SUBSEQUENT TIME CHECKLIST

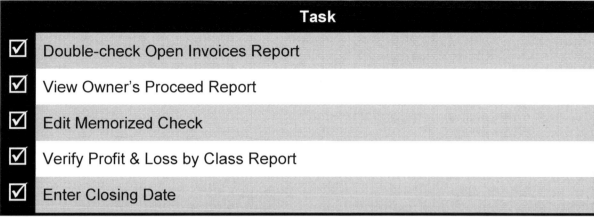

Checklist 20 Owner's Check - Each Subsequent Time

SUBSEQUENT OWNER'S PROCEED CHECK

To recall a memorized transaction for next month:

- Click **MemTx** on the Icon Bar
- Double-click the Property Owner under Owner's Proceed

Screen Shot 280 Memorized Transaction List

For each subsequent check, you only need to:

- Change the date
- Change the amount
- Click **Save & Close**

Commercial Property Management for Managers: QuickBooks Desktop

REPORT: OWNER'S PROCEED SUMMARY (AFTER)

Remember the objective is to have a Total Net Income of zero for all columns except Overhead.

To view the Owner's Proceed Summary report:

- Click **MemRpts** on the Icon Bar
- Double-click owner's name under Owner's Proceed

www.RealEstateAccounting.com
Profit & Loss by Class
November 2022

	Swamp Road (GKS Properties)	Fun Road 142 (GKS Properties)	Total GKS Propert...
▼ Total Rent			
Rental	2,500.00	5,000.00	7,500.00
Total Total Rent	2,500.00	5,000.00	7,500.00
Total Income	2,500.00	5,000.00	7,500.00
▼ Cost of Goods So..			
Property Repa...	2,750.00	1,598.00	4,348.00
Total COGS	2,750.00	1,598.00	4,348.00
Gross Profit	-250.00	3,402.00	3,152.00
▼ Expense			
Management F...	375.00	1,000.00	1,375.00
Total Expense	375.00	1,000.00	1,375.00
Net Ordinary Income	-625.00	2,402.00	1,777.00
Other Income/Expense			
▼ Other Expense			
Owners Proceed	-625.00	2,402.00	1,777.00
Total Other Expense	-625.00	2,402.00	1,777.00
Net Other Income	625.00	-2,402.00	-1,777.00
Net Income	0.00	0.00	0.00

Report 42 Owner's Proceed Summary

SECTION 12

IT'S A NO BRAINER!

There is always more to do than meets the eye. Performing miscellaneous and regular tasks will enable you to operate efficiently, put everything into action, and run a smooth and organized business! If you are stuck, please reach out and contact the author with any questions you may have.

The most challenging aspects of managing properties in QuickBooks are tackled in this section from owners 1099 to rent escalation and expense reconciliation.

At the end of the month, quarter, or the year, you may need to compare actual expenses with estimated expenses. Use QuickBooks to set up budgets and forecasts to easily make those comparisons. Also, at the end of each year, calculate escalations for rent and other expenses.

Truly, It's a no-brainer!

IT'S A NO BRAINER!

REPORTS CENTER

QuickBooks provides a set of default customized reports to let you track and analyze specific financial data. If none of the default reports suit your needs, you can customize an existing report refer to chapter Customizing Reports.

Use the Report Center to find standard, memorized, favorite, or recently run reports.

To view the Report Center:

- Click Reports on Menu Bar
- Select Report Center

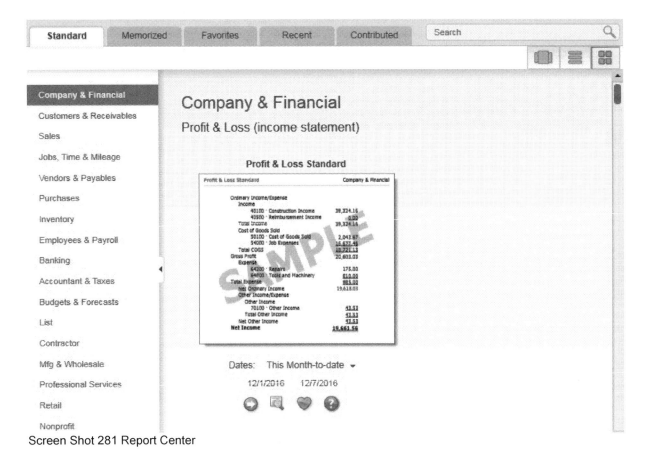
Screen Shot 281 Report Center

Chapter 69 1099 Forms

Review the current federal and state rules and regulations regarding when and to whom you should send 1099 Forms. Check www.irs.gov for current requirements, as the laws often change.

> **IMPORTANT**
> A W-9 Form and instructions at http://www.irs.gov/pub/irs-pdf/fw9.pdf
>
> You cannot print 1099-INT from QuickBooks.

Each and every year you are required to send a 1099 Form to all vendors and owners. Ask your vendors and owners to fill out a W-9, which captures their Tax ID number. This process also makes these individuals aware that they will receive a 1099 Form at the end of the year.

Objectives

Upon completion of this chapter, you will be able to:

- Prepare and review current file
- Create a 1099 file
- Issue 1099 forms
- Prepare, Print, and File 1099 Forms

1099 FORMS

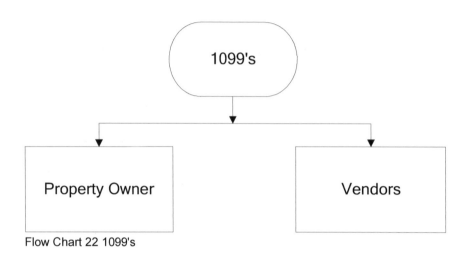

Flow Chart 22 1099's

> **IMPORTANT**
> There are two types of 1099 Forms: 1099-INT and 1099-MISC. For more information, go to http://www.irs.gov/uac/Form-1099-INT,-Interest-Income and http://www.irs.gov/uac/Form-1099-MISC,-Miscellaneous-Income.
>
> From QuickBooks, you can only print 1099-MISC forms, not 1099-INT forms; however, the author's team can help you.

Sample 1099 Form

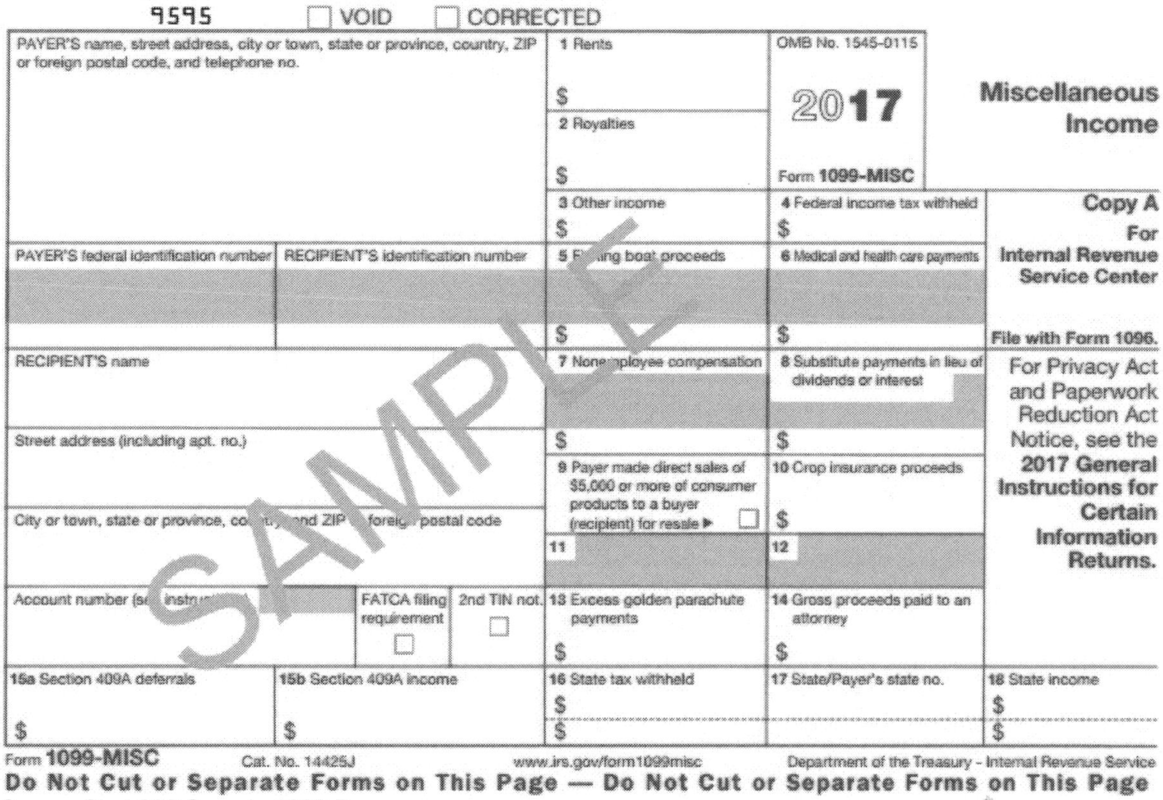

9595 ☐ VOID ☐ CORRECTED

PAYER'S name, street address, city or town, state or province, country, ZIP or foreign postal code, and telephone no.

1 Rents $

2 Royalties $

OMB No. 1545-0115

2017

Form 1099-MISC

Miscellaneous Income

3 Other income $

4 Federal income tax withheld $

Copy A For Internal Revenue Service Center

File with Form 1096.

PAYER'S federal identification number

RECIPIENT'S identification number

5 Fishing boat proceeds $

6 Medical and health care payments $

RECIPIENT'S name

7 Nonemployee compensation $

8 Substitute payments in lieu of dividends or interest $

For Privacy Act and Paperwork Reduction Act Notice, see the 2017 General Instructions for Certain Information Returns.

Street address (including apt. no.)

9 Payer made direct sales of $5,000 or more of consumer products to a buyer (recipient) for resale ▶ ☐

10 Crop insurance proceeds $

City or town, state or province, country, and ZIP or foreign postal code

11

12

Account number (see instructions)

FATCA filing requirement ☐

2nd TIN not. ☐

13 Excess golden parachute payments $

14 Gross proceeds paid to an attorney $

15a Section 409A deferrals $

15b Section 409A income $

16 State tax withheld $ $

17 State/Payer's state no.

18 State income $ $

Form 1099-MISC Cat. No. 14425J www.irs.gov/form1099misc Department of the Treasury - Internal Revenue Service

Do Not Cut or Separate Forms on This Page — Do Not Cut or Separate Forms on This Page

SAMPLE

Screen Shot 282 Sample 1099 Form

CHECKLIST TO 1099

Property managers must issue 1099 to the owner for the total amount of rent received. If you are keeping up with everything listed above, then it should only take about 30 minutes to create 1099's. Every year, you will have to create a new file to print 1099's. To issue 1099 to owners and vendors for the total amount of rent received and expenses paid, follow the checklist.

> **IMPORTANT**
> You will not be able to generate 1099 for owners from you existing file. As the rent is received by the Customer (Tenant) name, not the Vendor name.

1099 CHECKLIST

	Task	Refer to Chapter
☑	Prepare the existing file	
☑	Check the Open Invoices report	
☑	Print report for Rental Income	
☑	Print report for Vendor	
☑	Export the iif list and save the file	
☑	Download and save the "1099 File."	1099 Forms
☑	Restore the "1099 File."	
☑	Import the IIF File "1099 File."	
☑	Enter the income	
☑	Enter the expense	
☑	View reports	
☑	Print or eFile 1099	

Checklist 21 1099 Checklist

EXISTING QUICKBOOKS FILE

In the current QuickBooks file, update the owner and vendor addresses, Employer Identification Numbers (EIN), or Social Security Numbers (SSN). Refer to the chapter on Vendors in the Manage Names section.

REPORT: OPEN INVOICES

When you see a negative amount in the Open Invoices report, that amount will not reflect in the total rent received a report by property/owner.

IMPORTANT
You MUST review this report and apply the negative amounts to the appropriate invoices before recording property owner's rent income.

To apply the negative amount to an invoice, view the Open Invoices report and double-click on the negative amount to open the Receive Payments screen. Select the invoice to receive payment. Once all negative amounts have been applied to invoices, the rent will be accurate. Check the Open Invoices report under 1099.

REPORT: RENTAL INCOME FOR 1099

To determine the amount of 1099 to be issued **to the owners,** view the Profit & Loss by Class report, which reflects total rent for each property and each property owner. Compare the amounts to the amounts in the Rental Income for 1099 report.

To view and print 1099 reports:

- Click **MemRpts** on Icon Bar
- Double-click Rental Income for 1099 under 1099 and
- Print the report

REPORT: VENDOR EXPENSE FOR 1099

View the Vendor List report and the Vendor Expenses Summary report to ensure accuracy.

To view and print 1099 reports:

- Click **MemRpts** on Icon Bar
- Double-click on:
    - Vendor Expense Summary
    - Vendor Expense Detail
    - Vendor Expenses for 1099
- Print the report

EXPORT THE VENDOR LIST

To export the Chart of Accounts and Vendor List:

- Open your existing Company file and Switch to Single-user Mode
- Click **File** on the Menu Bar
- Select Utilities
- Select Export
- Click **Lists to IIF Files…**

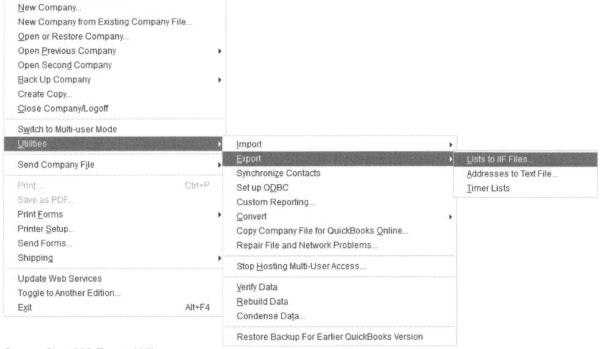

Screen Shot 283 Export Utility

1099 Forms

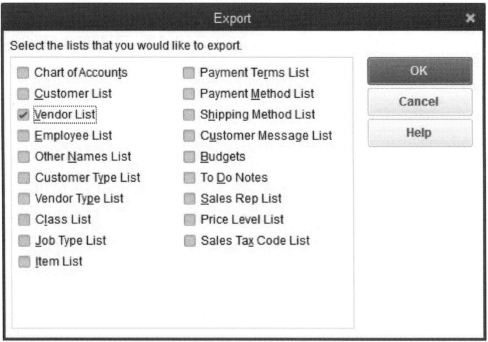

Screen Shot 284 Export Lists

- Select Vendor List
- Click **OK**
- Save to the accounting folder

Change Filename to "2022 Owner Vendor List 1099" using the year in the name.

1099 Forms

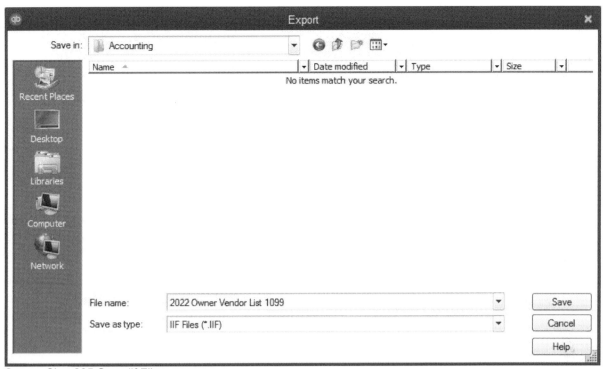

Screen Shot 285 Save iif File

- Click **Save**
- Click **OK**

Download "1099 File."

Download the "1099 File" from the portal and save it for next year in the accounting folder.

Restore "1099 File."

You should be a pro by now in backup and restore a file. Restore the 1099 File and rename with the year you are creating 1099 for.

1099 FORMS

IMPORT THE IIF FILE

To import the IIF File "2022 Owner Vendor List 1099" saved:

- Open File "1099 File."
- Click **File** on the Menu Bar
- Select Utilities
- Select Import
- Click **IIF Files...**

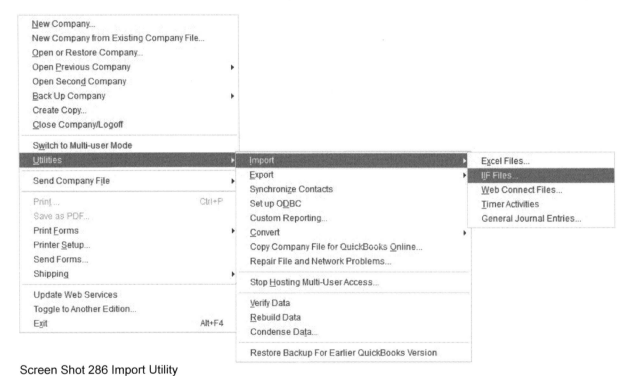

Screen Shot 286 Import Utility

- Browse and Double-click on the file name "2022 Owner Vendor List 1099."

After the import is complete, a pop-up message will appear.

- Click **OK**

Commercial Property Management for Managers: QuickBooks Desktop

ENTERING THE AMOUNTS

You will have to decide to issue 1099's to the property owner or by the property. To issue 1099 by the property owner, add the rent income of all properties. Otherwise, issue 1099's for rental income by the property and owner name for each property as a vendor.

To enter the owner's total rent received:

- Click **MemTx** on the Icon Bar
- Double-click "Owners 1099 Entry" and
- Double-click "Vendors 1099 Entry."

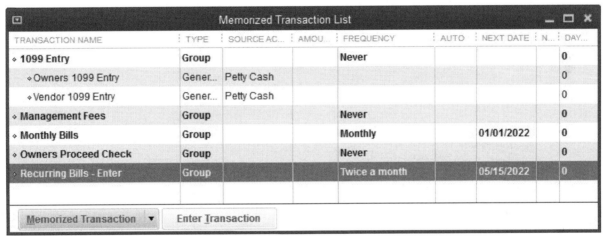
Screen Shot 287 Memorized Transaction List

1099 Forms

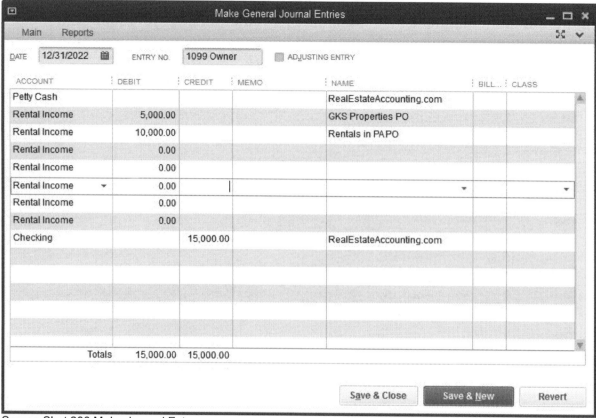

Screen Shot 288 Make Journal Entry

- Complete the fields as follows:

Field	Data
Date	Last day of the year
Entry No.	Year
Account	Debit: Rent amount received (from the printed report) (there will be a separate line entry for each owner or property) Credit: Total rent amount of all properties to a bank account
Memo	As needed
Name	Property Owner as a vendor
Billable?	Leave as is
Totals	Debits should equal Credits
Click **Save & Close**	

Table 73 Make Journal Entry

Prepare and File

QuickBooks calculates 1099 information for vendors, such as contractors, cleaning service providers, and suppliers. Collect the tax ID numbers for vendors receiving the 1099 Form.

To prepare 1099's for Vendors:

- Click **Vendors** on the Menu Bar
- Select Print/E-file 1099s…
- Click **1099 Wizard**

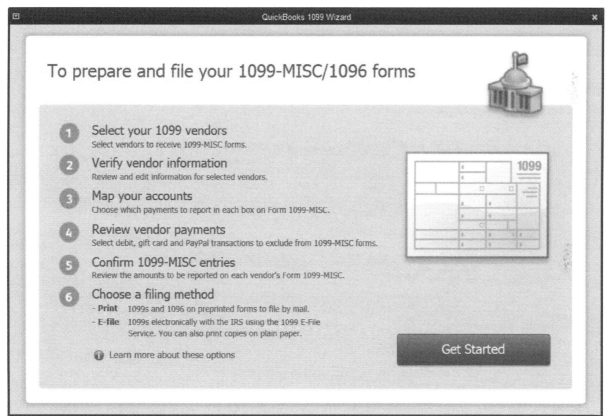

Screen Shot 289 1099 Wizard

- Click **Get Started**

1099 FORMS

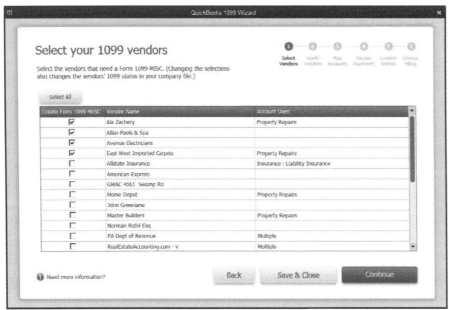

Screen Shot 290 Select your 1099 vendors

- Select the vendors to whom you wish to send 1099 Forms
- Click **Continue**

Screen Shot 291 Verify your 1099 vendors' information

- Ensure that the information is accurate
- Click **Continue**

1099 FORMS

The accounts used to pay vendors in the past year appear.

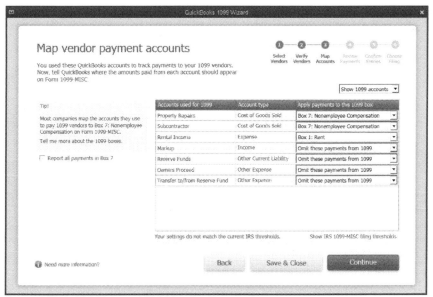
Screen Shot 292 Report 1099 Vendor Payments

- Choose which payments are applied to 1099
- Click **Continue**

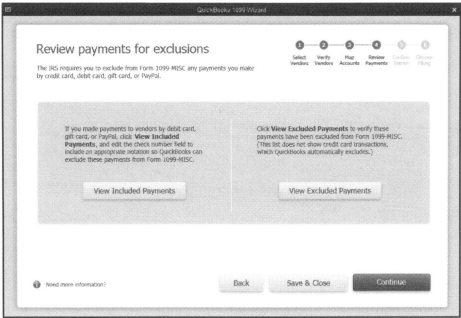
Screen Shot 293 Review payments for exclusions

- Review included and excluded payments, as needed

1099 Forms

- Click **Continue**

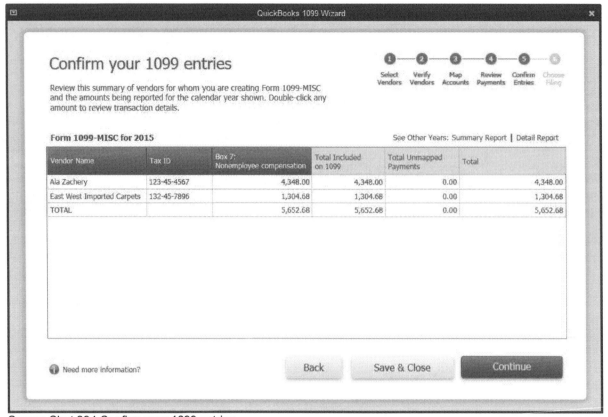

Screen Shot 294 Confirm your 1099 entries

- Confirm 1099 entries
- Click **Continue**

IMPORTANT
Efile save time and money. If you do you can: - Print the forms on plain paper and mail them to your vendor. Use plain envelopes - Do not require to submit 1096 form - Does my state participate? Click on the link on the screen and double check. Alternatively, you can just buy the forms and envelope, print and mail to the owners, vendors, federal and state authorities.

1099 Forms

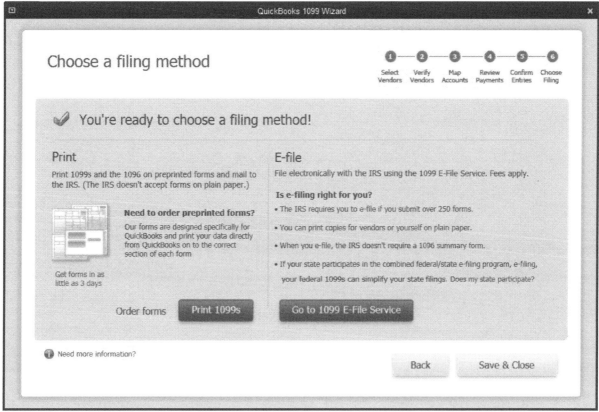

Screen Shot 295 Choose a Filing Method

- Choose Print 1099s or Got to 1099 E-file Service

If you choose to print the 1099 Forms, the following window appears:

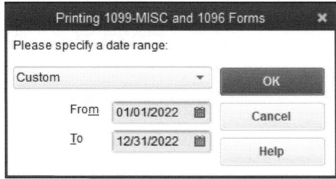

Screen Shot 296 Printing 1099-MISC and 1096 Forms

- Select the date range
- Click **OK**

Commercial Property Management for Managers: QuickBooks Desktop

1099 Forms

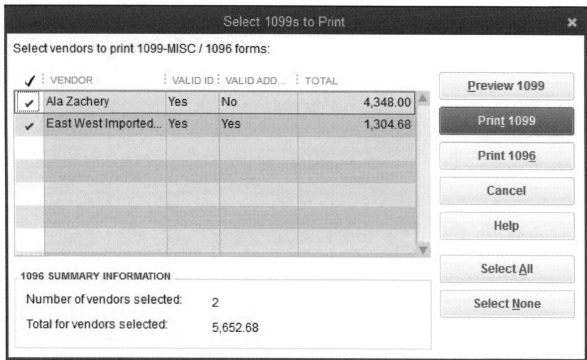

Screen Shot 297 Select 1099's to Print

- Select which vendors 1099-MISC/1096 forms you wish to print
- Click **Preview 1099**, **Print 1099**, **Print 1096**, or **Cancel**
- Remember to mail the forms

Report: 1099 Summary

To view the 1099 Summary report:

- Click **MemRpts** on the Icon Bar
- Double-click 1099 Summary under 1099s

www.RealEstateAccounting.com
1099 Summary
January through December 2022

	Box 1: Rents	Box 7: Nonemployee Compensation	TOTAL
Allen Pools & Spa	0.00	5,766.00	5,766.00
123-12-1234			
Avenue Electricians	0.00	0.00	0.00
99-9999999			
GKS Properties PO	5,000.00	0.00	5,000.00
12-3456789			
Rentals in PA PO	10,000.00	0.00	10,000.00
123-45-7896			
TOTAL	15,000.00	5,766.00	20,766.00

Report 43 1099 Summary

REPORT: 1099 DETAIL

To view the 1099 Detail report:

- Click **MemRpts** on the Icon Bar
- Double-click 1099 Detail under 1099s

www.RealEstateAccounting.com
1099 Detail
January through December 2022

Type	Date	Account	Paid Amount
Allen Pools & Spa			
123-12-1234			
General Journal	12/31/2022	Subcontractor	5,766.00
Total Allen Pools & Spa			5,766.00
GKS Properties PO			
12-3456789			
General Journal	12/31/2022	Rental Income	5,000.00
Total GKS Properties PO			5,000.00
Rentals in PA PO			
123-45-7896			
General Journal	12/31/2022	Rental Income	10,000.00
Total Rentals in PA PO			10,000.00
TOTAL			20,766.00

Report 44 1099 Detail

CHAPTER 70 RENT ESCALATION

Rent escalation is the adjustment of rent and operating expenses to cover changes in the cost of living and operating costs. The property owner and tenant agree on how rent escalation and operating expense escalation will be calculated in the lease. Below are a few terms to keep in mind when calculating escalation:

Rentable Space vs. Usable Space

Usable space is the area which is usable by the tenant. Rentable space includes usable space as well as common areas of the building.

Occupancy Rate

Divide occupied days by total days. Move-in and move-out days count as occupied.

Objectives

Upon completion of this chapter, you will be able to:

- Calculate Rent Escalation
- Calculate Operating Expense Escalation

CALCULATE RENT ESCALATION

Rent escalation can be calculated by increasing the rent amount by a percentage or a fixed amount, depending on the lease agreement between the property owner and tenant.

View your lease abstract, rent roll, budgets, and forecasts as a resource to calculate rent escalation.

By Percentage

If you calculate rent escalation by percentage, increase each year's rent by adding the percent to the previous year's rent.

The property owner and tenant agree upon an annual base rental rate of $50,000. The rent escalates by 3% for a 3-year lease. Therefore, the 2nd year's rental rate is 103% of the 1st year's base rental rate.

To calculate rent escalation:

Base Rental Rate	$50,000
	x 1.03
2nd Year's Rental Rate	$51,500
Base Rental Rate	$51,500
	x 1.03
3rd Year's Rental Rate	$53,045

For additional years, repeat the previous step.

Stepped Rent

Stepped rent is the most common way to escalate rent by increasing the rental rate by a certain amount each year.

The property owner and tenant agree to increase the base rent of $50,000 by $5,000 each year. Therefore, the 1st year's rent is $50,000, the 2nd year's rent is $55,000, and the 3rd year's rent is $60,000.

OPERATING EXPENSE ESCALATION

As these costs increase each year, leases include a clause for operating expense escalation. There are four major ways that operation expense escalation is calculated:

- Direct Pass-Thru Charges
- Consumer Price Index (CPI)
- Set Percentage Increases
- Porter's Wage Formula

Direct Pass-Thru Charges

The most common way to charge operating expenses escalation is Direct Pass-Thru Charges. The owner increases operating expenses by the actual cost increases per square foot. Each tenant is charged by the percentage of the property they occupy.

Invoice tenants for operating expenses each month based on prior year's actual cost. At the end of the year, reconcile the actual costs for that year with the total billed amount.

If the actual costs were greater than the estimated amount, invoice the tenants for the difference. If the actual costs were less than the estimated amount, credit the tenants for the difference.

The exact terms for operating expense escalation will be specified in the lease.

Consumer Price Index (CPI)

Operating expense escalation can be based on the increase in the Consumer Price Index. The Consumer Price Index measures the price change in the costs of goods and services.

Set Percentage Increases

Calculate operating expense escalation by increasing expenditure by an agreed upon percentage.

Porter's Wage Formula

Porter's Wage Formula is only used to calculate operating expense escalation in New York City. It increases the cost of operating expense per square foot as porters' wage increases. It serves as a proxy for owner costs.

EXPENSE STOP

Some lease agreements obligate the owner to pay expenses up to a stated amount known as an expense stop. The tenant is responsible for the remaining expenses.

CHAPTER 71 EXPENSE RECOVERY

In addition to the rent, you may invoice your tenants an estimated amount for CAM charges and for expenses that were originally paid by the Landlord or Management. At the end of the year, reconcile the actual expenses and CAM charges with the forecasted amount to either invoice or credit the tenant for the difference.

The calculation for the Expense Recovery depends on the lease type.

Setting up budgets and forecasts makes it easier to streamline the CAM reconciliation process. Use reports in QuickBooks to track variances and actual amounts for budgets and forecasts, manage CAM budgets, and even to send to the tenant.

Objectives

Upon completion of this chapter, you will be able to:

- View the Timeline for the Reconciliation Process
- Alternative Easy Approach
- Invoice or Credit Tenant
- Calculate Expense Recovery
- Customize and Memorize Budgets and Forecasts
- View Reports

RECONCILE CAM CHARGES

By entering budgets and forecasts, you can easily create reports to view CAM expenses and rental income.

The reports for budgets and forecasts can be seen in the latter portion of this chapter. Each report can be viewed by Tenan and Property depending on how you entered the data.

View reports either on cash or accrual basis.

Refer to chapter Budgets & Forecasts to create budgets and forecasts.

EXPENSE RECOVER CHECKLIST

	Year		Task by Tenant
	In	For	
☑	September 2021	2022	Set Up Budget for the Next Year • View Reports
☑	November & December 2021	2022	Set Up Forecast • Print Report • Write a Letter to the Tenant with Proposed Expenses for Next Year
☑	April 2022	2021	View Reports for Actual vs. Budget for Prior Year • Write a Letter to the Tenant Showing the Over or Under Payment Amount • Invoice the Tenant the Difference

Checklist 22 Expense Recovery

ALTERNATIVE EASY APPROACH

As long as you followed all the instructions, it is very easy to review reports. Use Microsoft Excel an easy alternative approach:

- Customize Profit & Loss by Job, review and reclassify as needed:
    - CAM Expenses for each property
    - Non-CAM Expenses for each property
- Print Profit & Loss by Job by Property on Accrual Basis for Tenant Invoices
- Export CAM report to Excel File
- Create an Excel file
- AND follow the steps below

You can contact me for the excel file and quick instructions.

Create or Export CAM Report to Excel

You have the option to create, export the report, update or type in the total amounts.

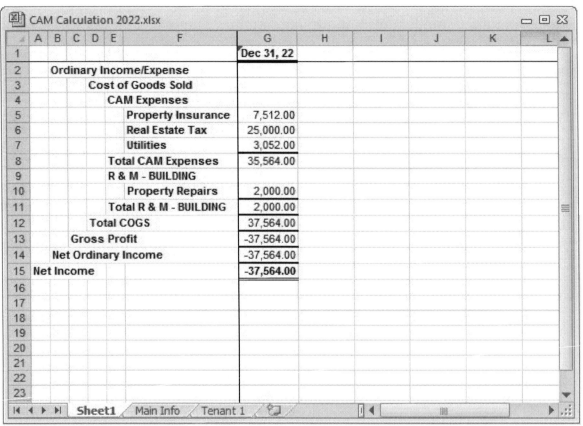

Screen Shot 298 Export QuickBooks Report to Excel

Update Excel File - Main Info Sheet

On the Main File sheet update the date and property name. All tenant sheets will automatically update.

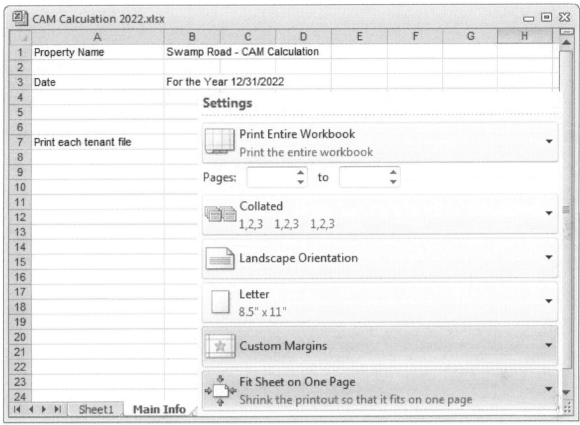

Screen Shot 299 Excel Main Info

Tenant's CAM Calculation

First time around create the tenant sheet exactly the way you want to print. To create your first tenant sheet:

On the Tenant Sheet update:

- Rename the sheet to tenant's name
- Update the heading with tenant's name
- Total Spend column add formula =+Sheet1!G5 to copy from Sheet1 G%
- Copy down to update the column
- Add Tenant % or $ in Tenant Share column
- Change the total amount Invoiced Tenant
- Tenant Credit/Invoice should auto populate.

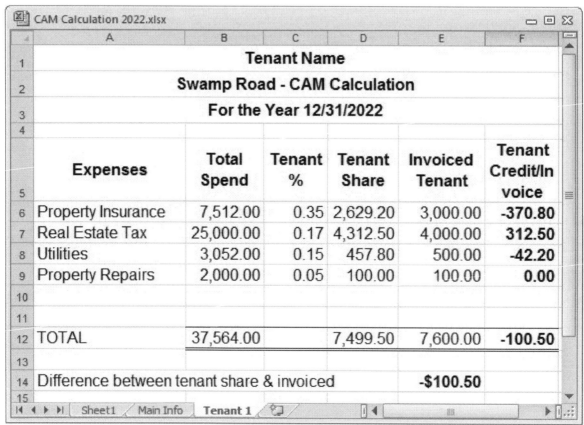

Screen Shot 300 CAM Calculation

EXPENSE RECOVERY

Duplicate Tenant Sheet

To keep the same format, copy the tenant sheet:

- Right-click on the Tenant 1 sheet
- Select (move to end)
- Checkmark Create a copy
- Start back again from "Tenant's CAM Calculation."

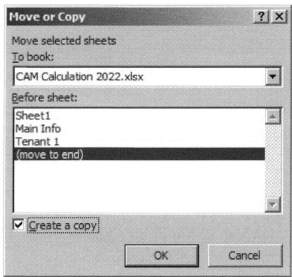
Screen Shot 301 Tenant Excel Sheet

Print CAM Calculation for Each Tenant

Calculation. Done? Check. Now it is time to print all the excel sheet either on the printer or to PDF. View the setting above "Update Excel File - Main Info Sheet."

Either create an invoice or credit the tenant.

EXPENSE RECOVERY

CREATE AN INVOICE OR CREDIT

If the tenant owes you: create an invoice using each item and date it the last day of the year. Review your report to show an outstanding balance.

If the tenant has a credit: create a credit memo using each item and date it the last day of the year. Review your report to show a credit on account. You may:

- Write a check to the tenant or
- Apply it to an outstanding balance

ITEM	DESCRIPTION	PROPERTY NAME	AMOUNT
CAM:Insurance	Insurance	GKS Properties:Swamp Road	370.80
CAM:Taxes:Building Taxes	Building Taxes	GKS Properties:Swamp Road	-312.50
CAM:Gas Utility	Utility	GKS Properties:Swamp Road	42.20

Screen Shot 302 Credit or Invoice

BUDGET & FORECAST REPORTS

To customize the reports to display the accounts and customers you would like to include:

- Click **Reports** on the Menu Bar
- Highlight Budgets & Forecasts
- Select the report you would like to view
- Click **Modify Report...**
- In the Display tab, specify the subcolumns to show actual amount, $ Difference, and % of Budget
- In the Filters tab, choose the necessary filters to view the desired data
- In the Header/Footer tab, update as needed
- Click **OK** to save
- MEMORIZE the report for future use

Report: Budget by Tenant

Filter the report by the Rental Income account.

www.RealEstateAccounting.com
Profit & Loss Budget Performance
January through December 2022

	Jan - Dec 22	Budget	$ Over Budget	Jan - Dec 22	YTD Budget
GKS Properties					
Fun Road 142					
A Unit					
Delicious Pizza	0.00	36,000.00	-36,000.00	0.00	36,000.00
Total A Unit	0.00	36,000.00	-36,000.00	0.00	36,000.00
B Unit					
Wawa	40,000.00	0.00	40,000.00	40,000.00	0.00
B Unit - Other	0.00	48,000.00	-48,000.00	0.00	48,000.00
Total B Unit	40,000.00	48,000.00	-8,000.00	40,000.00	48,000.00
Total Fun Road 142	40,000.00	84,000.00	-44,000.00	40,000.00	84,000.00
Total GKS Properties	40,000.00	84,000.00	-44,000.00	40,000.00	84,000.00
TOTAL	40,000.00	84,000.00	-44,000.00	40,000.00	84,000.00

Report 45 Profit & Loss Budget Preformance by Unit and Tenant

Report: Budget for the Year

www.RealEstateAccounting.com
Profit & Loss Budget Performance
January through December 2022

	Jan - Dec 22	Budget	$ Over Budget	Jan - Dec 22	YTD Budget
GKS Properties					
Fun Road 142					
A Unit					
Delicious Pizza	0.00	36,000.00	-36,000.00	0.00	36,000.00
Total A Unit	0.00	36,000.00	-36,000.00	0.00	36,000.00
B Unit					
Wawa	40,000.00	0.00	40,000.00	40,000.00	0.00
B Unit - Other	0.00	48,000.00	-48,000.00	0.00	48,000.00
Total B Unit	40,000.00	48,000.00	-8,000.00	40,000.00	48,000.00
Total Fun Road 142	40,000.00	84,000.00	-44,000.00	40,000.00	84,000.00
Total GKS Properties	40,000.00	84,000.00	-44,000.00	40,000.00	84,000.00
TOTAL	40,000.00	84,000.00	-44,000.00	40,000.00	84,000.00

Report 46 Profit & Loss Budget Preformance YTD

EXPENSE RECOVERY

Report: Budget Year To Date

www.RealEstateAccounting.com
Profit & Loss Budget Performance
August 2022

	Aug 22	Budget	$ Over Budget	% of Budget	Jan - Aug 22	YTD Budget	$ Over Budget	% of Budget	Annual Budget
Ordinary Income/Expense									
Income									
Common Area Maintenance	1,410.59	8,625.00	-7,214.41	16.4%	11,284.72	69,000.00	-57,715.28	16.4%	103,500.00
Rent	59,052.85	1,133.30	57,919.55	5,210.7%	402,462.43	9,066.40	393,396.03	4,439.1%	13,599.60
Total Income	60,463.44	9,758.30	50,705.14	619.6%	413,747.15	78,066.40	335,680.75	530.0%	117,099.60
Gross Profit	60,463.44	9,758.30	50,705.14	619.6%	413,747.15	78,066.40	335,680.75	530.0%	117,099.60
Expense									
Admin Expense	4,440.65	2,200.00	2,240.65	201.8%	25,548.40	19,200.00	6,348.40	133.1%	28,000.00
Capital Expenditures	0.00				1,867.50	45,000.00	-43,132.50	4.2%	45,000.00
Contract Maintenance	4,453.59	6,079.50	-1,625.91	73.3%	54,833.28	52,042.86	2,790.42	105.4%	75,697.73
Debt Service	20,137.50	20,540.25	-402.75	98.0%	161,100.00	163,113.75	-2,013.75	98.8%	245,274.75
General Administrative	154.56	125.00	29.56	123.6%	6,496.59	4,550.00	1,946.59	142.8%	5,050.00
Other Maintenance	1,423.25	1,710.33	-287.08	83.2%	4,324.53	31,458.14	-27,133.61	13.7%	36,499.46
Payroll Expenses	18,001.61	8,312.95	9,688.66	216.5%	61,225.63	67,382.35	-6,156.72	90.9%	100,634.15
Taxes	0.00	29,300.00	-29,300.00	0.0%	32,249.20	58,300.00	-26,050.80	55.3%	58,300.00
Utilities	4,420.72	5,713.33	-1,292.61	77.4%	47,705.49	49,796.64	-2,091.15	95.8%	72,029.96
Total Expense	53,031.88	73,981.36	-20,949.48	71.7%	395,350.62	490,843.74	-95,493.12	80.5%	666,486.05
Net Ordinary Income	7,431.56	-64,223.06	71,654.62	-11.6%	18,396.53	-412,777.34	431,173.87	-4.5%	-549,386.45
Other Income/Expense									
Other Income									
Interest Income	499.64	375.00	124.64	133.2%	2,964.41	3,000.00	-35.59	98.8%	4,500.00
Total Other Income	499.64	375.00	124.64	133.2%	2,964.41	3,000.00	-35.59	98.8%	4,500.00
Other Expense									
Interest Expense	6,446.68	3,833.33	2,613.35	168.2%	31,256.43	30,666.64	589.79	101.9%	45,999.96
Late Fee Expense	35.00				115.00				
Total Other Expense	6,481.68	3,833.33	2,648.35	169.1%	31,371.43	30,666.64	704.79	102.3%	45,999.96
Net Other Income	-5,982.04	-3,458.33	-2,523.71	173.0%	-28,407.02	-27,666.64	-740.38	102.7%	-41,499.96
Net Income	1,449.52	-67,681.39	69,130.91	-2.1%	-10,010.49	-440,443.98	430,433.49	2.3%	-590,886.41

Report 47 Profit & Loss Budget Preformance

Report: Budget Year To Date

www.RealEstateAccounting.com

Profit & Loss Budget Overview
January through December 2022

	Jan - Dec 22	Budget	$ Over Budget	% of Budget
Ordinary Income/Expense				
Income				
Common Area Maintenance	53,710.38	103,500.00	-49,789.62	51.9%
Rent	600,801.71	13,599.60	587,202.11	4,417.8%
Total Income	654,512.09	117,099.60	537,412.49	558.9%
Gross Profit	654,512.09	117,099.60	537,412.49	558.9%
Expense				
Admin Expense	46,735.88	28,000.00	18,735.88	166.9%
Capital Expenditures	1,867.50	45,000.00	-43,132.50	4.2%
Contract Maintenance	78,759.28	75,697.73	3,061.55	104.0%
Debt Service	241,650.00	245,274.75	-3,624.75	98.5%
General Administrative	10,812.31	5,050.00	5,762.31	214.1%
Other Maintenance	16,998.04	36,499.46	-19,501.42	46.6%
Payroll Expenses	81,110.29	100,634.15	-19,523.86	80.6%
Taxes	64,293.19	58,300.00	5,993.19	110.3%
Utilities	74,164.25	72,029.96	2,134.29	103.0%
Total Expense	616,390.74	666,486.05	-50,095.31	92.5%
Net Ordinary Income	38,121.35	-549,386.45	587,507.80	-6.9%
Other Income/Expense				
Other Income				
Interest Income	3,964.52	4,500.00	-535.48	88.1%
Total Other Income	3,964.52	4,500.00	-535.48	88.1%
Other Expense				
Interest Expense	41,585.32	45,999.96	-4,414.64	90.4%
Late Fee Expense	165.00			
Total Other Expense	41,750.32	45,999.96	-4,249.64	90.8%
Net Other Income	-37,785.80	-41,499.96	3,714.16	91.1%
Net Income	335.55	-590,886.41	591,221.96	-0.1%

Report 48 Profit & Loss Budget Overview

www.RealEstateAccounting.com
Profit & Loss Budget vs. Actual
January through December 2022

	CJ Bazu			TOTAL		
	Jan - Dec 22	Budget	$ Over Budget	Jan - Dec 22	Budget	$ Over Budget
Ordinary Income/Expense						
Income						
Common Area Maintenance	39,450.00	39,600.00	-150.00	39,450.00	39,600.00	-150.00
Rent	350,261.38	514.83	349,746.55	350,261.38	514.83	349,746.55
Total Income	389,711.38	40,114.83	349,596.55	389,711.38	40,114.83	349,596.55
Gross Profit	389,711.38	40,114.83	349,596.55	389,711.38	40,114.83	349,596.55
Expense						
Other Maintenance	166.19	-141.84	308.03	166.19	-141.84	308.03
Total Expense	166.19	-141.84	308.03	166.19	-141.84	308.03
Net Ordinary Income	389,545.19	40,256.67	349,288.52	389,545.19	40,256.67	349,288.52
Net Income	389,545.19	40,256.67	349,288.52	389,545.19	40,256.67	349,288.52

Report 49 Profit & Loss Budget vs. Actual

www.RealEstateAccounting.com
Profit & Loss Budget Overview
January through February 2022

	Jan 22	Budget	$ Over B...	% of Bu...	Feb 22	Budget	$ Over B...	% of Bu...	Jan - Feb ...	Budget	$ Over Budget	% of Budget
Ordinary Income/Expense												
Income												
Common Area Maintenance	1,333.33	8,625.00	-7,291.67	15.5%	1,333.33	8,625.00	-7,291.67	15.5%	2,666.66	17,250.00	-14,583.34	15.5%
Rent	49,052.85	1,133.30	47,919.55	4,328.3%	49,052.85	1,133.30	47,919.55	4,328.3%	98,105.70	2,266.60	95,839.10	4,328.3%
Total Income	50,386.18	9,758.30	40,627.88	516.3%	50,386.18	9,758.30	40,627.88	516.3%	100,772.36	19,516.60	81,255.76	516.3%
Gross Profit	50,386.18	9,758.30	40,627.88	516.3%	50,386.18	9,758.30	40,627.88	516.3%	100,772.36	19,516.60	81,255.76	516.3%
Expense												
Admin Expense	2,704.28	2,200.00	504.28	122.9%	65.72	2,200.00	-2,134.28	3.0%	2,770.00	4,400.00	-1,630.00	63.0%
Contract Maintenance	9,796.58	8,558.12	1,238.46	114.5%	3,578.14	5,954.50	-2,376.36	60.1%	13,374.72	14,512.62	-1,137.90	92.2%
Debt Service	20,137.50	20,137.50	0.00	100.0%	0.00	20,137.50	-20,137.50	0.0%	20,137.50	40,275.00	-20,137.50	50.0%
General Administrative	271.63	125.00	146.63	217.3%	3,435.86	3,675.00	-239.14	93.5%	3,707.49	3,800.00	-92.51	97.6%
Other Maintenance	303.00	1,670.33	-1,367.33	18.1%	772.23	1,880.83	-1,108.60	41.1%	1,075.23	3,551.16	-2,475.93	30.3%
Payroll Expenses	697.00	8,488.70	-7,791.70	8.2%	0.00	8,488.70	-8,488.70	0.0%	697.00	16,977.40	-16,280.40	4.1%
Utilities	6,216.59	8,033.33	-1,816.74	77.4%	6,832.93	7,833.33	-1,000.40	87.2%	13,049.52	15,866.66	-2,817.14	82.2%
Total Expense	40,126.58	49,212.98	-9,086.40	81.5%	14,684.88	50,169.86	-35,484.98	29.3%	54,811.46	99,382.84	-44,571.38	55.2%
Net Ordinary Income	10,259.60	-39,454.68	49,714.28	-26.0%	35,701.30	-40,411.56	76,112.86	-88.3%	45,960.90	-79,866.24	125,827.14	-57.5%
Other Income/Expense												
Other Income												
Interest Income	552.63	375.00	177.63	147.4%	307.33	375.00	-67.67	82.0%	859.96	750.00	109.96	114.7%
Total Other Income	552.63	375.00	177.63	147.4%	307.33	375.00	-67.67	82.0%	859.96	750.00	109.96	114.7%
Other Expense												
Interest Expense	3,892.60	3,833.33	59.27	101.5%	7,163.80	3,833.33	3,330.47	186.9%	11,056.40	7,666.66	3,389.74	144.2%
Total Other Expense	3,892.60	3,833.33	59.27	101.5%	7,163.80	3,833.33	3,330.47	186.9%	11,056.40	7,666.66	3,389.74	144.2%
Net Other Income	-3,339.97	-3,458.33	118.36	96.6%	-6,856.47	-3,458.33	-3,398.14	198.3%	-10,196.44	-6,916.66	-3,279.78	147.4%
Net Income	6,919.63	-42,913.01	49,832.64	-16.1%	28,844.83	-43,869.89	72,714.72	-65.8%	35,764.46	-86,782.90	122,547.36	-41.2%

Report 50 Profit & Loss Budget Overview

CHAPTER 72 CUSTOMIZE YOUR REPORTS

In the template file, we have provided 100+ customized reports for your business. However, you may need to personalize a few of those reports further. Customize and memorize reports to quickly access the information you need.

Objectives

Upon completion of this chapter, you will be able to:

- Checklist
- Change Report Format
- Create a Report Group
- Customize Reports
- Memorize Reports

CUSTOMIZE YOUR REPORTS

REPORT FORMAT PREFERENCE

You can default the report formatting to all the reports. To make any additional changes:

- Click on **Edit**
- Select Preferences
- Click on **Reports & Graphs**
- Select Format

Customize further by selecting the tabs: Header/Footer and Fonts/Numbers

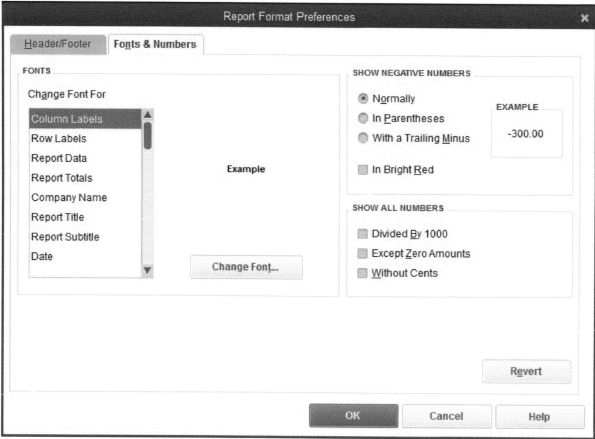

Screen Shot 303 Report Format Preferences

CUSTOMIZE YOUR REPORTS

GROUP REPORTS

Create a group for anything and everything to keep your reports organized and easy to find. Grouping the reports will let you select one or all reports and change dates. With one click you can display, print or email all selected reports. It cannot be any easy.

Memorized Group will keep your reports organized and easily accessible.

To create a new group in the Memorized Reports List:

- Click **Reports** on the Icon Bar
- Select Memorized Reports
- Click **Memorized Report List**
- Click **Memorized Report** on bottom left
- Click **New Group**

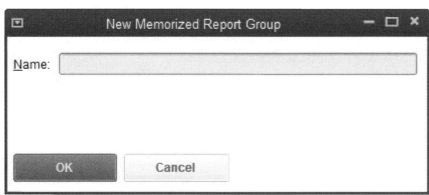

Screen Shot 304 New Report Group

- Enter a new group name in the Name field
- Click **OK**

Double-click on the Group Name to view and print all reports listed in the group.

CUSTOMIZE YOUR REPORTS

CUSTOMIZE REPORTS

Customize reports fitting your business needs.

To customize reports:

- Open the report you would like to customize
- Click **Customize Report** in the upper left-hand corner

Display

The first tab is used to specify what data will be included in the report and how it is sorted. Customize the reports by choosing specific fields.

The image below only displays some of the available customization features.

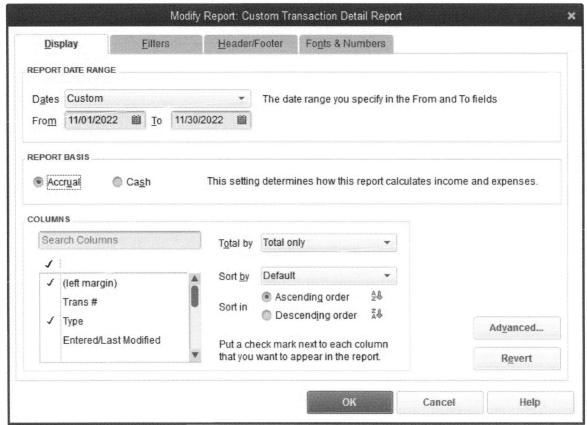

Screen Shot 305 Display Tab

Commercial Property Management for Managers: QuickBooks Desktop

CUSTOMIZE YOUR REPORTS

- The most frequently used fields are as below:

Field	Data
Report Date Range	Select the dates to display the data within the desired range
Report Basis	Select Accrual or Cash
Columns	Select each field you would like to appear in the report. Custom fields will be displayed in the list.
Total by	Select how you would like the total calculated
Sort by	Select how you would like the transactions sorted
Sort in	Select Ascending order or Descending order
Advanced…	Specifies the way QuickBooks selects data for the report. Select In Use to display the accounts affected by transactions in the given date range Screen Shot 306 Advance Options
Click **Filters** tab	

Table 74 Display Tab

CUSTOMIZE YOUR REPORTS

Filters

- The Filters tab allows you to specify the data.

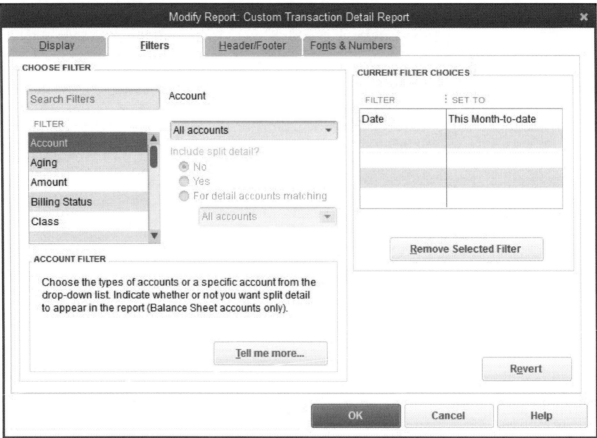

Screen Shot 307 Filters Tab

- The most frequently used fields are as below:

Field	Data
Filter	Select the field you would like to filter
	To the right, you will have the option to specify how you would like that data filtered
	On the bottom, it will describe how the selected filter will change the report. Click **Tell me more** for more details.
Current Filter Choices	All selected filters
Click **Header/Footer** tab	

Table 75 Filters Tab

Commercial Property Management for Managers: QuickBooks Desktop   558

CUSTOMIZE YOUR REPORTS

Header/Footer

The Header/Footer tab allows you to change the text displayed on the header and footer of the report.

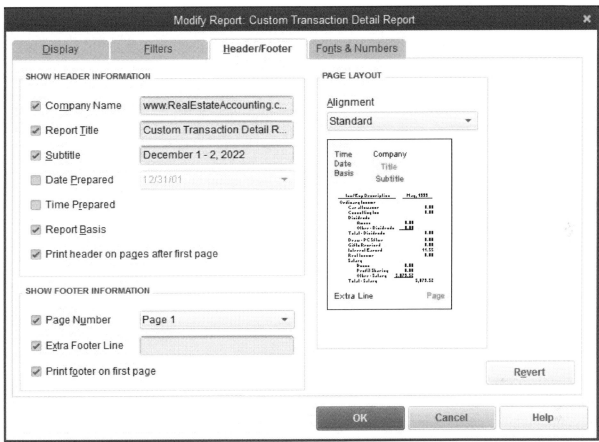

Screen Shot 308 Header/Footer Tab

- The most frequently used fields are as below:

Field	Data
Show Header Information	Select the text to be displayed
Show Footer Information	Select the formatting options
Page Layout	Choose the alignment and view where the text will be displayed on the report
Click **Fonts & Numbers** tab	

Table 76 Header/Footer Tab

Commercial Property Management for Managers: QuickBooks Desktop

CUSTOMIZE YOUR REPORTS

Fonts & Numbers

The Fonts & Numbers tab allows you to change fonts and choose how numbers are displayed in the report.

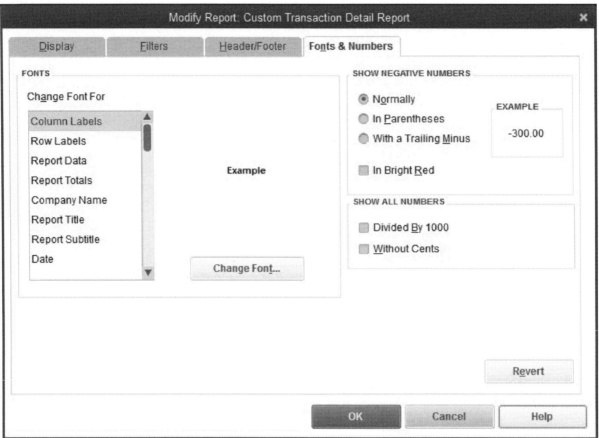

Screen Shot 309 Fonts & Numbers Tab

- The most frequently used fields are as below:

Field	Data
Fonts	Select the element to view the existing font Click **Change Font** to change the font, style, size, effects, and color
Show Negative Numbers	Select how you would like negative numbers to appear
Show All Numbers	Select how you would like all numbers to appear
Click **OK**	

Table 77 Fonts & Numbers Tab

CUSTOMIZE YOUR REPORTS

MEMORIZE REPORTS

Memorize reports after selecting and filtering your data to avoid repeating customization steps each time.

NOTE
When memorizing a report, the Report Title automatically appears as the Report Name.

To memorize reports:

- Click **Memorize**
- Click **Replace** to replace the existing report OR click **New** to create a new report

Screen Shot 310 Memorize Report

- Enter a report name
- Select the report group
- Click **OK**

If you are memorizing a previously memorized report, the following screen appears.

Screen Shot 311 Memorize Report

Commercial Property Management for Managers: QuickBooks Desktop

CHECKLIST CUSTOMIZE YOUR REPORT

CUSTOMIZE YOUR REPORT CHECKLIST

	Task	Refer to Chapter
☑	Change Report Format Preference	
☑	Create a Memorized Report Group	

☑	Customize Report
	    Display
	    Filters
	    Header/Footer
	    Fonts & Numbers
		Customize Your Reports

☑	Memorize report in a Group	

Checklist 23 Customize Your Report

Chapter 73 Customized Reports For You

In the template file, we have provided over 100+ industry-specific reports, as well as customized Chart of Accounts and Items, for your business. The reports are over and above what QuickBooks provides when you start a file under the Report Center. Of course, you have the option to customize further anything we have provided.

> **NOTE**
> There may be some reports that are not available or that different display column in your version of QuickBooks.

Objectives

Upon completion of this chapter, you will be able to:

- Access the Report Center
- View the Memorized Reports List

CUSTOMIZED REPORTS FOR YOU

MEMORIZED REPORTS INCLUDED

The following reports are customized for rental accounting and management. There may be more reports in the file than are listed here. When we receive a request for additional reports, you will be notified of the updates via email.

1 CHECKLIST
- Lease Expiration
- Open Invoices
- Profit & Loss Unclassified
- Unbilled Costs by Tenant

1099
- 1099 Detail
- 1099 Summary
- Expenses by Vendor Summary
- Open Invoice Report
- Rental Income for 1099
- Vendor Expenses for 1099

Accountant
- Balance Sheet
- General Ledger
- Profit & Loss
- Profit & Loss by Property
- Profit & Loss for Your Company
- Trial Balance

Application Fees
- Applicants List
- Application Fees

Banking
- Bank Register - Last Quarter
- Bank Register - This Month
- Bank Register - This Quarter
- Bank Register - This Week
- Bank Register - This year
- Check Detail
- Checking Register - This year
- Deposit Detail
- Petty Cash Register - This year
- Savings Register - This year
- Security Deposit Register - This year
- Last Month Rent Register - This year

Budgets & Forecasts
- Click to view reports

CAM
- CAM Expenses & Rent for Prior Year
- Profit & Loss by Property (CAM Expenses)
- Profit & Loss by Tenant (Invoices)

Cash Flow
- Cash Flow Forecast
- Cash Flow Forecast by Month
- Cash Flow Forecast by Quarter
- Cash Flow Forecast by Year
- Statement of Cash Flows

Company
- Asset Accounts
- Balance Sheet
- Bank Accounts
- Credit Card Accounts
- Current Asset Accounts
- Current Liability Accounts
- Fixed Asset Accounts
- Liability Accounts
- Long Term Liability Accounts
- Other Asset Accounts
- Other Current Asset Accounts

Commercial Property Management for Managers: QuickBooks Desktop

CUSTOMIZED REPORTS FOR YOU

- Profit & Loss
- Profit & Loss by Property
- Profit & Loss for Overhead

Credit Card
- Credit Card Charges by Property

Employees
- Payroll Item Detail
- Payroll Liability Balances
- Payroll Summary

Equity Holders – Corporation
- Additional Paid in Capital
- Common Stock
- Loans from Shareholders

Equity Holders - Partnership
- Loans from Partners

Equity Holders - Sole Proprietorship
- Draws
- Equity Accounts
- Investment

Invoices
- Tenant Invoices by Month
- Tenant Invoices by Year
- Open Invoices
- This Month's Open Invoices
- Unbilled Costs by Property

Late Fees
- Open Invoices
- This Month's Open Invoices

Lease Commissions
- Lease Commission

Lease Expiration
- Lease Expiration
- Lease Expiration - Last Month
- Lease Expiration - Next Month
- Lease Expiration - Next Quarter
- Lease Expiration - Next Year

- Lease Expiration - This Month
- Lease Expiration - This Quarter
- Lease Expiration - This Year

Lists
- Multi-Unit Tenant List
- Owner List
- Property List
- Property List - All
- Property List - Former
- Tenant List
- Tenant List - All
- Tenant List - Former
- Unit List

Management Fees
- Open Invoices
- Rent for Management Fees
- Management Fees

Notes
- Tenant Notes
- Owner Notes
- Property Notes
- To Do Notes
- Unit Notes
- Vendor Notes

Owners Proceed
- Owner Proceed Summary
- Owner Proceed Detail
- Open Invoice

Rent Due
- A/R Aging Summary
- Tenant Balance Detail
- Tenant Balance Summary
- Open Invoices
- Rent Due 10 Days and on
- Rent Due 3 Days and on
- Rent Due 5 Days and on
- This Month's Open Invoices

Commercial Property Management for Managers: QuickBooks Desktop

Rent Roll
- Rent Roll
- Rent Roll - All Tenants
- Rent Roll - Old Tenants
- Rent Roll for Vacant Units

Reserve Funds
- Funds - Unpaid
- Reserve Funds
- Reserve Funds in Detail

Sales Tax
- Sales Tax Liability
- Sales Tax Payable
- Sales Tax Payments
- Sales Tax Revenue Summary

Security Deposits
- Deposits - Unpaid
- Security Deposit
- Security Deposit in Detail

Tenant
- Tenant Contact List
- Open Invoices
- Options
- Rent Escalation Date
- Transaction List by Tenant

Tenant Credits
- Checks Issued for Credits
- Credit Memo - Not Refunded
- Credit Memo - Refunded
- Credit Memo Details

Timesheets
- Time by Name by Property
- Time by Property Detail
- Time by Property Summary
- Time by Work Performed by Property
- Time by Work Performed for YOUR COMPANY

To Do List
- To Do Notes
- To Do Notes - Active
- To Do Notes - All
- To Do Notes - Completed
- To Do Notes - Not Active
- To Do Notes - Not Completed

Units Leased
- Lease Expiration
- Rent Escalation Date
- Units Not Vacant
- Units Rented

Vacancy
- Units Vacant
- Vacancy Rent Loss

Vendors
- A/P Aging Summary
- Bills by Due Date
- Bills Entered
- Checks and Bill Payment
- Expenses by Vendor Detail
- Expenses by Vendor Summary
- Transaction List by Vendor
- Unpaid Bills by Property
- Unpaid Bills Detail
- Vendor Balance Detail
- Vendor Balance Summary Vendor Contact List
- Vendor Phone List

Work Orders
- All Work Orders
- All Work Orders by Property
- Closed Work Orders
- Closed Work Orders by Contractor
- Closed Work Orders by Property
- Open Work Orders
- Open Work Orders by Contractors
- Open Work Orders by Tenant
- Work Orders by Contractor

INDEX

#

1099, 515

A

Abbreviated Names, 150
Account
   Chart of, 91, 112
   Numbers, 92
Accrual Basis, 90
Application Fees, 263
   Applicant, 159
   Credit Rent, 265
   Paid to Owner, 265
   Retained by Manager, 265
Asset
   Chart of Accounts, 92
   Opening Balances, 249

B

Backup
   Automatic, 19
   Files, 14
   Schedule, 19
Bad Debt, *see Write Off*
Balances
   Checklist, 244
   Opening, 245, 248
   Sheet, 97
   Tenants, 246
   Vendors, 247
Bank
   Online, 465
   Opening Balances, 248
   Reconciliation, 472
   Register, 64, 382
   Service Fee, 333
Basis Cash and Accrual, 89
Batch Invoicing, 81
Bills
   Against Work Order, 388
   Credit Card Balances, 247, 393
   Opening Balances, 247
   Recurring, 71, 402
   Reimbursable Expenses, 387
   Time, 400
   Utility Bills, 420
   Without a Work Order, 390
Billable? , 143
Bounced Tenant Check
   Bank Service Fee, 333
   Record, 334
   Re-invoice, 336
Bounced Vendor Check, 447
Budget, 251

C

CAM
   Budgets and Forecast, 546
   Excel File, 541
   Expense Recovery, 539
   Invoice or Credit, 546
   Prior Balance, 257
   Reconcile, 540
   vs. non-CAM, 144
Calendar, 68
Cash
   Basis, 90
   Cash Flow, 96
   Petty Cash, 64, 382
Center
   Collections, 344
   Customers, 262
   Employees, 52
   Leads, 49
   Report, 514
Chart of Accounts, 91, 112
Check
   Bounced Tenant, 331
   Bounced Vendor, 447
   Credit Tenant, 337
   Credit Vendor, 423
   Enter, 376
   Electronic Signature, 37
   Management Fee, 481
   Owner's Proceed, 507
   Print, 433
   Void, 443
Checklist
   1099, 518
   Company Information, 99
   Customize Your Report, 562
   Exercise the Option, 273

INDEX

Expense (CAM) Recovery, 540
Investment or Loan From, 454
Leases New, 270
Management Fees, 483, 493
Owner's Proceed, 504, 511
Property, 151, 187
Property Owner, 151
Property Owner's Report Customization, 177
Reimbursement, Draw, or Personal Loan, 454
Renewal, 271
Rent Escalation, 272
Reserve Fund, 497
Required Document, 100
Tenants, 152
Terminated Lease, 274
Units, 152
Your Company Financials, 244
Class, 143
   List, 47
   Property, 189
   Property Owner, 164
Closing Date, 110
Collections Center, 344
Commission Lease, 293
Company
   Class, 114
   Customer:Job, 114
   File, *see File*
   Information, 104
   Name, 114
   Snapshot, 32
Contractors, 354
Corporation, 103, 155
Credit
   Credit Card, 423
   Opening Balances, 246, 247
   Tenant, 337
   Vendor, 423
Credit Card
   Accounts, 113
   Bill, 397
   Charges, 393
   Pay Balance, 397
   Reconcile, 476
   Refund, 423
   Register, 64

Custom Fields, 115
Customize
   Fields, 115
   Forms, 128
   Letters, 119
   Reports, 553, 563
   Statement, 343
   Template File, 7

D

Date
   Closing, 110
   Lease, 220
Deposits, *see Security Deposit*
Deposit Personal, 454
Document Management, 41
Download File, 7
Draw, 455

E

Entity Type, 103, 155
Equity
   Account, 93
   Deposit, 454
   Reimburse, 455
Escalation, 535
Excel CAM, 541
Expenses
   Accounts, 92, 94
   Apply to Vendor Deposit, 406
   CAM vs. non-CAM, 144
   Categorize, 137
   Fixed vs. Variable, 140
   Items vs., 141
   Organizational, 139
   Petty Cash, 64, 382
   Prepaid, 409
   Recovery, 539
   Reimbursing, 387, 455
   Start-up, 139
   Stop, 538
   Tab, 141
   Variable, 140
Expiration Lease, 220

INDEX

F

Favorites Manu, 38
Fees
 Late, 116
Fields Custom, 115
File
 Accountant's Copy, 15
 Backup, 14
 CAM Excel, 541
 Copy, 14
 Extensions, 8
 Existing, 249
 For Each Owner, 3
 One or Multiple, 3
 Open, 102
 Portable, 15
 Property Management, 3
 Restore, 10
 Schedule, 19
 Template, 7
 Your Company, 3
Finding Answers, 25
Forecast, 251
Forms, *see Customize*

G

Gita's
 Best Friends, 28
 Naming Rules, 234
 Transaction Rules, 140
Group
 Reports, 555
 Transactions, 73

H

Help, 26
History, 34
Home Page, 31
How to Use Manual, xii

I

Icon Bar, 30
Inactive, 60
Investment or Loan From, 454

Investments, *see Equity*
Invoices, *see Rent*
Items
 Add, 55
 Delete, 60
 Edit, 60
 Group, 58
 Inactive, 60
 Tab, 141
 Types, 54, 142

J

Job, *see Customer*
Journal Entry, 35

K

Keyboard Shortcuts, 42

L

Landlord, *see Property Owner*
Last Month Rent, *see Security Deposit*
Late Fees, 116, 319
Layout Designer, 132
Lead Center, 49
Lease
 Commissions, 293
 Exercise the Option Checklist, 273
 Expiration Date, 220
 New Checklist, 270
 Options, 220
 Renewal Checklist, 271
 Rent Escalation Checklist, 272
 Start Date, 220
 Sublease, 215
 Terminated Checklist, 274
Lease Abstract (Summary)
 Create, 280
 Edit, 279
 Group, 277
 Items, 278
 Update, 282
Letters and Envelopes, 119
Liabilities
 Chart of Accounts, 93
 Opening Balances, 249

INDEX

Line of Credit, 457
Lists
  Activate Names, 61
  Chart of Accounts, 45
  Class, 47
  Customer (Tenants) Center, 50
  Employee Center, 52
  Lead Center, 49
  Lists of Lists, 44
  Item, 46, 54
  Merge, 62
  Other Names, 48
  Property, 189, 191
  Property Owner, 163, 164, 166
  Tenants, 216
  Units, 105
  Vendor Center, 51
Loan, 453

M

Management Fees
  Calculate, 483
  Checklist, 483
  Flat Fees, 483
  Leave Income in Same Account, 492
  Subsequent Check, 493
  Transfer Funds, 491
Markups, 415
Memorized Reports, 563

Memorized Transactions
  Clean Up, 79
  Delete, 79
  Enter, 75
  Frequency, 78
  Group, 73
  List, 78
  Owner's Proceed Check, 510
  Update, 79
Menu
  Bar, 30
  Favorites, 38
Merge, 62
Multi-unit, 205
Multi-unit Tenant, 227

N

Names
  Abbreviated, 150
  Activate, 61
  Applicant, 159
  CAM and non-CAM, 201
  Company, 114
  Delete, 112
  Edit, 112
  Equity Holder, 153
  Inactivate, 60
  Merge, 62
  Move Other, 63
  Multi-Unit Tenants, 227
  Properties, 185
  Property Owners, 161
  Rules, 234
  Tenants, 213
  Units, 203
  Vendors, 231
Non-Sufficient Funds NSF, 333
Notes, 65

O

Online Banking Center, *see Online Services*
Online Bank Services, 465
Opening Balances, 243
Open Screen, 33
Organizational Expenses, 139
Other
  Expenses, 92, 94
  Income, 92, 94
  Merge Names, 62
  Move Names, 63
Overdue
  Invoices, 309
  Notes, 65, 344
Overhead, *see Your Company*
Owe
  What Others Owe You, 87
  What You Owe Others, 87
Owners, *see Property Owner*
Owner's Proceed
  Check, 507
  Checklist, 504

Memorize Check, 510
Subsequent Checks, 511

P

Partnership, 103, 155
Pass Thru Charges, 323
Passwords, 105
Pay Bills, 427
    Entered in QuickBooks, 429
    Not Entered in QuickBooks, 428
Payment - Vendor
    By Selecting Assign check number, 434
    By Selecting To be printed, 434
    Credit Card, 435
    Methods, 428
    Tax, see Tax
Personal Loan, 553
Petty Cash
    Record Expenses, 381
    Register, 382
    Withdraw Money, 380
Prepaid Expenses, 409
Print
    Checks, 433
    Envelopes, 119
    Letters, 119
Profit & Loss, 97
Property Owner
    1099, 515
    Class, 164
    Customize Report, 176
    Customer, 166
    Group, 175
    Vendor, 163
    View Information, 174
Property
    Checklist, 187
    Customer, 197
    Group, 199
    Job, 191
    Memorize Report, 200
    Subclass, 189
    Transfer Deposit Between, 408
    Transfer Funds Between, 462
Purchase Orders, see Work Orders

Q

QuickBooks, see File also
    Best Friends, 28
    Close Screen, 33
    Company Snapshot, 32
    Customer Center, 50
    Custom Fields, 115
    Document Management, 41
    Electronic Signature, 37
    Employee Center, 52
    Existing File, 249
    Favorites Menu, 38
    File Extensions, 8
    History, 34
    Home Page, 31
    Icon Bar, 30
    Items, 278
    Journal Entry, 35
    Lead Center, 49
    Lists, see Lists
    Menu Bar, 30
    Notes, 65
    Payment Methods, 428
    Passwords, 105
    Reminders, 65
    Restore, 10
    Saving Transactions, 34
    Screens (Windows), 33
    Search Feature, 39
    Shortcuts, 42
    Software Versions, 6
    Tenant Center, 50
    To Do List, 69
    Transaction History, 34
    Vendor Center, 51

R

Receive Items against Work Order
    With Bill, 363
    Without Bill, 360
Receive Payment, 311
Reconcile
    Bank Account, 472
    CAM, 539
    Credit Card Account, 476
    Deposit, 478

INDEX

Recurring Bills, 71, 402
Recurring Transactions, *see Transactions, Memorized*
Refund
  Credit Card, 423
  Deposit, 289, 290
  Last Month Rent, 291
  Tenant, 337
  Vendor, 424
Register
  Bank, 64
  Credit Card, 64
  Petty Cash, 64, 382
Reimbursable Expenses, *see Pass Thru Charges*
Reminders, 65
Renewal Lease, 271
Rent
  Credit, 337
  Credit Issue a Refund Check, 337
  Escalation, 535
  Memorize, 307
  Monthly, 305
  Paid in Advance, 304
  Pro-Rated, 304
  Prior CAM Rent, 257
  Received, 311
  Vacancy Loss, 347
  Write-off, 337
Rent Roll, 297
Reports
  Center, 514
  Checklist, 562
  Customize Your Reports, 553
  Customized For You, 563
  Format, 544
  Group, 555
  List of Memorized Reports, 563
  Memorize, 561
  Owner's Proceed, 175, 506, 512
  Properties, 175, 200, 506, 512
Reserve Funds, 495
  Opening Balances, 246
Restore
  QuickBooks File, 10

S

Sales Tax, *see Tax*
Save
  Save & Close, 34
  Save & New, 34
Screens
  Close, 33
  Open, 33
Search, 39
Security Deposit, 283
  Apply Last Month Rent, 291
  Credit Memo, 291
  Deposit Payable to Owner, 285
  Enter, 286
  Flow Chart, 284
  Forfeit, 290
  Full Refund, 289
  No Refund, 290
  Opening Balances, 246
  Partial Refund, 289
  Reconcile, 478
  Receive Payment, 288
  Transfer Funds, 291
Service Fee, *see Bank Charge*
Shortcuts, 42
Signatures, 37
Software Install, 6
Sole Proprietorship, 103, 155
Splits, 98
Start-up Cost, 139
Statements, 343
Subclass, 189
Sublease, 215
Supplies, 354

T

Tab, 141
Table of Contents, iii
Tasks, 65
Tax
  Code, 147
  Discount Adjust, 149
  Group, 148
  Liability Report, 438
  Opening Balances, 247
  Record Payments, 440

INDEX

Revenue Summary, 442
Set Up, 146
Template
   CAM Excel File, 541
   File, 3, 7
   Forms, 128
   Letters and Envelopes, 119
   Restore, 10
   Statement, 133
Tenant
   Add, 216
   Bounced Check, 331
   Center, 50
   Collections, 344
   Credit, 337
   Deposit, 314
   Duplicate Invoice, 336
   Eviction Letter, 119
   Invoice, 303
   Lease Abstract (Summary), 275
   Lease Commission, 293
   Lease Dates, 220
   Last Month Rent, 283
   Multi-Unit, 227
   Notes, 65
   Opening Balances, 246
   Payments, 312
   Reimbursement, 387, 455
   Reinvoice bounced check, 336
   Rent Roll, 297
   Security Deposit, see Security Deposit
   Single, 215
   Statements, 343
   Status, 220
   Sublease, 215
Timesheet
   Copy Last, 370
   Enter Bill, 400
   Enter Weekly, 368
To Do, 69
Transactions
   Gita's Rules, 140
   Group, 73
   History, 34
   Memorized Group, 73
   Recurring, 71, 402
Transfer
   Deposit between Properties, 408

Funds between Properties, 462
Management Fee Income, 491
Manual (Paper), 464
Money between Bank Accounts, 291
Online, 463
Trial Balance, 96

U

Uncleared, 248
Undeposited Funds, 98, 314
Unit
   Multi-Unit Tenant, 227
   Single Unit Tenant, 203
Users
   Add, 106
   Admin, 105
   Change, 106
   Closing Date, 110

V

Vacant, 220
Vacancy Loss, 347
Vendors
   Bounce Check, 447
   Center, 51
   Check, 376
   Credit, 423
   Deposits, 403
   Enter, 383
   Markups, 415
   Multiple Accounts, 233
   Naming Rules, 234
   Opening Balances, 247
   Pay Bills, 427
   Prepaid, 409
   Property Owner, 163
   Refund, 424
   Reimbursable Expenses, 387, 455
   Unbilled Expenses, 419
   Utility Bills, 420
Void Check
   Check Method, 446
   Register Method, 445

INDEX

W

What Others Owe You, 87
What You Owe Others, 87
Work Orders
  Close Automatically, 364
  Close Manually, 365
  Create, 358
  Employees vs. Vendors, 357
  Receive Items with Bill, 363
  Receive Items without Bill, 360
Write Off Tenant Invoices, 337

Y

Your Company, *see Overhead also*
  Closing Date, 110
  Company Information, 99
  Enter Opening Balances, 249
  Financial Checklist,
  Late Fee Settings, 116
  Open, 102
  Passwords, 105
  Users, 106

YOUR NOTES

Made in the USA
Columbia, SC
05 July 2021